TEACHING OF
HISTORY II

TEACHING OF
HISTORY II

Arul Jothi
M.Sc., M.Ed.
Principal, Arcot Sri Mahalakshmi Women's Teacher Training Institute,
Villapakkam, Vellore Dist.-632521 T.N.

Dr. D.L. Balaji
B.Com., M.A., M.Phil., D.Lit.
Correspondent, Arcot Sri Mahalakshmi Educational Institutions,
Villapakkam, Vellore Dist.-632521 T.N.

Sunil Kapoor
B.A. (Gen.) M.A. (History) M. Phil.
Archeological Survey of India

CENTRUM PRESS
NEW DELHI-110002 (INDIA)

CENTRUM PRESS
H.O.: 4360/4, Ansari Road, Daryaganj,
New Delhi-110 002 (India)
Ph.: 23278000, 23261597
B.O.: No. 1015, Ist Main Road, BSK IIIrd Stage
IIIrd Phase, IIIrd Block,
Bangalore - 560 085 (India)
Tel.: 080-41723429
Visit us at: www.centrumpress.com

Teaching of History II

First Edition, 2009

PRINTED IN INDIA

Printed at Mehra Offset Press, Delhi

Contents

Preface

This book was developed for the students of B.Ed. who intended to make their careers in the field of History. The purpose of the book is to present a reasonably comprehensive account of sampling theory as it has been developed for use in sample surveys, with sufficient illustrations to show how the theory is applied in practice, and with a supply of exercises to be worked by the student.

As an indication of the level at which the book is directed, the minimum Language equipment necessary for an easy understanding of the proofs is a knowledge of History. On the statistical side, the book presupposes an introductory course, which includes such topics as Biography, Existence, Inventions, Events, Teaching Skills, Microteaching and Macro teaching with relevant Explanations.

Readers with advanced training in History may find the arguments by which the understanding of Knowledge of History will become easy. Such a development would be illuminating in clarifying the interrelationships between the different parts of the subject, and might prove a stimulus to further research and discovery.

This book contains more material than can be required for B.Ed. students However, the sections have been prepared so that many of them can be omitted, or condensed to a brief statement of the results, without detriment to later parts of the book. There are, for instance, numerous discussions of special topics, which attempt to answer questions that have been raised by alert sampling practitioners but which are not essential to a firm understanding of the fundamentals of the subject.

Author

Unit I

Contributions of Eminent Historians

GREEK HISTORIOGRAPHY

OVERVIEW

Herodotus was a Greek historian in the fifth century B.C.E. His birth was around B.C.E. References to certain events in his narratives suggest that he did not die until at least 431 B.C.E, which was the beginning of the Peloponesian War. In his later years, Herodotus traveled extensively throughout the Eastern Mediterranean. There, he visited the Black Sea, Babylon, Phoenicia, and Egypt. He is best known for his work entitled *Histories*. Because of this, Cicero claimed him to be the Father of History. *Histories* is the story of the rise of Persian power and the friction between Persia and Greece.

The battles that are described are the ones fought at Marathon, Thermopylae and Salamis. His story is the historical record of events that happened in his own lifetime. The first Persian War took place just before he was born, while the second happened when he was a child. This gave him the opportunity to question his elders about the events in both wars to get the details he wanted for his story.

Histories also contained information having to do with the country of Egypt. The history, geography and ethnography of Egypt are what Herodotus wrote about. The customs of Egyptians fascinated him because of their differences compared to Greek culture. He wrote about how the Egyptians did everything backwards in relation to the Greeks. Observations he made describe how the Egyptians wrote from right to left, instead of left to right. Activities like eating were done outside while doing their "easement" indoors. The reason he gave was that the Egyptians thought "unseemly but necessary things should be done in secret, and things not unseemly in the open."

Herodotus also wrote about the appearance of the priests. He noticed that the Egyptian priests had shaven heads, while priests from other lands kept their hair long. The Egyptians, in his opinion, were the most religious nation than any other he had known. The monuments that he witnessed also filled him with wonder. He even considered Egypt to have more monuments than any other country in the world. The Nile River was also a target for his writings, which were considered valuable. Before the beginning of Egyptology in the nineteenth century, Herodotus' writings were the main source of information pertaining to Egypt.

Although early Egyptologists regarded his chronicles of Egypt as a valuable source of information, the accuracy of some of Herodotus' writings have been challenged. His eyewitness accounts are thought of as accurate, but the stories told to him are questioned. Some researchers think the people who told Herodotus information could have forgotten parts, or just humored him with an interesting answer having nothing to do with the truth.

HISTORY

Herodotus was the first man to use investigation and research to write history. For this reason he has been dubbed the "father of history." He is known for his *Histories,* in which he tells about the history, customs and people of the lands he visited. The main theme of his work is the conflict between East and West. Besides being the first historical work written using research, it is important as the first long work in Greek prose and is confirmation the historical reliability of the Bible.

Herodotus was born in c. 484 in Halicarnassus in modern southwestern Turkey. To be born at this time and place meant to be born under the great Persian Empire. According to A. R. Burn growing up in this environment "may have helped to foster the breadth of vision with which Herodotus surveys the great conflict [The Persian Wars] from both sides."His family was wealthy and probably aristocratic. While he was still quite young, the tyrant Lygdamis drove the family out of town and they were forced to live in exile on the island of Samos.

Throughout his life Herodotus traveled extensively, probably as a trader, as his writings show great interest in the products of the various lands he visited, and very few people at that time would have been able to travel simply for pleasure. In his travels he visited Egypt and Cyrene, Palestine, Phoenicia, Babylonia, the north Aegean, the Black Sea, Scythia and many other Greek cities on the Mediterranean.

In the ancient and even modern Near East a traveller with a wealth of stories from foreign lands was and is often the recipient of spontaneous hospitality. No doubt such was also the case for Herodotus. He made good use of his traveling by talking to the people of the land. He would often seek out the most promising sources of information, such as priests, whom he mentions conversing with in Egypt. He frequently talked to eyewitnesses of the events he later wrote about.

Sometime before 454 Herodotus took part in overthrowing the tyrant Lygdamis in Halicarnassus. However, he soon found himself to be disliked, a common occurrence for Greek politicians, and so he left for Athens. It was there that he first began to work on his book *The Histories*, which in Greek means "inquiries" or "research" He is said to have given public readings of sections of his work while in Athens. He stayed in Athens for some time, but because of the law of that time he was unable to become a citizen. He thus chose to take part in the colonization of Thuria, a city founded by Athens in Southern Italy. He remained there for some time, possibly till his death between 430 and 424. It was there that he did most of his writing, compiling his travel notes and the historical material he had collected.

Herodotus' great work was the writing of *The Histories*. It was the first historical work ever written (as far as we know) as well as the first large, well-planned prose work in Greek. The purpose of his book was to "preserve the memory of the war [Persians Wars], to record the achievements of the Greeks and the Persians, and to explain why the conflict began."In order to achieve this goal, Herodotus presented all the information he had collected, weather or not he believed. The book is significant because in it Herodotus establishes the ideas that investigation and research are essential to history.

Its scope is also significant, covering the Eastern Mediterranean world from the time of the Lydian Empire(c. 672 BC) to the defeat of Xerxes in 479 BC. In his book Herodotus writes not only about the history of the lands he visited, but its customs and people.

According to the *Encyclopedia of World Biography,* Herodotus "had a remarkable gift of telling a story clearly and dramatically, often with a dry ironic sense of humour; the best of his stories have delighted, and will continue to delight, generations of readers.

Also important is that in many instances Herodotus' writings confirms the reliability of the Bible. In order to test that the Bible is reliable we can compare it to other records to see that it is accurate in reporting what was known at the time it was written. Herodotus' writings coincide with the Bible in numerous places. In Genesis 42:32 is says, "the Egyptians could not eat bread with the Hebrews, for that is loathsome to the Egyptians." Herodotus tells of the same contempt the Egyptians had for foreigners.

He writes, "no native of Egypt, will kiss a Greek, or use the knife of a Greek, or his spit, or his cauldron, or taste the flesh of an ox, known to be pure, if it has been cut with a Greek knife. The Bible and Herodotus also agree in their description of Babylon. In Isaiah 45:2 we hear of Babylon's "gates of bronze" and Herodotus declared there were "a hundred gates in the circuit of the wall, all of bronze. These are only a few of the numerous times when Herodotus "provides unwitting testimony of the accuracy of the Old Testament.

Herodotus was given the title "the father of history" by Cicero and became very popular, sparking an interest in history. But he was not the first person to use ethnology, geography, research and investigation to describe past events. He was also not the first writer to put together a long historical narrative in which the main thread is never completely lost. Although Herodtus demonstrated an amazing degree of neutrality, showing very little of the usual Greek bias, there was another historian that lived 1000 years eariler that reported with even better acuracy.

Herodotus wrote broad and informative descriptions of ancient Near East cultures. In one of those cultures lived Moses who wrote what is known as the Hebrew Torah. It traces the history of humanity back to the begining and then focuses on the family of Abraham (which grew into many nations including today's Arabs and Jews).

The vibrant and intriguing narrative of Moses takes the reader through the Exodus from Egypt without pretense to hide any blemishes in persons or culture. Although Herodotus was the first great European historian, Moses stands alone in the annals of world history for his meekness and honest reporting of a nation's response to their God.

In geography, history, and flowing literature, Moses is obviously an inspired author. Cicero labled Herodotus the "father of history". Jews, Christians, and Muslims recognize Moses as the man who spoke with the real Father of history, the Alpha and Omega.

Herodotus' main sources were 'what he has been told' and 'what he has seen'. This was probably the best he could do and it must have been hard to ascertain facts about a war that had acquired mythical dimensions in his own lifetime, and few of whose participants were still alive for comment. He had few, if any, written documents to rely on - he queried priests, leading citizens, interpreters, eyewitnesses, 'men with traditions' - often fragmentary and unreliable. He also did land surveys and inspected battle sites.

Unlike Thucydides, Herodotus focused primarily on the non-Greek world. We know little about his private life and in *Histories* he offers practically no biographical information. On his travels, he covered a large part of the Persian Empire: he went to Egypt, at least as far south as Aswan, and he also visited Libya, Syria, Babylonia, Susa in Elam, Lydia, and Phrygia. He journeyed up the Hellespont to Byzantium, went to Thrace and Macedonia, and traveled northward to beyond the Danube and to Scythia eastward along the northern shores of the Black Sea as far as the Don River and some way inland. These travels would have taken many years (some estimate twelve) and contributed to the almost encyclopedic scope of the *Histories,* and its aura of comparative anthropology.

About his method he says, 'For myself, my duty is to report all that is said; but I am not obliged to believe it all alike - a remark which may be understood to apply to my whole History.' For conflicting accounts, he often records more than one, sometimes adding, 'so have I heard but I cannot be certain,' or if the account seems incredulous, 'my own opinion in the matter is .'

Even when he records much that makes his work drift away from history, he still provides us valuable insights - as long as he believes in the truth of the stories he relates, and there's little doubt he was sincere and honest. In his own lifetime, his enthusiastic openness and tolerance for other cultures won him a derisive label - Barbarophile - reinforced centuries later by another famous Greek: Plutarch.

Herodotus neither questioned the mythical origins of the Greeks nor dwelled upon them much. During his travels, he merely tried to reconcile the regional discrepancies and contradictions in a few famous myths. For the distant past, he therefore rationalized the mythical lore - surely not a history in our sense - but for his own times he conducted a wholly rational investigation, surely a history.

His religious inclinations are best indicated by the ambivalence of the passage below - while distrustful of active divine causation for everyday events, he nevertheless was a pious man and believed that divine retribution could strike those who soared too high, were arrogant, or committed egregious moral acts.

Only in Athens could Herodotus have found the right climate and support for his enterprise. Pericles was the son of

Xanthippus, the general who defeated the Persians at Mycale. Herodotus realized the momentous significance of the Persian wars and seized his opportunity. Subconsciously adopting and echoing the Athenian mindset, he glorifies their contribution, perhaps more so being an immigrant - we know that he gave public readings from *Histories*.

This may be an inescapable side-effect of identity but one that must accompany any reading of his work - in response to his admiration of the Athenian present came the urge to glorify its past. It's unfortunate that we have no other non-Athenian account of the war. In fact, resentment from other city-states, which felt under-recognized or vexed by the lavish glory he heaped upon Athens at the expense of Sparta, led him to be branded *father of lies*. It is a history eminently suitable for the purposes of an empire.

He contrasts the Greek and the Persian character with this story: During Xerxes' early days in Greece when the Olympics were on, certain Greek deserters were brought before him and Mardonius. They were asked, 'And what is the prize for which they contend?' The reply: 'An olive wreath, sire, given to the man who wins.' Hearing this, Herodotus writes, a senior aide of Xerxes 'uttered a speech which was in truth most noble [if not of the best timing] - Good heavens! Mardonius, what manner of men are these against whom you have brought us to fight - men who contend with one another, not for money, but for honor!'

Herodotus' Persians are the royalty and the aristocrats. His account projects a one-sided image of fawning courtiers, concentrated riches, minimal social mobility, and the most enlightened deeds coexisting with whimsical cruelty on the part of despots. This wasn't unusual in the extended Greek world either - there were storybook despots in Greek settlements, as in Sicily.

He undervalues a host of Persian achievements and their common humanity with the Athenians. However, writing for the Athenians to whom his emotional loyalty is axiomatic, Herodotus' gaze is on the 'barbarians' and while he carefully avoids passing judgment on cultural peculiarities that have few obvious moral disadvantages, in his choice and selection of material he could well qualify as the first Orientalist According to the modern classicist, Sir Moses Finley, 'His great discovery was that one could uncover moral problems and moral truths in history, in the concrete data of experience, in a discourse that was neither freely imaginative like that of the poets nor abstract like that of the philosophers.

That is what history meant to Herodotus; nothing could be more wrong headed than the persistent and seemingly indestructible leg-end of Herodotus the charmingly naïve storyteller.

Indeed a modern critique of Herodotus is that we often don't know whether to trust him. He retains a penchant for spicy, humorous, near-Homeric digressions, which, endearing and romantic as they often are, are hard to verify. They do, however, reveal his significant curiosity, tolerance, and compassion.

Perhaps those were his chief guiding principles, with little consciousness of the historical process as we articulate it today. On his solitary travels, he must have pondered the character of many cities and people, and felt intense moments of wonder and solitude.

We may never know, given his rising awareness of cause and effect, whether he ended up with a sinking feeling on the prospects of humanity, or, if he felt drawn to action alongside observation. He died a recluse, some believe in Italy. At one point in his narrative he soberly observes,

BOOKS BY HERODOTUS

Book 1

· Lydia, Medes, Persia, Cyrus

Mythical Origins of Conflict between Greeks and Asiatic peoples:

- Phoenicians abduct Io (Isis) daughter of king of Argos to Egypt (or did she go willingly?).
- Abduction of Tyre (in Phoenicia) king's daughter Europa by Greeks (Cretans).

- Abduction of Colchis king's daughter Medea by Greeks (Jason).
- Abduction of Helen of Lacedaemonia by Alexander (Paris) of Troy and subsequent destruction of Troy [34].

Croesus Of Lydia (560-546):

- First to subdue and enslave Ionians, Aeolians, and Dorians in Asia Minor. Ruled at peak of Lydian empire from Sardis.
- Predecessor Candaules displays his wife to Gyges, who kills Candaules at her insistence.
- Delphic Pythia foretells vengeance in the 5th generation of Gyges descendants [38].
- Tale of Arion saved by the dolphin [42].
- Visit of Solon of Athens: Tales of the men "most blessed of all" [45] "So, Croesus, man is entirely what befalls him... To me it is clear that you are very rich ..., but I cannot say of you of yet until I hear that you have brought your life to an end well."[47] Croesus sends him away.
- Croesus' son Atys killed by Adrastus accidentally in boar hunt, after Atys insists in going along. [51]
- Croesus seeks oracle whether of invade Persia- Delphi replies that "if he made war on the Persians he would destroy a mighty empire" [55] and that "whenever a mule [Cyrus] become sovereign king of the Medians" he should flee.
- Croesus inquires of status of Greek cultures to win friendship with- digression on Athenian Pisistratus [57-61] & Lacedaemonians/Spartans [61-5].
- Croesus ignores warning [65].
- Cr invades Syrian Cappadocia & is captured by Cyrus {546} [66-69].
- Tale of Scythians feeding Cyaxeres boy's meat and fleeing to Lydia [67].
- Sardis captured [72], Croesus' dumb son speaks out to save his father [73].
- Cyrus spares Croesus life when he calls out "Solon" on the burning pyre and tells his story [73].

- Croesus counsels Cyrus.
- The Pythia clarifies the oracles [76-7]
- Lydian customs and "facts".

Assyrian/Median/Persian History:

- Assyrians ruled 1229-709.
- Medes revolt & is united by Deioces ruling from Ecbatana (modern Iran) {704-647}.
- Phraortes {647-625}.
- Cyaxeres {625-585} (Scythians rule for 28 years {634-606}).
- Astyages (Median, rules {585-529}) fears a dream and marries his daughter to a Persian, Cambyses. Astyages orders her son (Cyrus) to be slain by Harpagus, but he turns Cyrus over to a shepherd.
- Young Cyrus acts like a king, is brought to Astyages. Harpagus is fed his son when Astyages learns of the deception.[88]
- Harpagus incites Cyrus to revolt against Media {559}
- Persian customs.

Persian Empire Expansions:

- Cyrus threatens the 12 Ionian cities of Panionium, first attacking Phocaea (attack led by Harpagus)- they flee to Corsica.[107]. Ionia enslaved by 545.[110]
- Carians, Caunians, Lycians.
- Cyrus attacks Assyria including Babylon (established 612 after fall of Nineveh, captured 538).
- Babylonian rulers: Semiramis, Nitocris.
- Babylonian customs- compulsory sex at the temple of Aphrodite.
- Cyrus attacks the Massagetae (on the Asian steppes W of the Caspian); their customs (get drunk on fruit). Queen Tomyris warns Cyrus as does Croesus, but he ignores them and is slain (529).

Book 2

Egyptian And African History, Customs, Geography:

- Cambyses, son of Cyrus, assumes rule in Persia. Attacks Egypt

- Egyptian religious beliefs [132].
- The Nile delta is the gift of the Nile- silting over geologic time periods [135].
- Why does the Nile flood? [139]
- Source of the Nile = "Libya" [141].
- Unusual African customs [145].
- Gods- Isis [148], phallic procession, Greek gods came from the Egyptians [153] and some rituals from the Pelasgians. Homer and Hesiod 400 yrs earlier [155].
- Skepticism of magic.
- Festivals of Bubastis, Ares, Busiris [158].
- Animals [160]- hippos, crocs, Phoenix, winged serpents [163].
- Astrology, funeral customs [165].
- Ancient history [171].
- Circumcision came from Egypt.[173]
- Helen in Egypt acc. to the Egyptians with Proteus-tale rejected by Homer [178].
- The thief steals from King Rhampsinitus [181] and is trapped, his body is rescued by his brother, is married to the kings daughter.
- Immortality of the soul through a 3000 yr cycle [185]
- Pyramids of Cheops [186].
- Mycinergus' incest with his daughter.
- Invasion by Ethiopia
- Sennacherib of Assyria defeated by mice [193].
- Psammetichus {663}, Necos {609} (tries to build canal to Red Sea), Psammis, Apries.
- Amasis {569} loved the Greeks and granted the town Naucratis.

Book 3

Cambyses Conquers Egypt; Cambyses' Death; Smerdis; Darius; 20 Persian Satrapies:

- Cambyses conquers Egypt and Amasis' son Psammenitus, ostensibly because Amasis sent him a spurious daughter for marriage. {525}
- The captured King Psammenitus shows pity on a beggar [216].

- Cambyses failed expedition against Ethiopia [219].
- Cambyses goes mad, kills his brother Smerdis and his sister-wife, has epilepsy, slays Prexaspes' son, tries to kill Croesus, opens tombs.
- Greek vs. Indian funeral custom- burying vs eating the dead. [228]
- Polycrates of Samos, allied with Amasis of Egypt, is attacked by Lacedaemonians, invites alliance with Cambyses. Polycratres sends untrusted exiles to Egypt ostensibly to help Cambyses. They instead escape to Lacedaemonia & plead for help to the taciturn Spartans.
- Sparta sends expedition against Samos (first Laced. exped. to Asia). Corinthians join because of grudge over Samian rescue of Corcyrean boys being sent to Persia for castration by Periander of Corinth (Corinth had colonized Corcyra) [233].
- Periander's despotism, kills wife, exiles his son Lycophron, who is later killed by Corcyreans.
- Magis plot against Cambyses with a false Smerdis.
- Cambyses wounds himself and dies; "Smerdis" succeeds but later is discovered because he has no ears.
- Prexaspes reveals the deception and kills himself.
- Darius slays the magis and Smerdis.
- Debate over whether to have a democracy or a tyranny [247]. Darius is elected king by his horse! {521} [251]
- 20 Persian satrapies summary- Indians eat their dead, ants as big as foxes, ...
- Oroetes of Sardis (a Persian) kills Polycrates [264] and is later killed on the order of Darius.
- Greek doctor Democedes heals Darius' twisted ankle
- Atossa, Darius' wife, urges him to attack Greece. He sends a spy mission to Greece- Democedes escapes.
- Darius orders attack against Samos. Otanes slaughters citizens after Charilaus fights back.

Maeandrius of Samos appeals to Sparta for help to no avail.

- Babylon revolts and is recaptured by Darius thanks to Zopyrus' heroism and self-sacrifice by self-mutilation.

Book 4

Europeans; Darius Fails To Conquer Scythia;

Greek Colonies In Libya (Cyrene, Barca); Persia Invades Libya:

- Scythia, nomadic, dependence on horses, mythical origins (Heracles and the half-woman half-snake have son Scythes), conflicts with Cimmereians and Massagetae. Other peoples: Issedones, Hyperboreans [290], goat-footed men, harsh winters, snow [290],
- Herodotus' world view, Phoenicians circumnavigate Africa [296], the Ister (Danube) [298],
- Scythian customs [302]- human sacrifice, scalping, blood oaths, funeral of the kings, cannabis, fear of Greek culture.
- Darius invades Scythia (N of the Black "Euxine" Sea & N of the Danube-Ister) [311]. Bridging the Bosporus with boats (Euxine Sea> Bosporos> Propontis> Hellespont). The Taurians [318], Neuri werewolves, Man-Eaters [319], Amazons [321], warrior women Sauromatians. Scythians stay ahead of Darius [325] and taunt him [327]. Darius sneaks back to the Ister. Histaeus prevents the Ionian guards from breaking up the bridge over the Ister (urged by the Scythians) and Darius escapes [311].
- Libyan colonial history [332]. Theras of Lacedaemonia colonizes Thera (in Cyclades); Battus of Thera colonizes Libyan coast 7th century - Cyrene.
- Conflict between Cyrene and Libyans, Arcesilaus killed [343], his mother Pheretime appeals to Persian viceroy of Egypt Aryandes for help.
- Sexual promiscuity of Libyans [344], Lotophagi [346]

- Inland Libyans: Ammonians, ..., Atlantes (near Mt Atlas); nomadic customs [350].
- Aryandes sends an expedition to conquer Libya [354], besieges Barca. Pheretimes commits atrocities and meets a bad end.

Book 5

Persia Conquers Thrace, Paeonians;
Ionian Revolt Under Aristagoras Of Miletus;
Former Athens-Sparta Conflicts;
Athenian Tyrants & Democracy;
Conflict Between Athens And Darius Begins:

- Megabazus lead invasion of Thrace [357], the "biggest nation of all"
- Thracian customs- sacrifice of favourite wives.
- Paeonians are enslaved and transported to Asia [361]
- Persians envoys are slain in the court of the Macedonian king Amyntas [364].
- Greek origins of the Macedonians [364].
- Darius moves to Susa.
- Otanes succeeds Megabazus as general and captures Byzantium, Lemnos, etc.
- Ionian revolt: Begins in Naxos and Miletus: Aristagoras asks Artaphrenes of Persia to invade Naxos, led by Megabates. Megabates warns the Naxians. Aristagoras plans to revolt from the Persians, encouraged by a secret messenger from Histaeus of Miletus [371]. Arist. Heads to Sparta for help from Cleomenes.
- Sparta history.
- Sparta refuses to help Aristagoras invade Persia [375].
- The road to Susa [376].
- Aristagoras appeals to Athens [378]. History of Athens Pisitratids.
- Origin of the Greek alphabet from Phoenicians [379].
- Past attacks of Sparta on Athens X4 [381-7], Athens attack on Boeotia and Chalcis.
- Athens value democracy [389].

- Origins of Enmity of Aegina and Athens [390].
- Corinth- Periander [397] {625}, the corruption of absolute power.
- Sparta tries to weakens Athens by forcing the return of the Pisistratid Hippias to power in Athens through Artaphrenes' intervention, but Athens refused and became enemies of Persia.
- Aristagoras appeals to Athens and wins their support to send ships fight the Persians. Aristagoras attacks and burns Sardis.
- The Ionians are defeated and Athens gives up supporting them. [402]. Cyprus revolts, defeated {497}
- Darius vows revenge on Athens.
- Aristagoras dies in Thrace.

Book 6

Miletus Conquered & Ionian Revolt Quelled;
Thrace, Athos, Macedonia Fall;
Rivalry Between Spartan Clemenes & Demaratus;
Athens-Aegina Conflict;
Athens & Plataeans Defeat Persia At Marathon Under Miltiades:

- Histiaeus flees from Darius to Chios.
- Persians attack Miletus. Problems of democracy and amateur fighters vs. Persian Military discipline [413]. Samos falls to Persia. Miletus falls {494}, women and children enslaved and taken to Susa. Ionians for the 3rd time are enslaved.
- Histaeus captured by Harpagus and killed [420].
- Miltiades, son of Cimon, rules the Chersonese.
- Mardonius launches land force {492}, enslaves Macedonia, shipwrecks at Athos, returns ingloriously.
- Darius demands submission from Greeks- Aegina submits (gave earth and water).
- Digression on Spartan kings' rights [428], Spartan descent from Egypt ?, Spartan culture.
- Rivalry of Demaratus and Cleomenes, kings of Sparta

[432]. Demaratus flees to Persia [426] and Leotychides succeeds him. Cleomenes' madness [438].

- Athens-Aegina conflict {490-480}, war {488-6}.
- Darius sends 600 warships under Datis and Artaphrenes son of Artaphrenes against Athens and Eretria, enslave Naxos, Delos, Eretria (on Euboea) [449].
- Battle at Marathon: Persians are guided by Hippias, son of Pistratus, to Attica, landing at Marathon. Athenians are led by Miltiades son of Cimon and 11 other generals. Athens appeals to Sparta [450], but they are preoccupied with a festival. Plataeans come to Athens aid. Miltiades persuades the other generals to fight. The Greeks charge the Persians at a run and win the victory {490}. Spartans arrive too late to help.
- Lineage of the Alcmaeonidae [458]- Cleisthenes of Sicyon, Alcmaeon, Megacles, Cleisthenes, Pericles etc.
- Miltiades' futile attack on Paros, later dies.

Book 7

Darius Dies—Xerxes King;
Invasion Of Thrace, Thessalia;
Athens And Sparta Unite;
Shipwrecks Of Persians;
Leonidas' Defeat At Thermopylae:

- Darius is enraged at Athenian victory and vows to march on Greece.
- Demaratus (from Sparta) promotes Xerxes to succeed his father Darius on Darius' death {485} Mardonius also promotes war on Greece.
- Egyptian revolt quelled.
- Xerxes vows to conquer Greece. Artabanus counsels against this [471] - "for the god loves to thwart whatever is greater than the rest... there is good in hesitation...." Xerxes angrily denounces this advice.
- A vision call Xerxes to war [474] and also comes to Artabanus.
- Campaign to Greece begun {480}. Out of arrogance,

X. orders digging of a channel separating Mt. Athos from the mainland [478]. March to Sardis. Sends heralds to Greece demanding earth and water. Bridging the Hellespont at Abydos [482] ends in destruction. Xerxes punishes the waters with lashes and fetters and beheads the supervisors! Pythius the Lydian asks to have his son left behind, and X orders he be cut in half. X comes to tears as he meditates on the shortness of life while viewing his great army and ships. [486] Artabanus voice of caution, warning of the Ionians lack of loyalty. X prefers to take risks.

- Hellespont crossed [p. 489] {490}
- The army [492], the navy [498] includes Artemisia - 5,000,000 men in all [503].
- Thessaly [510], Thebans, Melians pledge loyalty to the Persians ("Medize").
- Spartans prefer freedom to slavery [513] but Herodotus ascribes the saving of Greece to the Athenians [514].
- Oracle says a wall of wood and Salamis will save Athens- Themistocles orders ship building.
- Greeks peoples unite (mostly) [518] (Argos sides with Persia; Gelon of Syracuse (Sicily) refuses to help unless he can lead, which offends the Spartans, leading to his final refusal; Corcyra dissembles [528], Crete refuses).
- Greeks decide to fight (against overwhelming odds) at the narrow pass of Thermopylae.
- Storm wrecks 400 Persian ships on coast of Magnesia [537].
- Battle of Thermopylae {480} c. 6000 Greeks (no Athenians) commanded by Leonidas, King of Sparta. Xerxes' spies are amazed that the Greeks are making their heads beautiful in preparation for war. Hydarnes leads forces around the mountains to encircle the Greeks. Free Greeks fight slaves [550]. Leonidas dies. Aristodemus of Sparta survives but is scorned at home.

Book 8

Battle At Artemesium;
Attacks On Phocis, Boeotia, Delphi, Plataea, Athens;
Victory At Salamis:

- More Persian shipwrecks off Euboea. Sea fights near Artemisium (concurrent with Thermopylae) {480}.
- Themistocles appeals to the Ionians and Carians fighting for Persians [564].
- Persians pillage Phocis, Boeotia Medizes [568]. Attack on Delphi [569]. Greeks flee Athens and navy gathers at Salamis. Thespiae and Plataea burned, Athens captured [573], Acroplis burned [574].
- Themistocles advocates battle at Salamis rather than Isthmus of Corinth.
- Artemisia tries to stop Mardonius from wasting his ships in battle.
- Peoples of the Peloponnese [581].
- Battle of Salamis: Greeks debate their desperate situation [582], surrounded by the enemy at Salamis. {490}. Battle of Salamis. Artemisia rams her own allies but Xerxes thinks she has rammed an enemy. Xerxes fears for his safe return [591], sends ships to guard the bridge at the Hellespont. Greeks decide not to follow in pursuit.
- Xerxes retreats with his army, leaving Mardonius to winter in Thessaly and his ships to overwinter in Cyme and Samos.
- Mardonius tries to persuade the Athenians to Medize.

Book 9

Greek Victories At Plataea (Mardonius Killed); Greeks Attack Thebes; Victory At Mycale, Siege Of Sestos:

- Mardonius reinvades Boeotia {479}, retakes Athens and burns it. Sparta delays in helping but finally sends troops under Pausanias.
- Battle at Plataea {479} 110,000 Greeks against 700,000 barbarians + 50,000 allies. Greeks squabble. Mardonius' hubris. [638] Mardonius killed. Artabazus

flees. Persians retreat to their fort and are massacred. Pausanius refuses to desecrate the body of Mardonius. The booty is divided, including concubines.

- Greeks attack Thebes because they had supported Persia.
- Battle of Mycale won by the Greeks.
- Xerxes wife Amestris' atrocities against Masistes' wife whom Xerxes had fallen in love with).
- Athenians besiege Sestos.
- Athenians return home.
- Recollection of warning from Cyrus not to overexpand the empire when advised to move his people from their rocky lands- "from soft lands come soft men"

THUCYDIDES

INTRODUCTION

Thucydides, the Ancient Greek historian of the fifth century B.C., is not only the father of scientific history, but also of political "realism," the school of thought which posits that interstate relations are based on might rather than right. Through his study of the Peloponnesian War, a destructive war which began in 431 B.C. among Greek city-states, Thucydides observed that the strategic interaction of states followed a discernible and recurrent pattern. According to him, within a given system of states, a certain hierarchy among the states determined the pattern of their relations. Therefore, he claimed that while a change in the hierarchy of weaker states did not ultimatley affect a given system, a disturbance in the order of stronger states would decisively upset the stability of the system. As Thucydides said, the Peloponnesian War was the result of a systematic change, brought about by the increasing power of the Athenian city-state, which tried to exceed the power of the city-state of Sparta. "What made the war inevitable was the growth of Athenian power and the fear which this caused Sparta," Thucydides wrote in order to illustrate the resulting systematic change; that is, "a change in the hierarchy or control of the international political system."

Thucydides' realism has had a timeless impact on the way contemporary analysts perceive international relations. Adding to the works of Gilpin and Waltz, Leo Strauss of the University of Chicago viewed The Peloponnesian War as containing propositions that could be brought into a coherent framework and identified as "Thucydides' political philosophy" or serve even as the basis for a series of laws about the science of modern politics. In fact, political scientists have treated the work of Thucydides as a coherent attempt to communicate silent universals that have served as the basis for American foreign policy and security doctrine in the post World War II era.

Thus, on one hand, Thucydides was the first to describe international relations as anarchic and immoral. The "Melian dialogue" best exemplifies Thucydides' view that interstate politics lack regulation and justice. In the "Melian dialogue," he wrote that, in interstate relations, "the strong do what they have the power to do and the weak accept what they have to accept." For him, international relations allow the mighty do as they please and forfce the weak to suffer as they must. On the other hand, Thucydides illustrated the Cold War phenomenon of "polarization" among states, resulting from their strategic interaction.

The impact of Thucydides' work upon scholars of the Cold War period consists evidence for the relevance of his realist theory in today's world. In fact, while his Peloponnesian War is chronologically distant from the present, Thucydides' influence upon realist scholars in the post-1945 period, and in turn upon American diplomacy, is direct. Specifically, the foundations of American diplomacy during the Cold War with regard to the struggle between the two superpowers and the ethical consequences or problems posed for smaller states caught in the vortex of bipolar competition are derived from his work.

Writings of the early Cold War years often derive their inspiration from Thucydides' work. This period has spawned a significant body of theoretical literature which finds in the Athenian-Spartan rivalry a precedent to the Soviet-American bipolar competition. Structural realists such as Kenneth Waltz and Robert Gilpin found that the Hellenic world, and particularly the relationship between Athens and Sparta, as Thucydides describes it, provided an allegory for the Cold War polarization.

In 1947, Secretary of State George Marshall had called attention to the significance of the Peloponnesian War for an understanding of the contemporary world. "I doubt seriously whether a man can think with full wisdom and with deep convictions regarding certain of the basic issues today who has not at least reviewed in his mind the period of the Peloponnesian War and the fall of Athens," he said.

Moreover, during the polarization of the Cold War period, policy-makers equated America's power to Ancient Athens' glory, as told in The Peloponnesian War. Thus, in 1952, Louis J. Halle, at the time Director of the State Department's Policy Planning Staff, wrote that "the present, in which our country finds herself, like Athens after the Peloponnesian wars, called upon to assume the leadership of the free world brings him [Thucydides] virtually to our side... It seems to me that since World War II Thucydides has come still closer to us so that now he speaks to our ear."

Throughout the Cold War, scholarly work focused on the conclusions which Thucydides drew from his study of power and competition in bipolar systems. The contemporary interpretation of the Peloponnesian War paraphrases what realists have come to term the "security dilemma": as the power of a subordinate state in a relatively stable international system increases disproportionately, it is brought into conflict with the dominant state(s). The struggle between these contenders for preeminence and their accumulating alliances lead to a bipolarization of the international system. In the language of game theorists, a zero-sum situation results, in which one state's gain is the other state's loss. As bipolarization proceeds, the system becomes increasingly unstable, and so does the likelihood of system-changing conflict.

Indeed, the study of polarity in the Hellenic world in the period between the Persian and Peloponnesian wars has influenced the work of realist authors such as Robert Gilpin, Kenneth Waltz, Joseph Nye, and John Mearsheimer. In turn, this scholarship has influenced American diplomacy as reflected in the work of Louis Halle in the 1950s, and Henry Kissinger, not only in the doctoral thesis, but in his tenure as Secretary of State in the 1970s. Specifically, reference of the parallel bipolarity of th Peloponnesian and Cold wars influenced the manner in which the U.S. saw the superpower world, and the manner in which it treated political developments and cultures in non-western regions.

As a result of his study of the Peloponnesian War, Thucydides drew a fundamental distinction between the mode of politics within a certain state and the pattern of political interaction among several states. This distinction that is still the subject of intense debate in foreign policy circles. Within a state, citizens enter a community based on a form of social contract, which provides the protection of laws at the expense of some individual freedom. As a result of the legal equality with which the social contract provides the citizens, the weak are able to withstand the strong and ethical considerations are respected. In the international realm, however, there is no social contract among citizens of different states, and, consequenlty, there are no laws to defend legality and morality of state interactions.

Thus, in interstate relations, it is the strong who decide how the weak should be treated, as moral or ethical judgments are virtually nonexistent. This distinction between the ethics of domestic and international relations are implicit in the "Melian dialogue." Here, Thucydides had Demosthenes, the Athenian orator, specifically contrast the affairs of a city-state, where laws (nomoi) and customs exist to treat weak and powerful equally, with international disputes (en tois Hellenikois dikaiois), where the strong coerce the weak.

Demosthenes is not the only one, however, to identify the place of justice and ethics in domestic relations and their absence in interstate relations. In his Politics, Aristotle accused individuals for having double standards. While they might restrain from behaving in an unacceptable way with regard to their fellow citizens, in the case of outsiders it is a different case entirely. He wrote, "most people seem to think sheer domination is what is appropriate in the political sphere; and they are not ashamed to practice in regard to outsiders what they recognize is neither just nor expedient in their dealings with each other as individuals. For their own affairs, among themselves, they demand an authority based on justice: but in regard to outsiders justice is no concern of theirs."

Moreover, later writers have endorsed Thucydides' argument that "might makes right." Later realists, such as Machiavelli and Hobbes, agree with Thucydides that "might makes right" is an intoxicating precept for states to indulge in. Also, like Thucydides, these later realists suggest that, although Ethics has its own proper sphere within the community of a certain state, the attempt to regulate interstate relations according to similar precepts contains the risk of justifying cases of intervention in a sovereign state. To paraphrase the contemporary theorist Hans Morghenthau, the mixture or morality and foreign policy is a very dangerous one. Indeed, in the early days of the Cold War, Morgenthau disapproved of the U.S. policy to view any region or political development, no matter how far-flung or inconsequential, as a linchpin of the contested balance of power.

Throughout the Cold War period, as a result of America's zero-sum competition with the Soviet Union for the worldwide balance of power, the US justified intervention in regions such as Latin America, the Middle East, Africa, Asia, and the Mediterranean, with the objective of denying communist influence.

The critical importance of interventions for American interests overrode any sense of "immorality" that American support for anti-communist and often brutally undemocratic regimes may have caused. In short, concern for the customs and privileges of civil society in the United States was often not extended to cultures and countries whose political allegiance risked to upset the Cold War bipolar balance. One need only refer to American (mis)adventures in Iran, Greece, Egypt, El Salvador, Guatemala, and Nicaragua, to name a few.

Thucydides may have been the father of a cruel realist view of international reations, but this does not mean that Thucydides himself endorsed the immorality of the international realm. Rather, if one accepts the distinction between internal and external affairs in The Peloponnesian War, it becomes clear that, when Thucydides deals with the relations of individuals within the state, he is indeed ready to make moral judgements. In his reproduction of Pericles' funeral oration, the historian does not hesitate to comment on the tragedy of the plague that befalls Athens.

Furthermore, in the debate prior to the Sicillian expedition, Thucydides did not hesitate to compliment Nicias for his sense of morality, by saying that "[Nicias] had ordered his whole life by high moral standards." Of Nicias's cruel and unjust opponent Alcibiades, he wrote, "his way of life made him objectionable to everyone as a person, and thus [the Athenian people] entrusted their affairs to other hands." Finally, of the oligarchic coup that swept Athens after the exiled Alcibiades collaborated with the Persians and Spartans to dissolve democracy, Thucydides stated that democracy had been, in his experience, the best government Athens had had; its composition, of the few as well as the many, had been truly representative.

There have been, however, some misleading misinterpretations of Thucydides. For instance, Thomas Hobbes, great admirer of Thucydides, grieviously misinterpreted the historian when it suited his political interests to do so. He wrote, in fact, that the ancient historian "least of all liked democracy" and "best approved of regal government." Moreover, some classical scholars are uneasy with the conclusions that have been drawn by contemporary international relations theorists from the fifth century B.C. and the Peloponnesian War in the stark hues of the Cold War. "We have been presented lately with an up-dated version of the Thucydidean thesis that the war was the inevitable outcome of the division of the Greek world into two power blocs. In its new guise, the Thucydidean view is fortified with the weapons of modern social science. The condition that troubled the Greek world and brought on the war is discovered to the 'bipolarity.' Typically, such words are borrowed from the physical sciences to lend an air of novelty, clarity, and authority to a shopworn, vague, or erroneous idea."

Actually, while the use of Thucydidean scholarship in international relations theory is useful and accepted in the political science community, the lack of ease with which classical scholars consider such a relationship justifies the examination of realist Balance of Power precepts as derived from Thucydides. The significance of such an examination is found in the parallels that have been made between the Peloponnesian War and the Cold War, and the practical consequences of such scholarship on American diplomacy in the Cold War era with regard to the relationship between the superpower balance and regional politics in regions of contested influence.

Finally, the end of the Cold War requires a re-examination of Thucydidean scholarship and the theories of interstate behaviour which are derived from his work. Furthermore, if there is to be a new world order, the United States must recognize that the dynamics of interstate relations are constantly fluctuating. While there may be certain constants in the behaviour of states and individuals, the possibilities for interaction, cooperation, and conflict are always constant, and often present themselves in new and previously unknown forms. In this case, the study of history is only a guide, not a prescription. If the work of Thucydides is considered in these terms, it will truly be considered a possession for all time, just as the author had intended.

HISTORY

Thucydides' response to his literary predecessors has been explored with some frequency in recent years. Several articles have appeared even since Simon Hornblower recently wrote that 'two areas needing more work are Thucydides' detailed intertextual relation to Homer and to Herodotus'. In these discussions, Thucydides tends to be seen as inheriting a wide range of specific narrative techniques from Homer, and as alluding to particular passages in epic through the use of epic terms and through the broader structuring of his story. It has also been stressed that Thucydides' relationship with Homer should be studied in the light of the pervasive Homeric charge found in the work of Herodotus, the greatest historian before Thucydides. Nor is Thucydides' debt to Herodotus merely a matter of his taking over Herodotus' Homeric features: it is seen, for instance, in his modelling of his Sicilian narrative after Herodotus' account of the Persian Wars, and in his assuming knowledge of events described by Herodotus.

Nonetheless, no apology is needed for making another contribution to this topic: by drawing together and examining some of the recent explorations of Thucydidean intertextuality, I hope to establish more firmly how Thucydides alluded to his predecessors; and by looking beyond the worlds of epic and Herodotus that have dominated recent discussions, I hope to present a more rounded image of the literary milieu of the early Greek historians.

The Sicilian narrative is the section of Thucydides' work on which I will focus. It is also the section that has, more than any other, been mined for intertextual allusion in recent years. This intensity of focus is a reflection of the particular richness of the Sicilian narrative as a whole. But after criticizing some of these recent treatments, will analyse in detail a passage that seems unique in the richness of its allusions to different genres: Thucydides' closing assessment of the importance of the Sicilian expedition. Scholars have seen allusions in this one paragraph not just to Homer and Herodotus, but also to tragedy and to epigrams commemorating the Persian Wars. I shall examine further possible links with epigrams, and suggest that Thucydides may have been alluding to Simonides' lost poem on the battle of Salamis.

Examining Thucydides' allusions to earlier writers raises several interesting questions. Firstly, one must ask about the point of alleged allusions. When Hornblower notes 'the density of Homeric echoes in the epic Sicilian, he is implying that the manner and frequency of Thucydides' allusions are conditioned by Thucydides' perception of his subject-matter. (Hornblower has also pointed out how Thucydides uses an unusual number of epic words in his description of Brasidas, the 'new Achilles'.) These echoes evidently strengthen the traditional view that Thucydides' account of the Sicilian expedition is marked out as epic by the breadth of his coverage and by his inclusion of such features as a catalogue of the opposing forces.

Other scholars have taken the further step of stressing the context of alleged allusions: Allison, for instance, suggests that Thucydides' use of a particular word may gain an ironic resonance from the use of that word in Homer. At a broader level, attempts to spot epic allusions in Thucydides raise questions about attitudes in fifth-century Athens to Homeric epic and to the 'mythical' past represented in Homeric epic, and about the status and self-definition of historiography at an early stage in its development.

I shall answer these various questions - or at least discuss the issues that they raise - by turning to explore some specific passages. I start with isolated allusions, move on to broader parallels of story-pattern, and finally return to the abundance of isolated allusions that can be detected at the very end of the Sicilian narrative.

'ADDRESSING HIM BY HIS FATHER'S NAME'

In his account of the preparations for the final sea battle at Syracuse, Thucydides describes how the Athenian general Nikias delivers a formal speech of encouragement to the army as a whole, and then continues to made personal appeals as the men board the ships: 'he called forward each one of the trierarchs once more, addressing him by his father's name, his own name, and his tribe' (*patrothen te eponomazon kai autous onomasti kai phulen*). Already the scholia on Thucydides alluded here where Agamemnon tells Menelaus to summon the leading Achaians to a council, 'addressing each man by his father's name and by his family' (*patrothen ek genees onomazon andra hekaston*). The allusion appears to be supported not just by the verbal closeness (*patrothen te eponomazon ~ patrothen . . . onomazon*), but also by the fact that the passages cited are the only occurrences of the adverb *patrothen* in both Homer and Thucydides.

What is the significance of the echo? Hornblower simply takes the passages as evidence for a shared genealogical interest in Homer and Thucydides (and fifth-century culture more broadly). Some scholars, however, stress Agamemnon's involvement in the Homeric passage. Zadorojnyi thinks that the echo is but one of a number of links between Nikias and Agamemnon (see further below), while Allison sees the identification of Nikias with Agamemnon - who 'despite his bumbling, eventually succeeded' - as 'ironic'.

But there is an important difference between the Homeric and Thucydidean passages which tells against this 'identification': Nikias is using patronymics himself, Agamemnon is merely instructing someone else to use patronymics (rather as Xenophon instructs his troops to call on each other by name, *onomasti*: *Anab.*). The 'identification' of the two men would be more convincing if Agamemnon were himself calling on his troops in the midst of battle. (One could press for an ironic identification of Nikias and Menelaus - but Homer does not describe Menelaus carrying out Agamemnon's instructions.)

Lateiner finds the fact that a Homeric echo is attached to Nikias more revealing than the context of the Homeric passage: 'the Homeric reminiscence underlines the obsolete quality of Nicias' efforts.' (Compare Connor's argument that an allusion to Aeschylus *Persae* 402-5 later in Nikias' speech 'emphasizes how old-fashioned Nicias' approach is'.) It is true that Thucydides does say that Nikias' appeals showed that he was not 'guarding against appearing to speak in platitudes [*archaiologein* - lit. 'to speak in an old-fashioned way']'. But this refers to the content of Nikias' appeals rather than to the way he addresses the trierarchs. To take the Homeric echo as an indication that Nikias' rhetoric was obsolete is to underestimate the continued cultural significance of the Homeric poems in the fifth century: is Melesippos to be branded anachronistic for his remark that 'this day will be the beginning of great misfortunes for the Hellenes' an echo of two Iliadic passages?

To brand Nikias as anachronistic, it would be better to cite: Kleisthenes 'made the men living in each deme fellow-demesmen of one another, so that they should not use their fathers' names (*patrothen*) and make it obvious who were the new citizens but should be named after their demes: this is why the Athenians still call themselves after their demes'. There are, however, good reasons to doubt the historicity of this alleged attempt to stamp down on patronymics - not least the abundant evidence for their continued use. Thucydides himself often names people *patrothen*, and never by their demotic.

The suggestion of an anachronistic Nikias is further undermined by the fact that he addresses the trierarchs not just by patronymic (as Agamemnon tells Menelaus to do), but also by tribe. This is one of the few references in Thucydides to the ten tribes established at Athens by Kleisthenes, the basis of military organization at Athens.

Zadorojnyi, however, does find a Homeric archetype for Nikias' appeal: Nestor's advice to Agamemnon to 'divide your men by tribes and by clans, so that clan can support clan and tribe help tribe' (note *kata phula* and *phula de phulois*).But 'tribes are wholly foreign to the [Homeric] poems. *phule,* the standard word for tribes as subdivisions of the Greek states, is not used at all, and Homer's *phulon* is either wider . . . or more particular'; *Il.* 2. 362-3 is in fact 'the only passage in Homer where *phulon* must have a sense something like that of the classical *phule*', and there is no Homeric parallel at all for naming by tribe. Nikias' appeal is not a loaded Homeric allusion, but telling evidence of the emotional pull of the Kleisthenic tribes less than a century after their institution. It is significant that Thucydides alludes to the tribes elsewhere in his description of the annual public burial of the Athenian war-dead and that the tribes help to bring out 'the democratic or "isonomic" ("equally-sharing") character of the institution'.

Nikias' appeal to the trierarchs differs in two important

respects, then, from the Homeric passage alleged as a parallel: he is making an actual appeal, not enjoining someone else to make an appeal, and he appeals to people by the name of their tribe as well as by their own and their father's name. These differences were suggested against efforts to identify Nikias with Agamemnon or to depict his appeal as old-fashioned. We should rather see the Homeric reminiscence - like the unique appeal to tribe names - as underlining the seriousness and increasing the emotional impact of Nikias' appeals.

It is worth asking whether Thucydides' epic use of *patrothen* is found in Herodotus too: if so, this would make readings which stress the particular context in Homer even less attractive. Herodotus does use *patrothen* three times - and once in the very phrase *patrothen onomazon* (a nicely ironic use, because the patronymic is wrong: Amasis has deceived Kambyses by sending as his future bride not his own daughter, but the daughter of the previous king of Egypt). Perhaps Thucydides' phrase is simply an epic usage mediated through Herodotus.

Herodotus' other two uses of the word *patrothen* cast doubt on the very idea that Thucydides' phrase is much of a Homeric reminiscence at all. The word is used of the naming of individuals in inscriptions (the monument in Samos devoted to the trierarchs who did not desert the Greek cause at the battle of Lade) or in other forms of writing (a list of the trierarchs in the Persian fleet who were seen by Xerxes performing courageously at Salamis note that the list combines the patronymic with mention of their cities - that is, the personal is not at the expense of the civic). The contexts in these two Herodotean passages are close to that in Thucydides - where it is also trierarchs who are being called by their fathers' names. This could be seen as another point of similarity between Thucydides' account of the final battle at Syracuse and Herodotus' account of Salamis.

But it is more plausible to see it simply as a sign of how commonplace the term is. Indeed, it is frequently found in inscriptions with the same verb, *anagraphein,* that is used in the two Herodotean passages, in instructions for names, *onomata*, to be written up *patrothen kai tou demou* or *kata demous* - 'by father's name and by deme'.

Thucydides' use of *patrothen* should not be isolated from the word's use in epigraphic and other day-to-day contexts. Allison, though perhaps right to call it a 'formal word', is surely wrong to suspect that it had 'an archaic ring when found in a literary context'. Indeed, the fact that the word only occurs once in Homer makes it a very weak epic usage. The Thucydidean scholiast doubtless did well to remember the one passage where it does occur - but this may tell us more about education and scholarship in the centuries after Thucydides than about Thucydides himself.

FALSE WITHDRAWALS: NIKIAS AND AGAMEMNON

Zadorojnyi bases his attempt to connect Homer's Agamemnon and Thucydides' Nikias not just on the slender allusion, but also on the way they respond to the troubles faced by the Achaian force at Troy and the Athenian force in Sicily. He suggests that the 'provocative strategy' of the letter which Nikias writes to the Athenians suggesting withdrawal from Sicily is based on that of the speech in which Agamemnon suggests withdrawal from Troy Nikias' strategy is 'provocative', he argues, because his letter is as much a feint as Agamemnon's speech (Agamemnon's aim was really to encourage the Greek force to stay at Troy): 'By playing up hardships it eventually prompts the Athenians to a positive decision that might change the campaign to the better That is what Nicias really wants, not permission to withdraw from Sicily. The irony is that Nicias pretends to be as clever as Agamemnon, while actually geminating his folly.

Zadorojnyi's bold analysis seems to come unstuck on some important points of difference between Agamemnon's speech and Nikias' letter. For one thing, the audiences are different: Agamemnon is addressing the suffering troops at Troy, Nikias the Athenians at home. More importantly, Nikias explicitly presents the Athenians with an alternative: 'it is necessary either to recall the troops in Sicily or to send over just as many to reinforce them'. If he is repeating Agamemnon's trick, at least he does not dissemble. Even more telling is the fact that Nikias has been presented as hostile to the expedition's aims: why should his proposal to withdraw not be sincere? It is only when the reinforcements have arrived that he changes his tune slightly (but note that even here he is also concerned about the practicalities of withdrawal). Zadorojnyi's reading of Nikias' motivation destroys a paradox: it is to some extent the mere fact that reinforcements have been sent that sways Nikias' view of the chances of success and increases the force of his appeal to the threat of punishment by the Athenians at home.

I prefer, then, to take the similarities Zadorojnyi detects as a sign of the realities of naval warfare and distant campaigns (ship-timber does get wet) and of Thucydides' depicting those realities in an 'epic' manner. It is, rather, Nikias' second speech in the assembly at Athens (6. 20-3) that offers a good parallel to Agamemnon's disingenuous rhetoric: just as Agamemnon tries to stiffen the Achaians' resolve to capture Troy by a meek suggestion that they withdraw, so too Nikias tries to deter the Athenians from attacking Sicily by suggesting that they increase the size of the force they are due to send.

It is not just the shared rhetoric of Nikias and Agamemnon, but also the frustrated prospect of an early withdrawal, that contributes to the epic resonance of Thucydides' Sicilian narrative. The motif of an early withdrawal is prominent elsewhere in epic notably when a despondent Agamemnon repeats his proposal to withdraw, now in earnest The obvious difference is that whereas the Achaians are saved from a dishonourable retreat, the Athenians are in fact magnifying their eventual disaster. But it is the similarity which underlies this difference that in both cases increases readers' emotional engagement with the story (an engagement magnified by our knowledge of the different endings): we are encouraged to imagine how close the Achaians came to throwing away all their toil at Troy and how easily the Athenians could have avoided disaster.

The occurrence of the motif of an early withdrawal in the

epic cycle may point to an enlightening parallel with another scene in Thucydides. Proclus' summary of the *Cypria* reports a scene in which 'Achilles restrains the Achaeans when they are eager to return home'. This may bring to mind Thucydides' description of what he calls the first good deed that Alkibiades did Athens: 'when the Athenians at Samos were eager to sail against their own people [i.e. against the oligarchs at Athens], in which case it is absolutely clear that the enemy would immediately have seized Ionia and the Hellespont, he prevented it.

And at that moment not one other man would have had the power to restrain the crowd' Unfortunately nothing is known of the context of Achilles' similar deed in the *Cypria.* Proclus does report it immediately after a scene in which Achilles met Helen in person, and some scholars have been tempted to see a connection between the two scenes. A selfish Achilles would seem to contrast with an Alkibiades who is performing his first good service for his country. But it might further hint at the underlying self-interestedness of Alkibiades' actions. It is rash, however, to infer a link with the Helen scene from Proclus' concise summary. But it is still tempting to see an allusion to Achilles' masterful leadership - an allusion that adds some nuance to Thucydides' presentation of Alkibiades' enigmatic and destructive brilliance.

One of the grounds for withdrawal suggested in Nikias' letter further hints at how the shaping of Thucydides' narrative is rooted in epic: the claim that the Athenians are now besieged rather than besiegers This reversal (which is also found in Thucydides is common in later historians. And it is evidently grounded in the conditions of ancient warfare - the difficulty of taking walled cities by siege and the difficulty of securing supplies. The theme goes back to the *Iliad*: with Achilles' withdrawal from the fighting, the Trojans' successes lead to their camping out in the plain and pressing to destroy the Greek ships with fire. The parallel is particularly close when Nestor addresses the Achaians in terms more appropriate to people whose land is being attacked than to invaders: 'Be men, my friends, and put pride in your heart for the regard of others.

And think, every one of you, of your children and your wives, your property and your parents'. So too Nikias appeals to the Athenian army in Sicily with the thought that they are fighting for their fatherland.

AN *ODYSSEY* IN REVERSE?

The third proposal I will discuss for a detailed intertextuality in Thucydides' Sicilian narrative is also based on similarities at the broader level of story-patterning. What is surprising is that correspondences are sought not with the *Iliad*, the poem of war, but with the *Odyssey*, the poem of the exotic and the domestic. Thucydides, Mackie has argued, uses an 'inverted Homeric pattern' in his construction of the Athenian expedition to Sicily: whereas Odysseus has his adventures with the Cyclops, the Laistrygonians, and Charybdis before he arrives at Scheria, the Athenians sail from Corcyra (which is associated with Scheria), cross the Strait of Messene (which is identified with Charybdis at 4. 24. 4), and arrive at Sicily (whose 'earliest inhabitants are said to have been the Cyclopes and Laistrygones').

Mackie takes this pattern as 'a self-conscious recognition that the Athenian débâcle has its mythical parallel in the adventures of Odysseus'; 'the Athenian confrontation with death takes on epic proportions, and they are shown to endure miseries and loss of life greater even than in myth' - with the difference that 'the Athenian suffering is tragically real'. Mackie further argues for cases of '*direct* intertextuality' later in the Sicilian narrative: he compares the harbour at Syracuse with the harbour of the Laistrygonians, its barrier with the rock in the Cyclops' cave, and the quarry at Syracuse with the Cyclops' cave itself.

Mackie's thesis is certainly ingenious; and he is surely right to stress that the explicit allusions to Charybdis, the Cyclopes, and the Laistrygonians do mould the reader's impression of Sicily. But it is important to note that the allusion to the strait between Rhegion and Messene as the 'Charybdis where Odysseus is said to have sailed through' occurs only in the narrative of Athens' first intervention in Sicily; and that the connection of Corcyra with the Homeric Scheria does not occur in a Sicilian context at all. It is slightly disturbing, too, that Thucydides implies some doubt as to the historicity of the Cyclopes and the Laistrygones with a tone that has often been felt to be dismissive (he adds that 'I have no idea what their race was, where they came from, or where they went; what has been said by the poets and what any person may know of them must suffice'). The other detailed correspondences are also strained: they seem to diminish (rather than to draw out through contrast) the pained sense of unique and unrelenting actuality that makes Thucydides' narrative of events in Sicily so pathetic.

The allusions to the world of Odysseus, I would argue, should not encourage us to draw detailed comparisons between Thucydides' narrative and the *Odyssey*. Instead, they define Sicily as a distant land with a mythical aura - an aura that explains the 'longing for faraway sights' felt by the young men at Athens when they voted to invade Sicily. This 'longing' (*pothos*) for a spectacle associated with myth recalls Xerxes' 'desire' (*himeros*) to see Troy, and anticipates Alexander's 'longing' (*pothos*) to see everything (but in particular places associated with the divine and with his heroic predecessors, Dionysos and Herakles). And it is the contrast between the mythical projection of Sicily and the reality that is so effective.

This reading of Thucydides' allusions to the *Odyssey* makes even less attractive Mackie's search for a detailed intertextual relationship. Similarly strained is his comparison between Alkibiades' escaping from Sicily in a single ship and Odysseus' escaping in a single ship One could just as easily stress differences. Odysseus escapes when all the other ships are lost, and he is the only one of his companions to return home. Alkibiades flees at an early stage in the expedition, escaping a danger from his own side; he does not seek to return home in his single ship; and at the close of the expedition some of the Athenians do return home. That the seductive habit of drawing comparisons and contrasts between patterns in epic and patterns in Thucydides runs the danger of proving rather facile is suggested by the fact that Frangoulidis is able to point to an allegedly ironic *contrast* between Odysseus and two other Athenian generals in Sicily, Demosthenes and Nikias (Odysseus survives, the Athenian generals die).

What has emerged is the need for caution in the search for Homeric archetypes for scenes and phrases, and the danger that claims of implausibly detailed correspondences may in fact distract attention from the subtlety of Thucydides' exploitation of his literary predecessors. I turn away now from the narrative as such to Thucydides' closing assessment of the Sicilian expedition. I shall argue that this passage has a range of register and allusion that adds depth to Thucydides' contextualization of the Sicilian expedition. I shall start by pursuing further the theme of epic reminiscence, and by looking at how Thucydides evokes the return home that eluded most of the Athenian force.

'AND THIS HELLENIC EVENT': THUCYDIDES

'And this Hellenic event turned out to be the greatest connected with this war and, at least in my opinion, of Hellenic events we have heard of, the most splendid for those who won and the most wretched for those who were ruined. For after having been completely defeated in every respect and suffering no little misery at every point in, as the saying is, total destruction, army and navy, nothing was not lost, and few out of many returned home. This was what happened concerning Sicily.'

'FEW OUT OF MANY RETURNED HOME'

Thoughts of epic have been raised by the verb Thucydides uses to describe the Athenians' return home, *apenostesan*: as the only appearance in Thucydides of a verb that is 'Homeric, but rare in tragedy and prose (except, significantly, in Herodotus)', it 'perhaps suggests the sufferings and *nostoi* or "Returns" from Troy of wandering Greeks like Odysseus: *nostoi* is the name of a whole literary genre describing such returns'. Indeed, Thucydides' allusion to the Athenians' *nostos* has been seen as the culmination of a theme that starts with the reference to Odysseus' return implied by mention of the

Cyclopes and Laistrygones with the two passages offering a 'heroic frame' to the Sicilian narrative.

Allison takes the further step of arguing that the contexts of Homer's six uses of the verb *aponostein* help us to appreciate Thucydides' own use of the word. The word is used once in Homer of a successful return: Allison argues that here 'the intertextual message of the History is gloomy; the Athenians will not realise an Odyssean *nostos*'. In the other five Homeric passages she sees a 'tension between the hope of return and the reality of impending death'; where the verb is used of Patroklos' failure to return to the Greek camp, for instance, she argues that 'it is the foreboding sense of imminent loss . . . now predicted by Achilles, that Thucydides seems to impart into his account'.

It is hard to feel satisfied with Allison's 'no-lose' model of literary allusion: if Homer uses *aponostein* of a successful return, then Thucydides is drawing a contrast; if Homer uses it of an unsuccessful return, then Thucydides is suggesting a parallel. And further objections can be made, for instance, there is no 'foreboding sense of imminent loss' in Homer; rather, Homer is drawing out the pathos of the contrast between Achilles' expectation that Patroklos would return and the reality that Patroklos is already dead.So too there is no 'foreboding sense of imminent loss' in Thucydides: the main destruction of Athenian troops has already occurred; the men who return home are 'few' out of the 'many' who set off from the Piraeus, not few out of the men who actually left Sicily or even few out of those who were sold into slavery in Sicily. A further problem with seeking explicit allusion is that three of the Homeric uses of *aponostein* refer not (as is required for the parallel with the Athenians in Sicily to hold) to the return of the Greeks from Troy, but to the return of warriors from the battlefield to the city of Troy or to the Greek camp.

Even if one allows that Thucydides is alluding to *nostos* as a general theme, the allusion does not seem primarily to be to the *Odyssey* or to the poem in the epic cycle called *Nostoi*. Those poems described the difficulties experienced by some of the Achaian leaders at Troy during their return journeys across the sea, and after their arrival back home; the *Nostoi* also related how some of the heroes returned by land. Thucydides does not say anything about *how* the survivors from the Athenian force returned to Athens. In the *Anabasis,* by contrast, Xenophon does implicitly assimilate the return of the Ten Thousand to Greece to the return of Odysseus to Ithaca (see the references to the Lotus-eaters and to Odysseus); but he only uses *nostos*-words once, to refer to a report that no one at all returned from a Persian army which attacked the mountain-dwelling Kardouchoi (*ouden' aponostesai*).

Though it seems unhelpful to see Thucydides' use of *apenostesan* as alluding either to specific Homeric uses of *aponostein* or to the genre of epic *nostoi,* we should not dismiss the Homeric resonance altogether. At one level, it reinforces the sense created by Thucydides' other epic words that the Athenian expedition, and Thucydides' representation of it, are epic in scale and ambition. More particularly, it evokes the emotive force that the idea of *nostos* has in epic: the bitterness of separation from home, the longing for the day of return, the *nostimon emar*, and the joy when that day arrives.

Thucydides' evocation of the *nostos* theme seems the more poignant because the Athenians had been so sure they would come home in safety, and because they (or at least most of them) do not just fail to return, they do not even achieve anything to compensate for their loss of *nostos*. In the *Iliad,* by contrast, the idea of return is regularly linked with the sacking of Troy: what Agamemnon (and Menelaos) have been promised by the gods, and by their troops, is that they will return after sacking well-walled Troy (*Ilion ekpersant' euteicheon aponeesthai*.

A brief look at Herodotus' more plentiful uses of the verb *aponostein* will offer an interesting comparison with Thucydides' technique of epic allusion. Herodotus evokes the epic associations of the *nostos* theme in a broader, but equally general way. At one point, for instance, he describes the sufferings undergone by some of the heroes from Troy *after* their return home: 'the Cretans proved themselves by no means the most despicable champions of Menelaus; their reward for this service on their return home (*aponostesasi*) was famine and plague for both men and cattle'; this recalls one strand in the epic *nostoi* (see e.g. *Nostoi, Arg.* Bernabé for the murder of Agamemnon). Particularly rich in its evocation of this strand is Herodotus' account of the fate of Pheretima, ruler of Cyrene: 'No sooner had she returned to Egypt after her revenge upon the people of Barca, than she died a horrible death . . . So true it is that excess in taking revenge draws down on humans the anger of the gods'.

In epic, too, it seems that the excesses committed by the Achaians in the sack of Troy (notably Aias' rape of Kassandra and Neoptolemos' killing of Priam at the altar of Zeus) were responsible for their sufferings during and after their return home. Another sign of Herodotus' closeness to epic is that he does recount the sufferings of the Persians on their return home; Thucydides, as we saw, glosses over the details of the Athenians' return from Sicily.

Again, Herodotus' pathetic focus on the clash of expectation and reality in the story of Adrastus and Atys seems close to the *nostos* theme as it is elaborated in the *Iliad* (the main epic model, I have argued, on which Thucydides drew): Adrastos promises Croesus that his son Atys will return home safe from the boar hunt (*aponostesein* - last word of the speech) - when it will be Adrastos himself who unwittingly kills him. At a more general level, it is the expected delight of the soldier's *nostos* that makes more startling the two stories in Herodotus which illuminate the typically Spartan shame of survival (the suicide of the sole Spartan survivor of the Battle of the Champions; cf. on the two Spartans who miss the battle of Thermopylai).

While Herodotus' canvas has more room than Thucydides' for the full range of association that the epic theme of *nostos* conveys, it would evidently be as rash to claim for Herodotus as it would for Thucydides that the force of his *nostos* words ever depends on the reader's recollection of any single passage. Indeed, if we are to claim a narrower range of allusion for Thucydides' use of *apenostesan*, it is in Herodotus, not in epic, that this should be sought. Herodotus uses the word several times to express how only a small number of an original group survived: 'the Chians sent a chorus of one hundred young men to Delphi; only two of them returned home' - note the pathetic juxtaposition of *hekaton duo*; out of 1,000 Argive volunteers who went to Aigina, 'most did not return home' (*hoi pleones ouk apenostesan*)). And once his expression is almost exactly the same as Thucydides': 'few of them returned home to Egypt', *oligoi tines auton apenostesan es Aigupton*): all this is lacking here is the explicit *apo pollon*. So while Herodotus draws on epic, Thucydides draws not just on epic, but also on epic as its themes are reflected in, and transformed by, Herodotus' *History*.

Both Herodotus and Thucydides, moreover, seem to be using a mode of rhetoric already found in tragedy: 'All who survived and won to safety, when they had made their way through Thrace, as they best could, with grievous hardships, escaped and reached - and few they were indeed (*ou polloi tines*) - the land of hearth and home; so that the city of the Persians may well make lament in regret for the best beloved youth of the land' (Aesch. *Pers.* trans. Weir Smyth). Since there are other echoes of Aeschylus' depiction of Salamis in the *Persae* in the closing sections of the Sicilian narrative, Thucydides' *oligoi apo pollon* can plausibly be read as an allusion to this very passage of the *Persae*. These allusions reinforce the broader pattern of allusions to Herodotus' depiction of the Persian Wars: I turn now to explore how that pattern is itself reinforced by Herodotean elements in Thucydides' grand closure to the Sicilian narrative.

HERODOTUS CONCLUSION

Thucydides' claim that the Sicilian expedition was 'the greatest . . . at least in my opinion, of Hellenic events we have heard of' seems to evoke several typical Herodotean phrases. First, the limiting phrase 'at least in my opinion' (*dokein d' emoige*). Herodotus uses the phrase 'seem(s) to me' (*dok- (e)moi*) some 99 times, often in ethnographic contexts, or else to express uncertainty over motivation, to stress the subjectivity of hypothetical statements, or to tone down superlatives.

Thucydides uses the expression 'seem(s) to me' far more rarely - only 14 times. It is most frequent when he is re-creating past events - in the *Archaeology*, the *Pentekontaetia*, and the tyrannicide digression. Elsewhere it is used of Thucydides' interpretation of an oracle and of his scientific speculation about the link between earthquakes and tidal waves.

The phrase occurs only three other times in his main war narrative. Thucydides' usage accords with his statement that he will not write 'as it seemed to me' as Marincola has brought out, this is not polemic against Herodotus' supposed use of arbitrary judgement in relating events, but a way of separating contemporary history from history about the past, where use of reasoned conjecture is acceptable. Herodotus claims to narrate *events* 'as they seem to me' only very rarely, when he is dealing with events of the distant past.

What is the force of the phrase at 7. 87. 5? Marincola reasonably states that 'the enormity of the claim probably motivates the qualification'. But we must also consider the phrase in the light of other Herodotean phrases in their context.

Thucydides' qualification that the Sicilian expedition was 'the greatest . . . of Hellenic events *that we have know of by report*' (*hon akoe(i) . . . ismen*) also has a Herodotean ring. Herodotus often restricts superlative clauses by adding *ton hemeis idmen*: Pausanias at the battle of Plataia 'won the most splendid victory of all that we know of' (*niken anaireetai kallisten apaseon ton hemeis idmen* the losses suffered by the peoples of Tarentum and Rhegion against the Iapygians of Messapia were 'the greatest Hellenic slaughter of all that we know of' (*phonos Hellenikos megistos houtos de egeneto panton ton hemeis idmen,* As with *dokei(n) !(e)moi,* it is in the *Archaeology* that most of Thucydides' uses of the Herodotean formula '[first/greatest] of those that we know of' are found (1. 4. 1, 13. 4, 18. 1: only the first of these has 'by report', *akoe(i)*).

The difference is that Herodotus does not combine the phrase with *akoe(i)*: his claims presumably have a slightly smaller chronological reach than Thucydides'. Herodotus does, however, offer a similar restriction to his claim that 'of all the armies we know of, [Xerxes' army that invaded Greece] was by far the largest': 'The army with which Darius attacked Scythia was tiny by comparison; so was the Scythian army which invaded Media on the heels of a Cimmerian force and succeeded in conquering and occupying almost the whole of inland Asia; and so, by all accounts (*kata ta legomena*), was the army with which the Atreidai attacked Ilion, and the army the Mysians and Teukrians raised - this was before the Trojan War - with which they crossed the Bosporus ' though note that he concludes with an undiluted claim.

Both *dokein d' emoige* and *hon akoe(i) . ismen*, it could be objected, are standard expressions for toning down authorial claims. The important point, however, is that it is only with regard to the Sicilian expedition that Thucydides uses these phrases to extend a claim about the uniqueness of an event in the Peloponnesian War to cover previous wars too. And he makes this extension in the same competitive spirit shown by Herodotus at 7. 20. 2.

The expeditions which Herodotus compares with Xerxes' all involve crossings from Asia to Europe or from Europe to Asia. Thucydides adopts the same manner as Herodotus while shifting the focus of the claim to greatness from conflicts between Asia and Europe to a conflict of Greek against Greek. At the same time he uses as a criterion of greatness not size, as Herodotus had done, but the destruction done to the invading force and the glory won by the defenders.

Thucydides also lays a direct stress on the Greekness of the Sicilian expedition: 'this *Hellenic* event turned out to be the greatest connected with this war and, at least in my opinion, of *Hellenic* events'. The repetition of 'Hellenic' (*ergon touto Hellenikon, hon akoe(i) Hellenikon ismen*) has, however, been found strained. Arnold found the first *Hellenikon* 'unnecessary': 'for what great events took place in the Peloponnesian war in which Greeks were not the principal actors?' Krüger first proposed deleting it, and almost all editors have followed him (Dover finds it 'stylistically objectionable'). Steup is the exception: he argues that there *were* some important activities undertaken by barbarians during the twenty-seven years of the Peloponnesian War (the expedition of Sitalkes, the

Carthaginian invasions of Sicily) which could have prompted Thucydides to restrict his claim by adding *Hellenikon.* But Thucydides' claim surely applies to the events, rather than to the period, of the Peloponnesian War. And we may, in any case, doubt whether Thucydides would have felt compelled by the Carthaginian invasions to impose the apparent restriction he makes on the greatness claimed for the Athenian invasion.

'The repetition if authentic is obsessive. And it is perhaps the nature of Thucydides' obsessiveness which guarantees the authenticity of the repetition. It is not just that The Herodotean feel of Thucydides' use of 'Hellenic' seems to be confirmed by the Herodotean feel of the phrase it accompanies - 'greatest event' (*megiston ergon*). This form of commemoration is typical of Herodotus. Yet Immerwahr has claimed that Thucydides differs from Herodotus in his use of *ergon*: Thucydides, for instance, rejected Herodotus' concept of monuments as *erga* which are, as much as deeds, a criterion of greatness.

The problem comes with Immerwahr's further claim that Herodotus saw the two types of *erga* - deeds and monuments - as parallel: 'the conception of fame underlying both monuments and deeds is exactly the same'; 'Herodotus looks at a deed as if it were a monument' that is, he analysed the effects of deeds not in terms of their direct historical consequences but in terms of honour and fame. Immerwahr claims that in Thucydides, by contrast, '*ergon* almost always refers to an activity rather than an achievement, and to a fact rather than a deed'. Especially relevant for 7. 87. 5 is his further claim that in Thucydides 'a *mega ergon* means simply "great trouble", or "an important event", and never "a great deed" in the Herodotean sense'.

The distinction between Herodotus and Thucydides drawn by Immerwahr, though not without justification, is too sharp. There are passages where Thucydides uses *ergon* in its 'Herodotean' sense where the Chaonians rush ahead of the Spartans in the advance against Stratos, 'thinking they would take the city at one blow and the deed (*ergon*) would be all theirs'). When Thucydides calls the Sicilian expedition the greatest *ergon* of the war, and perhaps of Greek history, he is not just referring to its historical importance: as the phrase 'most splendid (*lamprotaton*) for those who won' shows, he is thinking in terms of fame and glory. He is echoing, indeed, the assessment of the Syracusan speaker Hermokrates 'whether we go on to defeat them or send them away without achieving their objective . . . the outcome will provide us with a most glorious deed, and the basis for that assessment - the fame the Athenians had won by defeating the Persians.

I conclude that Thucydides' closing assessment of the Sicilian expedition has the sort of commemorative tone that we usually associate with Herodotus; that this tone is conveyed by phrases that we also associate with Herodotus; and that this Herodotean manner is itself part of the way in which Thucydides sets the greatness of the Sicilian expedition against the greatness of Xerxes' expedition. I shall argue below, indeed, that the language of *ergon . . . lamprotaton* evokes the epigrams set up by the Greeks to commemorate their victory over Persia. It is enough here to conclude that Thucydides does regard the Sicilian expedition as the most important event of the war in historical terms, but that he also regards it as a source of great fame for the Syracusans.

It remains to consider the possibility that a word Thucydides uses later in our passage is a direct allusion to a specific passage in Herodotus. Thucydides calls the Athenian defeat 'as the saying is, total destruction' (*panolethria(i) de to legomenon*); Herodotus had described how Troy was doomed - 'the gods were arranging things so that in their total destruction (*panolethrie(i)*) the Trojans might make it completely clear to others that the severity of a crime is matched by the severity of the ensuing punishment at the gods' hands'. The echo which was already noted in the eighteenth century has been ignored by most commentators on Thucydides. What has more recently been claimed is that Thucydides is not just alluding to the Herodotean passage, but also injecting Herodotus' theodicy into his account of the Athenians' destruction in Sicily.

How plausible is the allusion to Herodotus, the basis for

the startling theological reading of Thucydides? The passage of Herodotus is the only place where the noun *panolethria* is found before Thucydides. But the argument from silence is dangerous when so much early literature is lost: Hornblower has raised the possibility that there was a common source in epic for *panolethria*. And need Thucydides' use of *to legomenon* imply a specific allusion to the noun *panolethria* - as opposed, for instance, to the adjective *panolethros*?

That adjective is common in tragedy; it also appears in a mock-tragic passage. In any case, *to legomenon* ('as the saying is') can plausibly be taken as an argument against the Herodotean allusion: it should flag a conventional phrase rather than a specific passage. There is also a negative argument: elsewhere Thucydides does echo specific passages in Herodotus without signalling the echo explicitly.

It seems possible, nonetheless, that Thucydides' use of *to legomenon* signals the commonness of the phrase without removing the chance of a specific allusion. There is a possible parallel in Xenophon's use of the verb *dekateuein* ('tithe') as a euphemism for 'destroy'. The word is twice used by speakers in the *Hellenica,* both times with the phrase *to legomenon,* alluding to an oath to tithe Thebes allegedly made during the Persian Wars. Herodotus tells of an oath made at Thermopylai to 'tithe' medizing states.

The phrase is also found in fourth-century versions which present an oath at Plataia historians argue that it took on new life after 374, when the Spartans and Athenians began co-operating against Thebes, and when Thebes' medism could be resented all the more because of Theban agitation for the destruction of Athens in 404. So the association with the Persian Wars is certain: but how important it is for our interpretation of Xenophon that it occurs in the work of an earlier historian is far harder to determine.

With Thucydides' apparent allusion to Herodotus we are on slightly surer ground. But the question of the significance of the allusion remains open. The theological interpretation suggested for the destruction of the Athenian force in Sicily would be without parallel in the *History*. If it is right to stress the specific allusion to Herodotus' theodicy, it would be more attractive to see Thucydides as commenting sardonically on the failure of the divine plan that the Trojans should 'make it completely clear to others that the severity of a crime is matched by the severity of the ensuing punishment at the gods' hands'. But there is another way of reading the allusion that is also attractive: 'Thucydides' choice of words proclaims the parity of his subject, and his treatment of it, with both Herodotos and "Homeric" epic.'

This reading is perhaps supported not just by the epic features in Thucydides discussed above, but also by Thucydides' broader patterning of the Sicilian disaster after the Persian invasion of Greece: he could easily have been swayed by the way that the Persian invasion was often linked with the Trojan War in imaginative constructions. The specific allusion to the fall of Troy is all the more portentous if we recall Troy's status in tragedy as 'a permanent reminder of the fact that cities are mortal'. Perhaps the allusion reinforces Thucydides' repeated suggestions that Athens' defeat in Sicily foreshadows the fall of the city in 404.

This interpretation of Athens' 'total destruction' appears to be supported by the stress on the mortality of cities in later historians - notably in Appian's (and perhaps Polybius') account of the destruction of Carthage:

'Scipio, when he looked upon the city as it was utterly perishing and in the last throes of complete destruction (*panolethrian eschaten*), is said to have shed tears and wept openly for his enemies. After being wrapped in thought for long, and realizing that all cities, nations, and authorities must, like men, meet their doom; that this happened to Troy, once a prosperous city, to the empires of Assyria, Media, and Persia, the greatest of their time, and to Macedonia itself, the brilliance of which was so recent, . he said: 'A day will come when sacred Troy shall perish, and Priam and his people shall be slain' And when Polybius . . . asked him what he meant by the words, they say that without any attempt at concealment he named his own country, for which he feared when he reflected on the fate of all things human.'

Just as Thucydides portends Athens' destruction by evoking Herodotus' account of the fall of Troy, so too we find here an eloquent expression of the idea of a succession of mortal cities (and one that is even stronger because it is combined with the idea of a succession of empires).

Thucydides, I conclude, is dwelling on destruction rather than on the divine. Indeed, even if it is felt (reasonably enough) that the commonness of the adjective *panolethros* in tragedy militates against the interpretation I have proposed, and that Thucydides is simply evoking the atmosphere of tragedy, it is still on destruction that he is dwelling.

'And The Most Wretched for Those Who were Ruined': Tragedy

While Thucydides' use of the word *panolethria* can be plausibly taken as general tragic colouring, a more spectacular allusion to the genre of tragedy seems to be offered by the phrase 'and the most wretched for those who were ruined' (*kai tois diaphthareisi dustuchestaton*): 'a perfect, sombre iambic trimeter which implicitly likens tragic events to tragic myth in drama'.

Perhaps, indeed, Thucydides' trimeter evokes one element of tragic drama in particular: the messenger speech, with its typical gnomic closure (cf. e.g. Aesch. *Pers.* 'there never perished in a single day so great a multitude of men') he does not slip into one of the metres of the sung choral odes where the deepest tragic emotions are expressed. As elsewhere, Thucydides' allusions to other genres and other periods carry implications for his self-definition as narrator as well as for his perception of history.

Dover rightly stresses that Thucydides uses tragic vocabulary as well as a tragic metre: words with the root *dustuch-* are 'abundant in Euripides but not so common in prose'. Indeed, Thucydides' *dustuchestaton* picks up his comment that the Athenian general Nikias was 'the least worthy (*axios*) of the Greeks of my day to come to such misfortune (*dustuchias*)' a tragic refrain.

Thucydides' specific evocation of the form of Athenian

tragedy - as well as his broader construction of the Sicilian expedition along tragic lines - does not mean that the expedition is in a closed sense a 'tragedy'. Scholars are right to point out that Thucydides' perception of the significance of the Athenian disaster in Sicily must reflect the broader perception of contemporaries in Athens.Even so, there is always more than one story to tell - and not just because there is no natural way of separating off beginnings, middles, and ends, but also because there are different ways of reading stories with the same beginning and end. The event that is for the Athenians 'most wretched' is for the Syracusans 'most splendid' (*lamprotaton*).

The splendour of the Syracusans' achievement also adds to our sense of the Athenians' tragedy. Thucydides had described the Athenian force when it set off from the Piraeus as 'celebrated for its splendour (*lamproteti*) to look upon' and he had noted when it set off in retreat from Syracuse how 'from such splendour (*lamprotetos*) and vaunting at first they had reached such an end in humiliation'.

The shift of focus from the Athenians' physical splendour to the Syracusans' symbolic splendour furthers Thucydides' suggestion that the Athenian defeat in Sicily is a reversal; and this pattern of reversal is something that we associate with tragedy. The suggestion of reversal would be even stronger if Thucydides' phrase *ergon . . . lamprotaton* were an allusion to Simonides' description of the battle of Salamis - a (slight) possibility that I shall now raise.

The Most Splendid Event': Simonides and Salamis

Plutarch is describing the battle of Salamis in his *Themistokles*:

Then the rest, put on an equality in numbers with their foes, because the barbarians had to attack them by detachments in the narrow strait and so ran foul of one another, routed them, though they resisted till the evening drew on, as Simonides says, bearing away that fair and notorious victory, than which there has been performed upon the sea no deed more splendid (*hes outh' Hellesin oute barbarois enalion ergon eirgastai lamproteron*), either by Greeks or barbarians, through the manly valour and common ardour of all who fought their ships, but through the clever judgement of Themistokles.

Plutarch's account brings to mind Thucydides' closural assessment of the Sicilian expedition. 'No more splendid exploit' (*ergon lamproteron*) seems to echo Thucydides' phrase 'most splendid event' (*ergon . . . lamprotaton*). 'Either by Greeks or by barbarians' recalls (and surpasses) Thucydides' strong focus on the Greekness of the Sicilian expedition. And the description of Salamis as a deed performed 'upon the sea' recalls (and is surpassed by) Thucydides' stress on Sicilian disaster as a disaster both on land and at sea ('land-force and ships (*kai pezos kai nees*), nothing was not lost').

How are we to interpret these links? They could be regarded simply as a sign that Plutarch shared Thucydides' taste for amplification, and a sign of the frequency of certain motifs (land and sea, Greek and barbarian) in such rhetorical contexts. More ambitiously, they could be taken as a sign that Plutarch had picked up Thucydides' modelling of the Sicilian expedition on the pattern of the Persian Wars.

Plutarch would then be retrospectively anticipating Thucydides (so to speak) by applying to Salamis the claims Thucydides had made for the Sicilian expedition. It would be more interesting for our interpretation of Thucydides if Plutarch's assessment were derived from the source he mentions: Simonides' poem on the battle of Salamis. In that case we could say that Thucydides boosted a pattern he had already established (the modelling of the Sicilian expedition on the Persian invasion of Greece) by a forceful closural allusion to a famous poetic treatment of the Persian Wars.

To determine whether Thucydides could have been alluding to Simonides' poem on Salamis, we must first try to determine the scope and precision of Plutarch's citation in the *Themistokles* passage. An immediate problem is that scarcely anything is known about Simonides' poem: there is uncertainty about its form; and the passage of Plutarch quoted above is in fact the only certain citation. Translators and editors of Plutarch have tended to view the citation as extensive:

unmodified, Perrin's translation reads 'though they resisted till the evening drew on, and thus "bore away", as Simonides says, "that fair and notorious victory through the clever judgment of Themistocles."' The optimism of Plutarch's translators has been shared by various scholars: the passage of Plutarch has been taken as evidence that Themistokles' role at Salamis was seen as decisive as early as Simonides; as a sign of a friendly - and perhaps even politically fruitful - relationship between Themistokles and Simonides; and as evidence that Simonides (unlike Aeschylus in the *Persae*) mentioned Themistokles by name.Editors of Simonides have been more sceptical: West, for instance, prints the whole paragraph of Plutarch in the latest edition of *Iambi et Elegi Graeci*, but in earlier editions he cut it off at 'more splendid' (*lamproteron*) and at 'as Simonides says'.

Two things about Plutarch's citation are at least clear: it has no discernible metre, and it is not presented as precise (in the *de Herodoti Malignitate*, by contrast, he introduces verbatim quotations of Simonidean epigrams with *tade*). Modern translators who use quotation marks are misleading. But scholars have still been tempted to see some of Plutarch's phrases as accurate quotations: 'deed upon the sea' (*enalion ergon*) or 'deed more splendid' (*ergon lamproteron*), for instance. These interpretations would support the view that Thucydides may have been imitating Simonides. But perhaps the most common view among students of lyric is that only the phrase 'holding out until evening' (*mechri deiles antischontas*) is Simonidean; this view is supported by its placement directly before the phrase 'as Simonides says'.

One way of trying to establish more clearly the scope of Plutarch's citation is to consider the point of the citation. Doubtless translators have extended its scope because the mere detail 'holding out until evening' seems so banal. The grander claim about the greatness of Salamis seems more memorable, more worthy to be quoted. Aeschylus, too, presented Salamis as a battle that lasted 'until the eye of dark night took away [the slaughter]' And battles lasting until evening are common in epic and in historiography Perhaps, then, it was the Persians' 'holding out' that Plutarch found significant; their resistance doubtless helps to justify the greatness claimed for the battle. In Aeschylus, by contrast, the Persians did resist at first, but what continued until night was not their resistance but their slaughter; the stress falls (from the viewpoint of the defeated) on the magnitude of the slaughter ('there never perished in a single day so great a multitude of men'). Herodotus, on the other hand, does say that the Persians fought well but not how long the battle continued.

Plutarch's citation is effective, therefore, even if it only covers the phrase 'holding out until evening'. He seems, too, to have been fond of quoting the great Simonides; indeed, as Christopher Pelling suggests to me, his mere act of signalling that there was a poem on the battle of Salamis by Simonides promotes the glory of the battle. But there are reasons (other than the claim itself) why Plutarch might have cited Simonides for the grander claim, and for the role of Themistokles.

The relationship of Themistokles and Simonides is noted by Plutarch elsewhere in the *Themistokles*. He relates two anecdotes in which they converse, and cites a poem of Simonides which told of Themistokles' restoration and dedication of the *telesterion* (initiation-house) of the Lykomids at Phlya perhaps wrongly, he took this as evidence that Themistokles himself belonged to the Lykomid family. If the citation from Simonides does extend to the end of the paragraph, then it would be tempting to explain it through Simonides' link with Themistokles (and perhaps also through Themistokles' absence from Aeschylus' *Persae*).

A further Themistoklean link has been suggested as a basis for establishing the extent of Plutarch's use of Simonides. Plutarch relates that Lykomedes was the first Athenian to capture an enemy ship at Salamis, and that he dedicated the ensign to Apollo at Phlya (*Them.* 15. 3). Both the name Lykomedes and the association with Phlya suggest a connection with the Lykomid *genos*. We know that Simonides wrote about Themistocles' connection with the Lykomids: it has been suggested that Simonides was Plutarch's source for the detail about Lykomedes' feat at Salamis too. But Herodotus reports that Lykomedes was the first Athenian to capture a ship at Artemision: 'it is easier to explain [Plutarch's] statement as a simple confusion of the two great battles rather than as a separate tradition based ultimately on Simonides.'

It remains to consider whether there is anything distinctive about Plutarch's vocabulary which can help to determine his use of Simonides. Some words are certainly not poetic: in the phrase 'bearing away that fair and notorious victory', the word *periboetos* is prosaic (it is found 40 times in Plutarch's *Lives,* and 59 times in his *oeuvre* as a whole). Indeed, the expression 'that fair and notorious victory' (*ten kalen ekeinen kai periboeton*) itself has the mark of a distant perspective. But this distant perspective could be taken as a nod not just to a famous victory, but also to a description of that victory by a famous poet: that is, it might tell for, rather than against, the view that the quotation from Simonides is resumed in the clauses that follow.

The phrase 'bearing away victory' (*aramenoi niken*) is quite high language, but not exclusively so. The adjective *enalion* ('upon the sea') is poetic, but it is used in later prose. What about *lampros* - the word common to Plutarch and Thucydides? It is commonly used for the brilliant light of the sun and stars, and commonly extended to brilliant deeds in celebratory poems. But it is equally common in prose; it is worth noting that Plutarch applies the epithets *lampros* and *megas* to the former deeds (*erga*) of Gylippos, Spartan commander in Sicily.

While it is best to be cautious in reconstructing Simonides' poem, there are several reasons why it is at least worth considering the possibility of such an allusion. One reason is the light cast on the development of Greek historiography by the recent publication of Simonides' elegy on the battle of Plataia: the apparent suggestion in that poem of a continuity between the great deeds of epic and the Greek performance at Plataia is interesting in view of the more distant and competitive attitude to the Trojan War in Herodotus. Doubtless Herodotus' account of Salamis - as well, perhaps, as Thucydides' account of Syracuse - would be equally illuminated by the discovery of Simonides' poem on the battle of Salamis. Plutarch's account strongly suggests that it would have contained the motif of ships confined in the narrows that is the principal link between Salamis and Syracuse. There may be other, more surprising, echoes: Stephen Harrison has noted that both Herodotus and Aeschylus stress the bloodying of the water at Salamis, and speculated that Horace's description of the bloodying of water during the sea-battles in the Roman civil war may be an allusion to Simonides' use of this motif in his poem on Salamis. This is relevant because Thucydides too uses the motif - but he applies it not to the final battle at Syracuse, but to the final slaughter of thirsty Athenian troops in the river Assinaros.

To return to the 'most splendid event': either both Thucydides and Simonides/Plutarch are using a shared encomiastic vocabulary or there is a specific echo (whether it is Thucydides echoing Simonides or Plutarch echoing Thucydides). This problem returns when we consider the possibility that Thucydides was alluding to another possible sphere of literature - the epigrams inscribed on monuments commemorating the Greek success against Persia.

And this further possibility will suggest that it does not matter that the problem is intractable: Thucydides can still be recognized as using language that recalls celebrations of the Persian Wars even if he is not held to be evoking specific examples of that language (so too with Xenophon's use of *kalliston ergon* at *Anab.* where the stress on shared safety reproduces two other motifs familiar from Persian Wars contexts). The important thing is that he is using that language in the context of Athens' defeat in Sicily, and to suggest an inversion of the Persian Wars.

Persian Wars Epigrams

He started with a famous epigram ascribed in antiquity to Simonides and generally agreed to be a commemoration of the Cyprus campaign of

Since the time when the sea first separated Europe from Asia and wild Ares controlled the cities of mortals, no such deed of earthly men was ever carried out on land and sea at the same time: these men destroyed many Medes on Cyprus and then on the sea captured a hundred ships of the Phoenicians with their full complement of men; and Asia groaned loudly when struck with both hands by them with the strength of war.

One similarity with Thucydides lies in the use of *ergon* in the phrase 'no such deed of earthly men was ever carried out' (*oudama po kallion epichthonion genet' andron / ergon*). Another lies in the precision of 'on land and sea at the same time' (*en epeiroi kai kata ponton hama*): compare Thucydides' polar expression 'land-force and ships (*kai pezos kai nees*), nothing was not lost'.

This pairing of land and sea (which picks up the emphatic 7. 75. 7 - where part of the Athenians' reversal of fortune is that they leave 'on foot instead of on board ship', *pezous . . . anti naubaton*) is certainly different from the stress in the epigram on a simultaneous land and sea battle. But the difference is only one of degree; and the focus on land and sea recurs in other Persian Wars epigrams - for instance in an epigram of 'Simonides': 'These men once lost their splendid youth at the Eurymedon, spearmen fighting the vanguard of the Median archers both on foot and on swift-sailing ships (*pezoi te kai okuporon epi neon*), and when they died they left the finest memorial of their valour' (trans. D. A. Campbell; note that this poem is an *epitaph* - though also that Thucydides uses impersonal words, land-force and ships, where the epitaph has land-soldiers and men on board ships); and in an earlier Persian Wars epigram (*CEG* 2 = ML 26): 'The valour of these men shall beget glory for ever undiminished / so long as the gods allot rewards for courage. / For on foot and on their swift-moving ships (*pezoi te kai okuporon epi neon*) they kept / all Greece from seeing the dawn of slavery'.

Here, the focus on the preservation of Greek liberty on land and sea offers a pointed contrast with Thucydides' depiction of the destruction on land and sea that befell an expedition which had set out to enslave the Greeks of Sicily. And the parallel with Thucydides may be particularly close because the epigram may be commemorating not a joint land

and sea battle (like the epigrams for Eurymedon and Cyprian Salamis), but the various campaigns by land and sea in the years: 'on foot' would refer mainly to Plataia, 'on their swift-moving ships' mainly to Salamis (but Mykale could also be included). This would balance the destruction of 'land-force and ships' in the Sicilian campaign as a whole - a dichotomy that evokes, in any case, Herodotus' use of the land/sea dichotomy to structure his account of the Persian Wars.

Thucydides' dichotomy of land and sea is complicated by his presentation of the battles in the harbour at Syracuse as sea battles that are like land battles. This blurring is not just a way of linking Sicily with the fighting at Pylos, where the same confusion occurs; it also contrasts the confused fighting of the Peloponnesian War with the clear-cut battles of the Persian Wars - 'the greatest action of the past, yet it had a quick resolution in two battles on sea and two on land' and of later stages in the fighting against Persia The fighting on the island of Psyttaleia in his presentations of Salamis purely as a sea battle; Aeschylus, by contrast, links the two parts of the battle by having the men who have fought in the sea battle go on to slaughter the Persian nobles on the island.

Nor does he just simplify Salamis to increase the contrast between the Persian and Peloponnesian Wars: he further blurs the distinction of land and sea fighting in Sicily by postponing the motif of the bloodying of water - which, I have suggested, we might have expected in his account of the final sea battle at Syracuse - until his description of the slaughter of Athenian troops at the Assinaros.)

My suggestion that the polar expression 'land-force and ships' (*kai pezos kai nees*) at 7. 87. 6 recalls depictions of the Greek victory over Persia as a victory on land and sea is strengthened not just by Thucydides' own depiction of the Persian Wars in terms of the land/sea dichotomy, but also by the agonistic spirit that seems to bind the various Persian Wars epigrams. We have seen that the Eurymedon - or Cyprus - epigram quoted by Diodorus included the claim that 'no such deed of earthly men was ever carried out': Wade-Gery took this as a sign that 'the poem deliberately invited comparison with Mykale'; indeed, he took the phrase as one reason why the epigram had to refer to Eurymedon (if it referred to the victory at Cyprian Salamis, the precedent of Eurymedon would make the claim invalid). Gomme, by contrast, took the boastfulness of 'its implied comparison with Salamis and Plataia' as an argument against Wade-Gery's view that the epigram dates from the time of Eurymedon (he aptly compared Plut. *Kimon* 'though he had surpassed the victory at Salamis with an infantry battle and that of Plataea with a naval battle', trans. Perrin).Besides this, the use of the phrase *pezoi te kai okuporon epi neon* in both the Salamis (or Persian Wars) and the Eurymedon epigram, while doubtless a sign of the repetitiveness of epigrammatic language, could also be taken as another reflection of the tendency to present one battle in the light of another.

And the Salamis epigram itself has been (implausibly) linked with a 'battle of the battles': the addition to the monument on which the Salamis epigram was inscribed of an epigram which may refer to Marathon has been taken as the reaction of the Kimonian, hoplite, faction against the democratic exploitation of Salamis.

The grand heightening which Thucydides gives to the Sicilian expedition at its close belongs in this tradition. But the effect of his evoking the past of the Persian (and perhaps also the Trojan) Wars is rather different from what we find in other contexts. In contexts such as funeral orations, or Simonides' poem on the battle of Plataia, or the paintings on the Stoa Poikile, or the epigram on the Eion herms, past events are explicitly assimilated to the Greek resistance to Persia, as evidence of a continuity of bravery. The Persian Wars epigrams offers some evidence of a linking of battles, but also some rivalry. With Thucydides we have rivalry - but now no longer a continuity of bravery, but a contrast between success and total destruction.

SUMMARY

When he began this paper with a slightly sceptical treatment of some recent attempts to detect a detailed intertextual correspondence between Thucydides and epic. I went on to argue that readers' understanding of Thucydides' closing remarks on the greatness of the Sicilian expedition is enhanced if they are alert to a range of possible literary allusions: to epic, to tragedy, to earlier historiography, and perhaps also to lyric and epigram. The closure to the Sicilian expedition is, doubtless, the only passage in Thucydides where it is plausible to see so great a range of allusion in so short a space of text. But it will still be useful to draw some general conclusions from both the negative and the positive sections of this paper, by pointing to the differences between the approaches I have examined and the approach I have followed myself.

Some of the links which scholars have seen between Thucydides and earlier authors are instances of verbal repetition (*patrothen, panolethria*); others consist in shared plot-patterns (Nikias' letter and Agamemnon's speech, the Athenians' expedition to Sicily and Odysseus' return to Ithaca). My cautious treatment of some of the alleged links does not mean that I am hostile to the attempt to detect such potentially enriching patterns.

I have argued, indeed, that many of the links are indeed plausible, but that in interpreting them we should not subject them to more weight than they can bear. Often a tempting similarity may be blurred by more telling differences, or our response to an apparent verbal echo may be modified by a broader view of a word's application. Indeed, the picture that has emerged from both parts of my paper is that it is by defining intertextuality in a broad and accommodating way that our understanding of Thucydides is most likely to be enhanced.

I have, however, argued elsewhere for a detailed correspondence between Herodotus' narrative of the Persian invasion of Greece and Thucydides' narrative of the Sicilian expedition - a correspondence that is seen both in the choice of words and at a broader level of the structuring of the accounts, and indeed of the shaping of the works as a whole. And in this paper I have offered slightly different readings of some of the alleged links with epic, proposing some new points of contact with epic (including the epic cycle), and broadened my previous analysis of Thucydides' use of Herodotus' account of the Persian Wars by looking for possible links between Thucydides and other accounts of the Persian Wars. This broader analysis gives a better view of the horizons of expectation of a fifth-century audience.

Our tendency to place Herodotus and Thucydides at the beginning of the historiographical tradition runs the risk of obscuring the fact that they were writing in the context of - and to some extent competing with - other forms of commemorating the past. It is not that we should downplay the genuine striving for a new form of historical expression which we see in Herodotus and Thucydides; it is, rather, that we should see their receptiveness to other genres as part of the way they convey both the experience, and their own interpretations, of historical events.

XENOPHONE

OVERVIEW

Greek historian and man of letters, he was the son of a well-born Athenian named Gryllus. Xenophon approached manhood during the last turbulent years of the Peloponnesian War (431-404), in which he himself took part as a cavalryman; and perhaps he was also present at the sea battle of Arginusae (406). He got to know Socrates and became his keen admirer, though probably not his pupil, since he possessed no aptitude for philosophy himself. Xenophon was a man of right-wing political tastes, with a simple belief in the virtues of strong leadership; he probably found life uncomfortable when the short-lived oligarchic revolution came to an end and democracy was restored in Athens (403).

In any case, he moved away from the city. In 401 his Boeotian friend Proxenus invited him to join the expedition (anabasis, march up country) of Cyrus the Younger who was in rebellion against his brother King Artaxerxes II of Persia. After Cyrus had been defeated and killed at Cunaxa (401),

Xenophon was elected a general and played a major part in the evacuation of the Greek expeditionary force to Trapezus (Trabzon, northeastern Turkey). Then, after a brief period of service with the Thracian king Seuthes, he offered himself and his troops to Thibron—a general from Sparta, which was at war with Persia—and engaged as his ally, in operations that continued under Thibron's successor Dercylidas.

Although Xenophon was an Athenian, he spent much of his life in Sparta. When democracy was re-established in Athens in 401, Xenophon, a man of right-wing political opinions, turned his back on its new leaders and went abroad. He joined with ten thousand Greek mercenaries the expedition (anabasis, march up country) of Cyrus the younger into the hinterland of Asia Minor. However, Cyrus's real aim was to oust his brother King Artaxerxes II of Persia.

His plan failed - Cyrus lost his life in the battle of Cunaxa. The mercenaries were left leaderless on the plains between the Tigris and the Euphrates, over 1,600 kilometers (about 1,000 miles) from home. Xenophon was elected one of the generals. In this role he took the principal part in the struggle of the Greeks to return home through the "barbarian" world - the Greeks referred to the Persians as "barbarians". Less than 6,000 mercenaries survived. The *Anabasis* became not only an account of the expedition but also a tale of military virtues, discipline, leadership, and courage.

Xenophon wrote his book in the third person. The author himself rode casually onto the scene in the first book: "Cyrus, riding past at some distance from the lines, glanced his eye first in one direction and then in the other, so as to take a complete survey of friends and foes; when Xenophon the Athenian, seeing him, rode up from the Hellenic quarter to meet him, asking him whether he had any orders to give. Cyrus, pulling up his horse, begged him to make the announcement generally known that the omens from the victims, internal and external alike, were good." A famous part of the *Anabasis* is Xenophon's description of the Greeks, shouting "*Thalassa, thalassa*" (the sea, the sea) at the top of a great dune, when they saw the sea. "Thereupon they began running, rearguard and all, and the baggage animals and horses came galloping up. But when they had reached the summit, then indeed they fell to embracing one another - generals and officers and all - and the tears trickled down their cheeks."

Socrates was put to death in 399, and it seems probable that Xenophon was banished by Athens. After "the march of the 10,000" Xenophon entered the service of the Thracian king Seuthes and in 396-394 he served the Spartan king Agesilaus II, who defeated a coalition of Greek states at the Battle of Coronea in 394. About 365 Xenophon returned home, and settled with his wife Philesia and two sons at Scillus in Elis. There, during the following two decades, he probably composed most of his works.

Xenophon's experiences in cavalry and his love of horses prompted two books, *Hipparchikos* (Cavalry Officer) and *Peri hippikes* (On Horsemanship), the oldest surviving complete manual on this subject. Xenophon starts the latter work by explaining, how to avoid being cheated when buying a horse. In *Hieron,* a fictitious discussion between King Hiero I of Syracuse and the poet Simonides of Ceos, Xenophon presents his ideas on how an autocrat can secure his subjects' loyalty. *Agesialos,* one of the earliest Greek biographies, dealt with King Agelilaus II of Sparta.

After Sparta lost possession of Scillus, Xenophon moved to a new residence on the isthmus of Corinth. The sentence of his banishment from Athens was repealed. It is possible that before his death he lived in Athens; at least his sons Gryllus and Diodorus fought with Athens and Spartans against the Thebans. Xenophon died in Corinth. His last book was probably *Poroi e peri prosodon* (Ways and Means), in which he suggested methods for improvement of Athenian public finance, and advocated a policy of peace.

Xenophon's works had already started to become famous in the Roman imperial period. The Roman orator Cicero (106-43 B.C.) praised especially his *Education of Cyrus*. Its style perhaps inspired Julius Caesar's *Commentarii,* the unfinished histories of the Gallic and Civil wars. By the fifteenth century

Xenophon had secured his place among the great writers of antiquity, and from the 16th century his works were printed in many European languages. Xenophon's elegant style, clear and straightforward, sometimes rhetorical, is much admired, but at the same time he has not been regarded as a thinker. On the other hand, it has been argued that Xenophon's writings demand more serious philosophical analysis than they have received.

The *Anabasis* inspired the Swedish Nobel writer Gustaf Fröding's (1860-1911) poem 'Ur Anabasis'. The Italian writer Italo Calvino noted in his essay 'Xenophon's *Anabasis*' (1978), that the work is similar to the memoirs written by Italian Alpini troops on their retreat from Russia. Calvino also draws parallels between Xenophon, Hemingway's novels, and "the modern ethic of perfect technical efficiency".

In Xenophon's absence, however, at the time when Socrates had just been executed and his associates were discredited, the Athenians formally pronounced a sentence of exile upon him, involving the confiscation of his property. In 396-394 he fought against the Persian satrap Pharnabazus in the service of Agesilaus, king of Sparta (398-361), to whom he formed a strong attachment; and when Agesilaus was called home in 395 at the outset of the Corinthian War (in which Sparta was pitted against Thebes), Xenophon took part in the battle of Coronea (394), thus fighting against his own Athenian compatriots, who were in alliance with Thebes.

Subsequently, he settled with his family at Sparta. He was presented by the Spartans with an estate at Scillus in Elis (northwestern Peloponnese) where he spent the next two decades living the life of a literary country gentleman, dividing his time between hunting and writing.

The Spartans appointed him as their envoy (proxenos) to look after such of their citizens as visited Olympia nearby. When, after its defeat by the Thebans at the battle of Leuctra, Sparta lost possession of Scillus, Xenophon and his family moved to a new residence on the isthmus of Corinth. However, relations between Athens and Sparta having now improved, the Athenians repealed his condemnation to exile, and it seems likely that he returned to Athens and lived there. In 362 his sons Gryllus and Diodorus (by his wife Philesia) were members of an Athenian contingent fighting with the Spartans against the Thebans at Mantinea, and Gryllus was killed. Xenophon was probably on a visit to Corinth when he died.

POLYBIUS

INTRODUCTION

Polybius was born in Megalopolis, Arcadia, a Greek city that was an active member of the Achaean League, of which his father, Lycortas, was at one time leader. Polybius advanced politically in the League and reached a position from which he, too, could have become its leader. However, after the Romans conquered Macedonia, they stabilized their control of the area by purging Greek cities of their leaders. One thousand of the principal Achaeans were deported to Italy. Polybius was fortunate in that L. Aemilius Paulus interceded for him and made him tutor of his sons Scipio and Fabius in Rome. A friendship developed that led Scipio to take Polybius with him as an advisor on political and military matters.

Polybius was thus able to move in the highest circles in Rome and to witness major Roman military campaigns in the Mediterranean region. This gave him a unique opportunity as a Greek to analyse the successful expansion of Rome and to record the principles involved as a lesson for future statesmen, notably those in Greece, who he hoped would profit from his work. Polybius's analysis is contained in his Histories—forty volumes describing the constitution of Rome and the sequence of Roman conquests. It has a strong political slant and represents an early attempt at a universal history rather than the history of a single people. Polybius set out to show how many different regions were merged by the Romans into a single whole.

He was clearly aware of the dangers of accepting fables as history: he sought the truth rather than idle and unprofitable tales. Polybius remarked acidly of other historians that to believe things that were beyond the limits of possibility showed a childish simplicity or the mark of limited intelligence. His particular interest in how Rome could organize to gain control of the world around the Mediterranean led him to analyse different types of constitution and to propose a theory of how these change from one to another in an inevitable cycle (kingship, tyranny, aristocracy, oligarchy, democracy, mob rule, and tyranny again). He had great praise for the constitution of Rome, but seemed to think that it might eventually succumb like others, if not from conquest, then from internal sources.

OVERVIEW AND INVENTIONS

Greek historian, a native of Megalopolis in Arcadia, the youngest of Greek cities, which, however, played an honorable part in the last days of Greek freedom as a stanch member of the Achaean League. His father, Lycortas, was the intimate friend of Philopoemen, and on the death of the latter, in 182, succeeded him as leader of the league. The date of Polybius's birth is doubtful. He tells us himself that in 181 he had not yet reached the age (perhaps thirty years) at which an Achaean was legally capable of holding office.

We learn from Cicero that he outlived the Numantine War, which ended 132, and from Lucian that he died at the age of eighty-two. The majority of authorities therefore place his birth between 224 and 204 BC. Little is known of his early life. As the son of Lycortas he was naturally brought into close contact with the leading men of the Achaean League. With Philopoemen he seems to have been on intimate terms. After Philopoemen's tragic death in Messenia (182) he was entrusted with the honorable duty of conveying home the urn in which his ashes had been deposited.

In 181, together with his father, Lycortas and the younger Aratus, he was appointed, in spite of his youth, a member of the embassy which was to visit Ptolemy Epiphanes, king of Egypt, a mission, however, which the sudden death of Ptolemy brought to a premature end. The next twelve years of his life are a blank, but in 169 he reappears as a trusted adviser of the Achaeans at a difficult crisis in the history of the League. In

171 war had broken out between Rome and the Macedonian king Perseus, and the Achaean statesmen were divided as to the policy to be pursued; there were good reasons for fearing that the Roman senate would regard neutrality as indicating a secret leaning towards Macedon. Polybius therefore declared for an open alliance with Rome, and his views were adopted. It was decided to send an Achaean force to cooperate with the Roman general, and Polybius was selected to command the cavalry.

The Roman consul declined the proffered assistance, but Polybius accompanied him throughout the campaign, and thus gained his first insight into the military system of Rome. In the next year (168) both Lycortas and Polybius were on the point of starting at the head of 1200 Achaeans to take service in Egypt against the Syrians, when an intimation from the Roman commander that armed interference was undesirable put a stop to the expedition.

The success of Rome in the war with Perseus was now assured. The final victory was rapidly followed by the arrival in Achaea of Roman commissioners charged with the duty of establishing Roman interests there. Polybius was arrested with 1000 of the principal Achaeans, but, while his companions were condemned to a tedious incarceration in the country towns of Italy, he obtained permission to reside in Rome.

This privilege he owed to the influence of L. Aemilius Paullus and his two sons, Scipio and Fabius. Polybius was received into Aemilius's house, and became the instructor of his sons. Between Scipio (P. Cornelius Scipio Africanus the younger), the future conqueror of Carthage, and himself a friendship soon sprang up, which ripened into a lifelong intimacy, and was of inestimable service to him throughout his career. It protected him from interference, opened to him the highest circles of Roman society, and enabled him to acquire a personal influence with the leading men, which stood him in good stead when he afterwards came forward to mediate between his countrymen and Rome.

It placed within his reach opportunities for a close study of Rome and the Romans such as had fallen to no historian before him, and secured him the requisite leisure for using them, while Scipio's liberality more than once supplied him with the means of conducting difficult and costly historical investigations. In 151 the few surviving exiles were allowed to return to Greece. But the stay of Polybius in Achaea was brief. The estimation in which he was held at Rome is clearly shown by the anxiety of the consul Marcus Manilius (149) to take him as his adviser on his expedition against Carthage. Polybius started to join him, but broke off his journey at Corcyra on learning that the Carthaginians were inclined to yield. But when, in 147, Scipio himself took the command in Africa, Polybius hastened to join him, and was an eyewitness of the siege and destruction of Carthage.

During his absence in Africa the Achaeans had made a last desperate attempt to assert their independence of Rome. He returned in 146 to find Corinth in ruins, the fairest cities of Achaea at the mercy of the Roman soldiery, and the famous Achaean League shattered to pieces. All the influence he possessed was freely spent in endeavoring to shield his countrymen from the worst consequences of their rashness. The excesses of the soldiery were checked, and at his special intercession the statues of Aratus and Philopoemen were preserved.

An even more difficult task was that entrusted to him by the Roman authorities themselves, of persuading the Achaeans to acquiesce in the new regime imposed upon them by their conquerors, and of setting the new machinery in working order. With this work, which he accomplished so as to earn the heartfelt gratitude of his countrymen, his public career seems to have closed. The rest of his life was, so far as we know, devoted to the great history which is the lasting monument of his fame. He died, at the age of eighty-two, of a fall from his horse. The base of a statue erected to him by Elis was found at Olympia in 1877.

Of the forty books which made up the history of Polybius, the first five alone have come down to us in a complete form; of the rest we have only more or less copious fragments. But the general plan and scope of the work are explained by

Polybius himself. His intention was to make plain how and why it was that all the known regions of the civilized world had fallen under the sway of Rome. This empire of Rome, unprecedented in its extent and still more so in the rapidity with which it had been acquired, was the standing wonder of the age, and "who", he exclaims, "is so poor-spirited or indolent as not to wish to know by what means, and thanks to what sort of constitution, the Romans subdued the world in something less than fifty-three years?"

These fifty-three years are those between 220 (the point at which the work of Aratus ended) and 168 BC, and extend therefore from the outbreak of the Hannibalic War to the defeat of Perseus at Pydna. To this period then the main portion of his history is devoted from the third to the thirtieth book inclusive. This seems to have been his original plan, but at the opening of book III, written apparently after 146, he explains that he thought it desirable to add some account of the manner in which the Romans exercised the power they had won, of their temperament and policy and of the final catastrophe which destroyed Carthage and forever broke up the Achaean League. To this appendix, giving the history from 168-146, the last ten books are devoted.

Whatever fault may be found with Polybius, there can be no question that he had formed a high conception of the task before him. He lays repeated stress on two qualities as distinguishing his history from the ordinary run of historical compositions. The first of these, its synoptic character, was partly necessitated by the nature of the period. The various states fringing the basin of the Mediterranean had become so inextricably interwoven that it was no longer possible to deal with them in isolation. Polybius therefore claims for his history that it will take a comprehensive view of the whole course of events in the civilized world, within the limits of the period.

He thus aims at placing before his readers at each stage a complete survey of the field of action from Spain to Syria and Egypt. This synoptic method proceeds from a true appreciation of what is now called the unity of history, and to Polybius must be given the credit of having first firmly grasped and clearly enforced a lesson which the events of his own time were especially well calculated to teach. It is the great merit of his work that it gives such a picture of the 2nd and 3rd centuries BC as no series of special narratives could have supplied.

The second quality upon which Polybius insists as distinguishing his history from all others is its "pragmatic" character. It deals, that is, with events and with their causes, and aims at an accurate record and explanation of ascertained facts. This "pragmatic method" makes history intelligible by explaining the how and the why; and, secondly, it is only when so written that history can perform its true function of instructing and guiding those who study it. For the great use of history, according to Polybius, is to contribute to the right conduct of human life. But this it can do only if the historian bears in mind the true nature of his task.

He must remember that the historian should not write as the dramatist does to charm or excite his audience for the moment. He will aim simply at exhibiting events in their true light, setting forth "the why and the how" in each case, not confusing causes and occasions, or dragging in old wives' fables, prodigies and marvels.

He will omit nothing which can help to explain the events he is dealing with: the genius and temperament of particular peoples, their political and military systems, the characters of the leading men, the geographical features of the country, must all be taken into account. To this conception of history Polybius is on the whole consistently faithful.

It is true that his anxiety to instruct leads often to a rather wearisome iteration of his favourite maxims, and that his digressions, such as that on the military art, are occasionally provokingly long and didactic. But his comments and reflections are for the most part sound and instructive (e.g. those on the lessons to be learned from the revolt of the mercenaries in Africa, from the Celtic raids in Italy, and on the Roman character), while among his digressions are included such invaluable chapters as those on the Roman constitution, the graphic description of Cisalpine Gaul and the account of the rise and constitution of the Achaean League.

To his anxiety again to trace back events to their first causes we owe, not only the careful inquiry into the origin of the Second Punic War, but the sketch of early Roman history in book I, and of the early treaties between Rome and Carthage. Among the many defects which he censures in previous historians, not the least serious in his eyes are their inattention to the political and geographical surroundings of the history, and their neglect duly to set forth the causes of events.

Polybius is equally explicit as regards the personal qualifications necessary for a good historian, and in this respect too his practice is in close agreement with his theory. Without a personal knowledge of affairs a writer will inevitably distort the true relations and importance of events.

Such experience would have saved accomplished and fluent Greek writers like Timaeus from many of their blunders, but the shortcomings of Roman soldiers and senators like Q. Fabius Pictor show that it is not enough by itself. Equally indispensable is careful painstaking research. All available evidence must be collected, thoroughly sifted, soberly weighed, and, lastly, the historian must be animated by a sincere love of truth and a calm impartiality.

It is important to consider how far Polybius himself comes up to his standard. In his personal acquaintance with affairs, in the variety of his experience, and in his opportunities for forming a correct judgment on events he is without a rival among ancient historians. A great part of the period of which he treats fell within his own lifetime.

He may just have remembered the battle of Cynoscephalae , and, as we have seen, he was actively engaged in the military and political affairs of the Achaean League. During his exile in Rome he was able to study the Roman constitution, and the peculiarities of the Roman temperament; he made the acquaintance of Roman senators, and became the intimate friend of the greatest Roman of the day. Lastly, he was able to survey with his own eyes the field on which the great struggle between Rome and Hannibal was fought out. He left Rome only to witness the crowning triumph of Roman arms in Africa, and to gain a practical acquaintance with

Roman methods of government by assisting in the settlement of Achaea. When, in 146, his public life closed, he completed his preparation of himself for his great work by laborious investigations of archives and monuments, and by a careful personal examination of historical sites and scenes. To all this we must add that he was deeply read in the learning of his day, above all in the writings of earlier historians.

Of Polybius's anxiety to get at the truth no better proof can be given than his conscientious investigation of original documents and monuments, and his careful study of geography and topography — both of them points in which his predecessors, as well as his successor Livy, conspicuously failed. Polybius is careful constantly to remind us that he writes for those who are lovers of knowledge, with whom truth is the first consideration.

He closely studied the bronze tablets in Rome on which were inscribed the early treaties concluded between Romans and Carthaginians. He quotes the actual language of the treaty which ended the First Punic War, and of that between Hannibal and Philip of Macedon. He refers to a document which he had personally inspected in the archives at Rhodes, and to the monument on the Lacinian promontory, recording the number of Hannibal's forces. According to Dionysius, he got his date for the foundation of Rome from a tablet in the pontifical archives. As instances of his careful attention to geography and topography we have not only the fact of his widely extended travels, from the African coast and the Pillars of Hercules in the west, to the Euxine and the coasts of Asia Minor in the east, but also the geographical and topographical studies scattered throughout his history.

Next to the duty of original research, Polybius ranks that of impartiality. Some amount of bias in favour of one's own country may, he thinks, be pardoned as natural; but it is unpardonable, he says, for the historian to set anything whatever above the truth. And on the whole, Polybius must be allowed here again to have practiced what he preached. It is true that his affection for and pride in Arcadia appear in more than one passage, as also does his dislike of the Aetolians.

His treatment of Aratus and Philopoemen, the heroes of the Achaean League, and of Cleomenes of Sparta, its most constant enemy, is perhaps open to severer criticism. Certainly Cleomenes does not receive full justice at his hands. Similarly his views of Rome and the Romans may have been influenced by his firm belief in the necessity of accepting the Roman supremacy as inevitable, and by his intimacy with Scipio.

He had a deep admiration for the great republic, for her well-balanced constitution, for her military system, and for the character of her citizens. But just as his patriotism does not blind him to the faults and follies of his countrymen, so he does not scruple to criticize Rome.

He notices the incipient degeneracy of Rome after 146. He endeavors to hold the balance evenly between Rome and Carthage; he strongly condemns the Roman occupation of Sardinia as a breach of faith; and he does full justice to Hannibal. Moreover, there can be no doubt that he sketched the Roman character in a masterly fashion.

His interest in the study of character and his skill in its delineation are everywhere noticeable. He believes, indeed, in an overruling fortune, which guides the course of events. It is fortune which has fashioned anew the face of the world in his own time, which has brought the whole civilized world into subjection to Rome and the Roman Empire itself is the most marvellous of her works. But under fortune not only political and geographical conditions but the characters and temperaments of nations and individuals play their part. The Romans had been fitted by their previous struggles for the conquest of the world; they were chosen to punish the treachery of Philip of Macedon; and the greatest of them, Scipio himself, Polybius regards as the especial favourite of fortune.

In respect of form, Polybius is far the inferior of Livy, partly owing to his very virtues. His laudable desire to present a picture of the whole political situation at each important moment is fatal to the continuity of his narrative. Thus the thrilling story of the Second Punic War is broken in upon by digressions on the contemporary affairs in Greece and Asia. More serious, however, than this excessive love of synchronism is his almost pedantic anxiety to edify. For gace, and elegance of composition, and for the artistic presentation of events, he has a hardly concealed contempt. Hence a general and almost studied carelessness of effect, which mars his whole work.

On the other hand he is never weary of preaching. His favourite theories of the nature and aims of history, of the distinction between the universal and special histories, of the duties of an historian, sound as most of them are in themselves, are enforced with wearisome iteration; more than once the effect of a graphic picture is spoiled by obtrusive moralizing. Nor, lastly, is Polybius's style itself such as to compensate for these defects.

It is, indeed, often impressive from the evident earnestness of the writer, and from his sense of the gravity of his subject, and is unspoiled by rhetoric or conceit. It has about it the ring of reality; the language is sometimes pithy and vigorous; and now and then, we meet with apt metaphors, such as those borrowed from boxing, from cock-fighting, etc.

But, in spite of these redeeming features, the prevailing baldness of Polybius's style excludes him from the first rank among classical writers; and it is impossible to quarrel with the verdict pronounced by Dionysius of Halicarnassus, who places him among those authors of later times who neglected the graces of style, and who paid for their neglect by leaving behind them works "which no one was patient enough to read through to the end."

It is to the value and variety of his matter, to his critical insight, breadth of view and wide research, and not least to the surpassing importance and interest of the period with which he deals that Polybius owes his place among the writers of history. What is known as to the fortunes of his histories, and the reputation they enjoyed, fully bears out this conclusion. The silence respecting him maintained by Quintilian and by Lucian may reasonably be taken to imply their agreement with Dionysius as to his merits as a master of style. On the other hand, Cicero describes him as" bonus auctor in primis"; in the *De republica* he praises highly his accuracy in matters of chronology; and Cicero's younger contemporary,

Marcus Brutus, was a devoted student of Polybius, and was engaged on the eve of the battle of Pharsalia in compiling an epitome of his histories. Livy, however, notwithstanding the extent to which he used his writings, speaks of him in such qualified terms as to suggest the idea that his strong artistic sensibilities had been wounded by Polybius's literary defects.

He has nothing better to say of him than that he is "by no means contemptible", and "not an untrustworthy author." Posidonius and Strabo, both of them Stoics like Polybius himself, are said to have written continuations of his history. Arrian in the early part of the 2nd and Aelian in the 3rd century both speak of him with respect, though with reference mainly to his excellence as an authority on the art of war.

In addition to his *Histories* Polybius was the author of the following smaller works: a life of Philopoemen, a history of the Numantine War, a treatise on tactics. The geographical treatise, referred to by Geminus, is possibly identical with the thirty-fourth book of the *Histories*.

PLUTARCH

Mestrius Plutarchus was a Greek philosopher, biographer, and essayist. He was a Middle Platonist and was known to have written a number of philosophical treatises. While a large number of semi-philosophical writings survive under the title of *Memoria,* his more technical philosophical treatises were all lost. Consequently, Plutarch is far better remembered for his biographical works than philosophical contributions.

Among his works, the most important are the *Bioi paralleloi (Parallel Lives),* which describes the characters and recounts the noble deeds of Greek and Roman soldiers, legislators, orators, and statesmen. The biographies, which paired Greek and Roman subjects in comparisons which were sometimes rather forced, are an important source of historical information. Plutarch's *Lives* provided the material for many stories and poems during the Middle Ages, and influenced English and French literature from the sixteenth through the nineteenth centuries. Shakespeare and other Elizabethan dramatists used a translation by Thomas North as a source for many of their historical plays. The *Moralia,* or *Ethica,* is a series of more than 60 essays on philosophical, religious, ethical, political, physical, and literary topics.

LIFE

Plutarch was probably born in 46 C.E. in the small town of Chaeronea, in the Greek region known as Boeotia, probably during the reign of the Roman Emperor Claudius. His parents were wealthy people, and after 67 C.E., Plutarch traveled widely in the Mediterranean world, including two journeys to Rome. Plutarch studied philosophy, rhetoric, and mathematics at the Academy of Athens. He never became a staunch Platonist, but remained open to the ideas of other philosophical schools such as the Stoa and the school of Aristotle. It is thought that Plutarch was present when the emperor Nero, who visited Greece at this time, declared the Greek towns to be free and autonomous.

A wealthy aristocrat, Plutarch became a leading citizen of Chaeronea and is known to have represented his town on several occasions, including a visit to the governor of Achaea, and journeys to Alexandria and Rome. He had a number of influential friends, including Soscius Senecio and Fundanus, both important Roman senators, to whom some of his later writings were dedicated; and Lucius Mestrius Florus, a Roman consul during the reign of Vespasian, and Plutarch's guide during his visit to Cremona.

Lucius Mestrius Florus sponsored Plutarch as a Roman citizen and, according to the tenth century historian George Syncellus, late in life, the Emperor Hadrian appointed him procurator of Achaea, a position that entitled him to wear the vestments of a consul, a golden ring and white toga with a purple border. (The *Suda,* a medieval Greek encyclopedia, states that Hadrian's predecessor Trajan made Plutarch procurator of Illyria, but most historians consider that unlikely, since Illyria was not a procuratorial province, and Plutarch probably did not speak Illyrian.)

In the 90s, Plutarch, returned to his home town. Once, when asked why he had returned to the province, he explained that Chaeronea was in decline and that it would be even smaller if he did not settle there. For some time, he was mayor of Chaeronea. He was initiated into the mysteries of the Greek god Apollo, and served as the senior of the two priests of Apollo at the Oracle of Delphi (where he was responsible for interpreting the auguries of the Pythia). He led an active social and civic life and produced an extensive body of writing, much of which is still extant.

Plutarch's books brought him international fame, and his home became a private school for young philosophers. He was often visited by eminent Greeks and Romans. Plutarch died after his procuratorship, which was in 119, and before 125. The Delphians and Chaeroneans ordered statues to be erected in honor of their famous citizen.

MORALIA

The remainder of Plutarch's surviving work is collected under the title of the *Moralia* (loosely translated as *Customs and Mores)*, an eclectic collection of seventy-eight essays and transcribed speeches. It includes *On Fraternal Affection*—a discourse on honor and affection of siblings toward each other; *On the Fortune or the Virtue of Alexander the Great*—an important adjunct to his Life of the great king; *On the Worship of Isis and Osiris*—a crucial source of information on Egyptian religious rites; and *On the Malice of Herodotus*—which may, like the orations on Alexander's accomplishments, have been a rhetorical exercise, in which Plutarch criticizes what he sees as systematic bias in the work of Herodotus.

There are also more philosophical treatises, such as *On the Decline of the Oracles, On the Delays of the Divine Vengeance, On Peace of Mind;* and lighter fare, such as *Odysseus and Gryllus,* a humorous dialogue between Homer's Ulysses and one of Circe's enchanted pigs. The *Moralia* was composed earlier than the Lives, which occupied much of the last two decades of Plutarch's life.

Some editions of the *Moralia* include several works now known to be *pseudepigrapha*: Among these are the *Lives of the Ten Orators* (biographies of the Ten Orators of ancient Athens, based on Caecilius of Calacte), *The Doctrines of the Philosophers,* and *On Music.* One unknown "pseudo-Plutarch" is considered responsible for all of these works. Though the thoughts and opinions recorded are not Plutarch's and come from a slightly later era, they are all classical in origin and have value to the historian.

The *Moralia* includes a letter of consolation to Plutarch's wife, after the death of their two-year-old daughter, which gives a glimpse of his ideas on reincarnation:

The soul, being eternal, after death is like a caged bird that has been released. If it has been a long time in the body, and has become tame by many affairs and long habit, the soul will immediately take another body and once again become involved in the troubles of the world. The worst thing about old age is that the soul's memory of the other world grows dim, while at the same time its attachment to things of this world becomes so strong that the soul tends to retain the form that it had in the body. But that soul which remains only a short time within a body, until liberated by the higher powers, quickly recovers its fire and goes on to higher things.

It is clear that Plutarch's aim was the moral education of his readers. *Moralia* includes essays with titles such as *Checking Anger, The Art of Listening, How to Know Whether One Progresses to Virtue,* and *Advice to Bride and Groom.* Plutarch's central theme seems to have been the concept of a dualistic opposition between good and evil principles in the world. Later philosophers of the neoplatonistic school disagreed with this idea, and this may explain why several of Plutarch's more serious philosophical publications are now lost, leaving only some lighter works, together with his attacks on the Stoa and Epicureanism.

SUMMARY

46 A.D – He was born this year to a prominent family in Chaeronea, Boeotia. He was best known for his works Morallia and Parallel Lives.

66 A.D - Plutarch is believed to have had a liberal education at Athens, where he studied physics, rhetoric,

mathematics, medicine, natural science, philosophy, Greek, and Latin literature in this year.

68 A.D - Plutarch married Timoxena, daughter of Alexion, who bore him four sons, Soclarus, Chairon, Autobulus, and Plutarchus, and one daughter, Timoxena.

69 A.D - Among his friends was Lucius Mestrius Florus, a consul during the reign of Vespasian, and Plutarch's guide during his visit to Cremona, where two important battles had been fought in this year, the year of the four emperors Galba, Vitellius, Otho, and Vespasian.

75 A.D - He spent much time in Italy between this year and 90; he apparently never mastered the Latin language, though he gained the friendship of notable Romans. The latter half of his life, Plutarch enjoyed the intellectual benefits of the Pax Romana, mostly in Chaeronia.

90 A.D - Plutarch, who had seen much of the world, settled in his hometown. When asked to explain his return to the province, he said that Chaeronea was in decline and that it would be even smaller if he did not settle there. For some time, he was mayor. He held many civic positions, both high and low; the most notable one that of head priest of Delphi. He held with distinction for 20 years and elevated to an importance it had not had in his time.

105 A.D. - The Lives (often called Parallel Lives) are biographies of soldiers and political leaders of repute, generally presented in pairs of lives, first a Greek, then a Roman, followed by a comparison. Twenty-three of these have survived and four single lives; that is, four comparisons are lacking. There is no detailed chronology, but the Lives were probably published between this year and 115.

127 A.D – He passed away this year in Delphi, Phocis. During the latter part of his life, he is thought to have written most of the Lives and some portions of the Moralia.

ROMAN HISTORIOGRAPHY

CATO

Marcus Porcius Cato "Uticensis" (also known as Cato the

Younger) was many things, including the adamantine foe of the triumvirs Pompey, Caesar, and Crassus and the man whose undying enmity to Caesar in the Civil War led him to commit particularly violent suicide rather than give Caesar the pleasure of pardoning him in defeat. Austere, humorless, puritanical, incapable of compromise, he was a fanatic in defence of liberty and the Republic. Cato was deeply admired by Americans in the Revolutionary period; Addison's play *Cato,* in which Cato defies the tyrant Caesar in verse, was a favourite of George Washington. In his own time, while regarded as one of the greatest Romans, his implacable moral stands apparently stirred both reverence and exasperation:

UPBRINGING OF A STOIC

Cato inherited a famous name as the great-grandson of the famous Marcus Porcius Cato the Elder (the Censor), the inveterate foe of Carthage in the third Punic War. He was reared by his uncle, Marcus Livius Drusus, along with several full and half-siblings (including half-sister, Servilia, later Caesar's longtime mistress and mother of Brutus). Cato deeply admired his ancestor and imbibed early both the austere principles of the early Republic and the fonts of Stoic philosophy. He also appears to have absorbed his forebear's inability to compromise and his utter certainty of his own right action. Yet in his own time of universal political and financial corruption, Cato was perhaps the one man in Italy who could not be bought.

After the normal young Roman's army service as a tribune in Macedon in 67 BC, Cato was elected quaestor in 65. The position gave him a forum to gain a reputation for honest, even eccentric, frugality, as well as a much-publicized intemperance of the bribery and corruption seething in contemporary Rome. He returned to Rome and continued in politics, although he never scaled the offices of the *cursus honorum* with the single-minded ambition of his contemporaries, reaching no higher than tribune. His reputation soon outweighed his political rank.

During the trial of Catiline in 63, the up-and-coming Cato

first is known to have clashed with his great opponent, Julius Caesar. Cato's speeches during the drama of Catiline's conspiracy strongly supported Cicero and his actions in putting the alleged conspirators instantly to death. Cato also hinted that Caesar himself should be charged with the guilty conspirators.

When the debates over the punishment for the accused were at their height, Caesar spoke for their banishment, not execution, and seemed to have changed the Senate's mind on the verdict. At the very moment of victory, Cato stood again and spoke for death with such passion and persuasiveness that the entire Senate reversed itself. In the end, Cato's firmness was applauded, the conspirators died, and the stamp was set on Caesar's and Cato's future enmity.

CATO "UTICENSIS", 46 BC

Cato was in command at Utica. After word reached Utica of Caesar's definitive victory against Scipio's army at the Battle of Thapsus, Cato enjoined his son, with bitter pride, to surrender to Caesar; *"I grew up in freedom, with the right of free speech. I cannot change my ways in my latter years and accustom myself to servitude. But it is right that you, having been born and brought up in such conditions, should serve the divinity that governs your destiny."* Cassius.

His son would later fall at Philippi. Determined to die, Cato fell on his sword during an unwatched moment, claiming that, at last, he was free. However, he was discovered by those watching him and a doctor was called to bandage him tightly. Knowing that Caesar's arrival in the city was imminent, Cato ripped through his bandaged abdomen and bled to death, literally taking his life with his own hands rather than surviving to be pardoned by the man he viewed as the Republic's bane.

Cato's personal life was more than peculiar. One of his closest emotional attachments was to a young brother, Caepio, who died young in Thrace; the self-contained Cato, by all accounts, suffered a complete emotional breakdown. He put away his first wife for adultery. He divorced his second wife, marrying her to an aged patrician, Hortensius, and then remarried her when Hortensius died (and after she had inherited his property). He married his daughter, Porcia, to his political ally, Bibulus, and then to his nephew, Brutus. Ever puritanical in public, he was in private a notoriously heavy drinker. Caesar (as quoted by Pliny the Younger) wryly acknowledges Cato's legend even when drunk; a group of passersby, meeting the Great Man by chance when dead drunk, blush in embarrassment: *"You would have thought they had been found out by Cato, not Cato by them."* Pliny, *Letters,* III.12.

What Cato must have thought of his own sister being Caesar's favourite of many mistresses can scarcely be imagined; of course, Cato was one of many contemporaries whom Caesar was alleged to have cuckolded. Fanatical to embody the primitive example of a "pure" early Rome, Cato roused titters by appearing in public wearing nothing but a toga, without either shoes or tunic. But none of these domestic infelicities affected Cato's reputation as the foremost champion of the Republic.

Lucan wrote, in his Civil War epic, *The Pharsalia, "victrix causa diis placuit, sed victa Catoni"* ('The victorious cause pleased the gods but the defeated cause pleased Cato'). In death, Cato's obdurate determination was elevated to the high pantheon of Roman patriotism. Caesar appears to have disliked Cato as he disliked few men; it is impossible otherwise to account for Caesar's genuine resentment at Cato's untimely death. He is said to have spoken, as if to the living man, *"I envy you this death, for you envied [denied] me the chance to save you."*

Cassius Dio, *Roman History*I. When Cicero and Brutus published posthumous praises of Cato's noble qualities, Caesar published his *Anti-Cato,* which has not survived but which apparently was viewed disparagingly by his contemporaries. 90 years later, Cato could be seriously described by as having *"...a character nearer to that of gods than of men. He never did a right action solely for the sake of seeming to do the right, but because he could not do otherwise."*

It is difficult to warm to Cato, but it is possible to both admire and condemn him. Like some patriots of the American

Revolution - Patrick Henry come to mind - the very qualities of obdurate determination not to compromise is arguably ill-suited - even harmful - to the act of governing. The tale is told that, in the early days of the Civil War, Pompey and Caesar almost found a peaceable accommodation which might have changed Roman history, except that Cato, discovering that Pompey was negotiating with Caesar, persuaded him to fight him instead. Like all fanatics, Cato's inflexible convictions were more than slightly frightening. Yet Cato's very implacability, in the corruption of his own age, earns its own grudging admiration. He was viewed by his own contemporaries as one of the very greatest men of his time.

In the event, and by his death, he also earned the undying regard of Roman historians. The irony is that it may be his very obduracy which made the dictatorship of Caesar, the death of the Republic, and the Ides of March, inevitable. The conspirators, striking at Caesar, struck also for Cato.

CICERO

INTRODUCTION

Cicero was born on 3 January 106 BC. His family was from the town of Arpinum, about 70 miles south-east of Rome. The name Cicero means chickpea, and stemmed from an ancestor who had a wart at the end of his nose, which looked like a chickpea. Cicero studied literature, philosophy and law in Rome. His studies were interrupted by a spell of military service under Gnaeus Pompeius Strabo during the Social War (the war Rome fought (90-88) against its Italian allies which ended with the extension of Roman citizenship to the whole of Italy south of the Po). He claims to have supported Sulla in the upheavals of the 80s without actually taking up arms.

In 80, Cicero appeared as the advocate defending Sextus Roscius of Ameria against a charge of parricide. He defended Roscius by turning the accusation of murder back on one of Roscius' accusers, his relation Titus Roscius Magnus, and another relation, Titus Roscius Capito. What caused a sensation was Cicero's claim that Chrysogonus, one of Sulla's freedmen, had assisted in covering up the murder and, for his pains, had bought the lion's share of the dead man's property at a rock bottom price a claim that could easily be seen, despite all Cicero's protestations to the contrary, as an attack on Sulla himself. Sextus Roscius was acquitted and Cicero was famous. Soon afterwards, Cicero took on another politically sensitive case, that of a woman from Arretium, in which he criticised Sulla for depriving the people of Arretium of their citizenship. Cicero then left for Greece, perhaps for health reasons (his digestion was never good), or perhaps because he felt a discreet absence might be wise, or perhaps a bit of both.

He used this time to continue his studies of philosophy in Athens. Here he renewed his acquaintance with Titus Pomponius Atticus, who was to become a life-long friend and correspondent. Although he was attracted by Antiochus of Ascalon's lecturing style, Cicero's own philosophical leanings were towards the sceptical position of the philosophers known as the New Academy. Cicero did consider settling in Athens, but after the death of Sulla (78), he left for the Roman province of Asia (now Western Turkey) and Rhodes where he studied oratory. On his return to Rome (77) he resumed his career as an advocate.

In 75, he became quaestor and served in Sicily, securing the grain supply. The Sicilians' gratitude for his fair, if strict, administration led to their approaching Cicero to undertake the prosecution of Verres, who had just completed his term of office (73-71) as governor of Sicily, for extortion. Cicero did so (70), although he first had to argue before the courts that he, and not Quintus Caecilius Niger, who had been quaestor under Verres and was expected to put up only a token prosecution to ensure Verres' acquittal, should be the prosecutor.

Verres' strategy was to draw out the proceedings to the next year when Hortensius, Verres' defending advocate, would be one of the consuls, and one member of the Metelli family, who were supporters of Verres, would be the other consul and another the praetor presiding over the court where Verres was to be tried.

Cicero gathered his evidence more quickly than anyone

expected despite the efforts of yet another Metellus, who succeeded Verres as governor of Sicily. Nevertheless, because of the great number of festivals coming up, during which the courts would be closed, Cicero had to adopt an unusual strategy in court. The normal procedure in cases of extortion was for the prosecution to give an introductory speech and then one or more speeches arguing for the defendant's guilt. The defending advocates would then reply, and then witnesses would be called. After a two-day adjournment, the prosecution and defence would each give further speeches, and then the jury would vote by secret ballot.

Cicero's opening speech laid great stress on the political aspects of the case. Only senators could be jurors, but there were moves afoot to turn the courts over to the *equites* (rich non-senators) on the grounds that the senatorial juries were notoriously corrupt. Cicero warns the jury that if they do not convict Verres, who had frequently boasted that his money would guarantee an acquittal, they should not be surprised if the senate's privilege of sitting on juries is taken away.

Rather than making speeches arguing for Verres' guilt, Cicero then just presented his witnesses. Verres chose not to contest the case and went into voluntary exile from Italy. Cicero published the speeches he would have given if Verres had stuck it out. The next year the senators lost their exclusive right to sit on juries.

LIVY

TITUS LIVIUS, the most illustrious of Roman historians, was born at Pativium, (Padua,) 61 B.C., according to Cato, but according to Varro, in 59 B.C., the year of the great Caesar's first consulship. We know nothing of his early life, except that for some time he practiced as a rhetorician, and wrote on Rhetoric. It is probable that he did not commence his great historical work till he was drawing near middle age. He had ample time to finish it for he lived to see his eightieth year. His fame was so thoroughly established and widely spread even during his lifetime, that a Spaniard travelled from Gades to Rome only to see him. The Roman history of Livy is one of the greatest masterpieces of Latin, or of human composition. Originally it was comprised in 142 books, divided into tens or decades; but only 30 books, with the greater part of five more, now exist.

In classing Livy in his proper place among the great historians of the ancient and modern world, we must not think of him as a critical antiquarian writer - a writer of scrupluously calm judgment and diligent research. He is preeminently a man of beautiful genius, with an unrivalled talent for narration, who takes up the history of his country in the spirit of an artist, makes a free use of the materials lying handiest, for the creation of a work full of grace, colour, harmony, and a dignified ease.

The value of his history is incalculable even in the mutilated state in which we have it, as a picture of what the great Roman traditions were to the Romans in their most cultivated period. The literary talent most conspicuous in Livy, is that of a narrator.

He does not rival Tacitus in portraiture or in tragic power, but no writer has ever surpassed him in the art of telling a story; and the speeches which, acccording to the antique fashion, he puts into the mouths of his historic characters, are singularly ingenious, pointed, and dramatically real.

TACITUS

Publius or Gaius Cornelius Tacitus (born around AD 56 - died around AD 120), was a Roman historian. Born into a wealthy family living in Gaul. He was a friend of Pliny the Younger and married the daughter of Cnaeus Julius Agricola, who governed in Roman Britain . Tacitus received the best education available to a Roman from a good wealthy family. Public speaking skills, oratory and debate, which were considered the most important areas of study for a young man destined for a career in imperial service or senatorial office. Tacitus was a senator during the reign of Domitian. In AD 97 he was appointed substitute consul under Nerva, and in AD 112-113 he held the highest civilian governorship, that of the Roman province of Asia in Western Anatolia.

Tacitus objected to great concentration of power in the

hands of the early emperors. Though he hated imperial power and in his writings tries to paint every emperor as a corrupt despot, he hated civil war and anarchy even more. He had a particularly heavy bias against the emperor Tiberius, whom he portrayed as a sinister and cruel emperor, purging his opponents from the Senate by having them tried for treason and executed.

He showed scorn for Claudius and Nero, and even his writings about Augustus contained some belittling and snide remarks. His writing is full of tales of corruption, government scandal, and innocent people being destroyed or having their good names ruined because of the emperor's lust for power. It was Tacitus' belief that the emperor had so much power in his hands that no man could occupy the throne without being corrupted by that power.

Tacitus wrote at least 16 books, but books 7-10 and parts of books 5, 6, 11 and 16 are missing. Book 6 ends with the death of Tiberius and books 7-12 presumably covered the reigns of Caligula and Claudius. The remaining books cover the reign of Nero, perhaps until his death in June 68 or until the end of that year, to connect with the Histories.

The second half of book 16 is missing. We do not know whether Tacitus completed the work or whether he wrote any further associated books. Of the Histories only the first four books and 26 chapters of the fifth book have survived, covering the year 69 and the first part of 70. The work is believed to have continued up to the death of Domitian on September 18, 96. Tacitus also wrote three shorter works: the Agricola, a biography of his father-in-law Gnaeus Julius Agricola; the Germania; and the Dialogus.

The first of his works was the Dialogus [dialogue], a discussion of oratory in the style of Cicero, demonstrating to some degree why Tacitus was celebrated as an eloquent speaker; this work was long disputed, but his authorship is now generally accepted. Tacitus was primarily concerned with the balance of power between the Roman senate and the Roman Emperors. His writings are filled with tales of corruption and tyranny in the governing class of Rome as they failed to adjust to the new imperial régime; they squandered their cherished cultural traditions of free speech and self-respect as they fell over themselves to please the often bemused emperor.

Tacitus then wrote a biography of Agricola , expressing his admiration for his father-in-law as a good and able man. His small treatise De origine et situ Germanorum [concerning the origin and location of the Germans], commonly called the Germania, supplies (along with the earlier account of Julius Caesar) the principal written material on the Germanic tribes. His treatment of the Germanic peoples outside the empire is of mixed value to historians.

Tacitus uses what he reports of the German character as a kind of 'noble savage' as a comparison to contemporary Romans and their (in his eyes) 'degeneracy'. Despite this bias, he does supply us with many names for tribes with which Rome had come into contact.

Tacitus' information was not, in general, based on first-hand knowledge, and more recent research has shown that many of his assumptions were incorrect. In fact, contemporary historians debate whether all these tribes were really Germanic. He is also to blame for the misnaming of the Battle of the Teutoburg Forest, which did not quite take place in the saltus Teutoburgiensis, as he claimed in the Germania.

The moral purpose and severe criticism of contemporary Rome, fallen from the virtuous vigor of the old republic, also underlies his two long works, commonly called in English the Histories and the Annals. The surviving books of the Histories cover only the reign of Galba (AD 68-69) and the beginning (to AD 70) of the reign of Vespasian but give a thorough view of Roman life-persons, places, and events.

The surviving books of the Annals tell of the reign of Tiberius, of the last years of Claudius, and of the first years of Nero. The account contains incisive character sketches, ironic passages, and eloquent moral conclusions. The declamatory writing of the Dialogus is replaced in the historical works by a polished and highly individual style, a wide range of vocabulary, and an intricate and startling syntax. The Annals was Tacitus' final work, covering the period from the death of Augustus Caesar in AD 14.

MEDIEVAL HISTORIOGRAPHY

LIFE

Formative Period

Augustine, bishop of Hippo (Lat. Augustinus; the pr~enomen Aurelius given by Orosius, Prosper, and others, has no evidence in his own writings, or in letters addressed to him), is not only the most important of the Fathers of the early Church, but at the same time the one best known through a variety of specially full and useful sources. He was one of the most fertile writers of the early period, and the multiplication of his manuscripts has allowed his works to come down relatively complete in number.

Among these, the Confessiones and the Retractationes have a unique value for the history of primitive church life, while others are full of biographical details. Moreover, a countryman of his, Possidius, Bishop of Calama, who was in close relations with him for forty years and present at his death, has given us a life which deserves a place of honor in early hagiography.

We have thus remarkably satisfactory sources both as to Augustine's life and as to his literary work. He himself, in his Confessiones (written between 397 and 400), has described the events of his first thirty-three years; and for the rest of his life we have both the treatises and letters, which begin about the time when the Confessiones stop, as well as the biography by Possidius. For the historical understanding of his works, as well as for their dates and criticism, Augustine himself has left in the Retractationes (completed at the end of 427) a unique guide.

In this review he has taken up each one of his writings, except the letters and sermons, in chronological order, with the purpose of explaining things which might be misconstrued or of restating them in a better way; and Possidius has given us also a comprehensive and systematic list of all the writings, as an appendix to his biography.

Boyhood. Parental Influences

Augustine is the first ecclesiastical author the whole course of whose development can be clearly traced, as well as the first in whose case we are able to determine the exact period covered by his career, to the very day. He informs us himself that he was born at Thagaste (Tagaste; now Suk Arras), in proconsular Numidia, Nov. 13, 354; he died at Hippo Regius (just south of the modern Bona) Aug. 28, 430. [Both Suk Arras and Bona are in the present Algeria, the first 60 m. w. by s. and the second 65 m. w. of Tunis, the ancient Carthage.]

His father Patricius, as a member of the council, belonged to the influential classes of the place; he was, however, in straitened circumstances, and seems to have had nothing remarkable either in mental equipment or in character, but to have been a lively, sensual, hot-tempered person, entirely taken up with his worldly concerns, and unfriendly to Christianity until the close of his life; he became a catechumen shortly before Augustine reached his sixteenth year (369-370). To his mother Monnica (so the manuscripts write her name, not Monica; b. 331, d. 387) Augustine later believed that he owed what he became.

But though she was evidently an honorable, loving, self-sacrificing, and able woman, she was not always the ideal of a Christian mother that tradition has made her appear. Her religion in earlier life has traces of formality and worldliness about it; her ambition for her son seems at first to have had little moral earnestness and she regretted his Manicheanism more than she did his early sensuality. It seems to have been through Ambrose and Augustine that she attained the mature personal piety with which she left the world. Of Augustine as a boy his parents were intensely proud.

He received his first education at Thagaste, learning to read and write, as well as the rudiments of Greek and Latin literature, from teachers who followed the old traditional pagan methods. He seems to have had no systematic instruction in the Christian faith at this period, and though enrolled among the catechumens, apparently was near baptism only when an illness and his own boyish desire made it temporarily probable.

Schooling and Early Marriage

His father, delighted with his son's progress in his studies, sent him first to the neighboring Madaura, and then to Carthage, some two days' journey away. A year's enforced idleness, while the means for this more expensive schooling were being accumulated, proved a time of moral deterioration; but we must be on our guard against forming our conception of Augustine's vicious living from the Confessiones alone. To speak, as Mommsen does, of" frantic dissipation" is to attach too much weight to his own penitent expressions of self-reproach.

Looking back as a bishop, he naturally regarded his whole life up to the" conversion" which led to his baptism as a period of wandering from the right way; but not long after this conversion, he judged differently, and found, from one point of view, the turning point of his career in his taking up philosophy in his nineteenth year. This view of his early life, which may be traced also in the Confessiones, is probably nearer the truth than the popular conception of a youth sunk in all kinds of immorality.

When he began the study of rhetoric at Carthage, it is true that (in company with comrades whose ideas of pleasure were probably much more gross than his) he drank of the cup of sensual pleasure. But his ambition prevented him from allowing his dissipations to interfere with his studies. His son Adeodatus was born in the summer of 372, and it was probably the mother of this child whose charms enthralled him soon after his arrival at Carthage about the end of 370. But he remained faithful to her until about 385, and the grief which he felt at parting from her shows what the relation had been.

In the view of the civilization of that period, such a monogamous union was distinguished from a formal marriage only by certain legal restrictions, in addition to the informality of its beginning and the possibility of a voluntary dissolution. Even the Church was slow to condemn such unions absolutely, and Monnica seems to have received the child and his mother publicly at Thagaste.

In any case Augustine was known to Carthage not as a roysterer but as a quiet honorable student. He was, however, internally dissatisfied with his life. The Hortensius of Cicero, now lost with the exception of a few fragments, made a deep impression on him. To know the truth was henceforth his deepest wish.

About the time when the contrast between his ideals and his actual life became intolerable, he learned to conceive of Christianity as the one religion which could lead him to the attainment of his ideal. But his pride of intellect held him back from embracing it earnestly; the Scriptures could not bear comparison with Cicero; he sought for wisdom, not for humble submission to authority.

Comes Under Manichean Influences

In this frame of mind he was ready to be affected by the Manichean propaganda which was then actively carried on in Africa, without apparently being much hindered by the imperial edict against assemblies of the sect. Two things especially attracted him to the Manicheans: they felt at liberty to criticize the Scriptures, particularly the Old Testament, with perfect freedom; and they held chastity and self denial in honor. The former fitted in with the impression which the Bible had made on Augustine himself; the latter corresponded closely to his mood at the time.

The prayer which he tells us he had in his heart then, "Lord, give me chastity and temperance, but not now," may be taken as the formula which represents the attitude of many of the Manichean auditores. Among these Augustine was classed during his nineteenth year; but he went no further, though he held firmly to Manicheanism for nine years, during which he endeavored to convert all his friends, scorned the sacraments of the Church, and held frequent disputations with catholic believers.

Teaches at Thagaste

Having finished his studies, he returned to Thagaste and began to teach grammar, living in the house of Romanianus, a prominent citizen who had been of much service to him since his father's death, and whom he converted to Manicheanism. Monnica deeply grieved at her son's heresy, forbade him her house, until reassured by a vision that promised his restoration.

She comforted herself also by the word of a certain bishop (probably of Thagaste) that "the child of so many tears could not be lost." He seems to have spent little more than a year in Thagaste, when the desire for a wider field, together with the death of a dear friend, moved him to return to Carthage as a teacher of rhetoric.

Rejection of Manicheanism. Removal to Rome

The next period was a time of diligent study, and produced (about the end of 380) the treatise, long since lost, De pulchro et apto. Meanwhile the hold of Manicheanism on him was loosening. Its feeble cosmology and metaphysics had long since failed to satisfy him, and the astrological superstitions springing from the credulity of its disciples offended his reason. The members of the sect, unwilling to lose him, had great hopes from a meeting with their leader Faustus of Mileve; but when he came to Carthage in the autumn of 382, he too proved disappointing, and Augustine ceased to be at heart a Manichean.

He was not yet, however, prepared to put anything in the place of the doctrine he had held, and remained in outward communion with his former associates while he pursued his search for truth. Soon after his Manichean convictions had broken down, he left Carthage for Rome, partly, it would seem, to escape the preponderating influence of his mother on a mind which craved perfect freedom of investigation. Here he was brought more than ever, by obligations of friendship and gratitude, into close association with Manicheans, of whom there were many in Rome, not merely auditores but perfecti or fully initiated members. This did not last long, however, for the prefect Symmachus sent him to Milan, certainly before the beginning of 385, in answer to a request for a professor of rhetoric.

Life Under Ambrose at Milan

The change of residence completed Augustine's separation from Manicheanism. He listened to the preaching of Ambrose and by it was made acquainted with the allegorical interpretation of the Scriptures and the weakness of the Manichean Biblical criticism, but he was not yet ready to accept catholic Christianity. His mind was still under the influence of the skeptical philosophy of the later Academy.

This was the least satisfactory stage in his mental development, though his external circumstances were increasingly favorable. He had his mother again with him now, and shared a house and garden with her and his devoted friends Alypius and Nebridius, who had followed him to Milan; his assured social position is shown also by the fact that, in deference to his mother's entreaties, he was formally betrothed to a woman of suitable station.

As a catechumen of the Church, he listened regularly to the sermons of Ambrose. The bishop, though as yet he knew nothing of Augustine's internal struggles, had welcomed him in the friendliest manner both for his own and for Monnica's sake. Yet Augustine was attracted only by Ambrose's eloquence, not by his faith; now he agreed, and now he questioned. Morally his life was perhaps at its lowest point. On his betrothal, he had put away the mother of his son; but neither the grief which he felt at this parting nor regard for his future wife, who was as yet too young for marriage, prevented him from taking a new concubine for the two intervening years. Sensuality, however, began to pall upon him, little as he cared to struggle against it.

His idealism was by no means dead; he told Romanian, who came to Milan at this time on business, that he wished he could live altogether in accordance with the dictates of philosophy; and a plan was even made for the foundation of a community retired from the world, which should live entirely for the pursuit of truth. With this project his intention of marriage and his ambition interfered, and Augustine was further off than ever from peace of mind.

Attracted to Neoplatonism

In his thirty-first year he was strongly attracted to Neoplatonism by the logic of his development. The idealistic character of this philosophy awoke unbounded enthusiasm, and he was attracted to it also by its exposition of pure intellectual being and of the origin of evil. These doctrines brought him closer to the Church,. though he did not yet grasp the full significance of its central doctrine of the personality of Jesus Christ.

In his earlier writings he names this acquaintance with the Neoplatonic teaching and its relation to Christianity as the turning-point of his life, though in the Confessiones it appears only as a stage on the long road of error. The truth, as it may be established by a careful comparison of his earlier and later writings, is that his idealism had been distinctly strengthened by Neoplatonism, which had at the same time revealed his own will, and not a natura altera in him, as the subject of his baser desires. This made the conflict between ideal and actual in his life more unbearable than ever. Yet his sensual desires were still so strong that it seemed impossible for him to break away from them.

Conversion to Christianity

Help came in a curious way. A countryman of his, Pontitianus, visited him and told him things which he had never heard about the monastic life and the wonderful conquests over self which had been won under its inspiration. Augustine's pride was touched; that the unlearned should take the kingdom of heaven by violence, while he with all his learning, was still held captive by the flesh, seemed unworthy of him. When Pontitianus had gone, with a few vehement words to Alypius, he went hastily with him into the garden to fight out this new problem. Then followed the scene so often described. Overcome by his conflicting emotions he left

Alypius and threw himself down under a fig-tree in tears. From a neighboring house came a child's voice repeating again and again the simple words Tolle, lege, "Take up and read." It seemed to him a heavenly indication; he picked up the copy of St. Paul's epistles which he had left where he and Alypius had been sitting, and opened at Romans xiii.

When he came to the words, "Let us walk honestly as in the day; not in rioting and drunkenness, not in chambering and wantonness," it seemed to him that a decisive message had been sent to his own soul, and his resolve was taken. Alypius found a word for himself a few lines further, "Him that is weak in the faith receive ye;" and together they went into the house to bring the good news to Monnica. This was at the end of the summer of 386.

Baptism. Ordination in Africa

Augustine, intent on breaking wholly with his old life, gave up his position, and wrote to Ambrose to ask for baptism. The months which intervened between that summer and the Easter of the following year, at which, according to the early custom, he intended to receive the sacrament, were spent in delightful calm at a country-house, put at his disposal by one of his friends, at Cassisiacum (Casciago, 47 m. n. by w. of Milan). Here Monnica, Alypius, Adeodatus, and some of his pupils kept him company, and he still lectured on Vergil to them and held philosophic discussions.

The whole party returned to Milan before Easter (387), and Augustine, with Alypius and Adeodatus, was baptized. Plans were then made for returning to Africa; but these were upset by the death of Monnica, which took place at Ostia as they were preparing to cross the sea, and has been described by her devoted son in one of the most tender and beautiful passages of the Confessiones. Augustine remained at least another year in Italy, apparently in Rome, living the same quiet life which he had led at Cassisiacum, studying and writing, in company with his countryman Evodius, later bishop of Uzalis. Here, where he had been most closely associated with the Manicheans, his literary warfare with them naturally began;

and he was also writing on free will, though this book was only finished at Hippo in 391. In the autumn of 388, passing through Carthage, he returned to Thagaste, a far different man from the Augustine who had left it five years before. Alypius was still with him, and also Adeodatus, who died young, we do not know when or where.

Here Augustine and his friends again took up a quiet, though not yet in any sense a monastic, life in common, and pursued their favourite studies. About the beginning of 391, having found a friend in Hippo to help in the foundation of what he calls a monastery, he sold his inheritance, and was ordained presbyter in response to a general demand, though not without misgivings on his own part.

Presbyterate at Hippo

The years which he spent in the presbyterate (39 1-395) are the last of his formative period. The very earliest works which fall within the time of his episcopate show us the fully developed theologian of whose special teaching we think when we speak of Augustinianism. There is little externally noteworthy in these four years. He took up active work not later than the Easter of 391, when we find him preaching to the candidates for baptism.

The plans for a monastic community which had brought him to Hippo were now realized. In a garden given for the purpose by the bishop, Valerius, he founded his monastery, which seems to have been the first in Africa, and is of especial significance because it maintained a clerical school and thus made a connecting link between monasticism and the secular clergy.

Other details of this period are that he appealed to Aurelius, bishop of Carthage, to suppress the custom of holding banquets and entertainments in the churches, and by 395 had succeeded, through his courageous eloquence, in abolishing it in Hippo; that in 392 a public disputation took place between him and a Manichean presbyter of Hippo, Fortunatus; that his treatise DeJlde et symbolo was prepared to be read before the council held at Hippo October 8, 393;

and that after that he was in Carthage for a while, perhaps in connection with the synod held there in 394.

Beginnings of Polemic Activity

The intellectual interests of these four years are more easily determined, principally concerned as they are with the Manichean controversy, and producing the treatises De utilitate credendi (391), De duabus animabus contra Manichceos (first half of 392), and Contra Adimantum (394 or 395). His activity against the Donatists also begins in this period, but he is still more occupied with the Manicheans, both from the recollections of his own past, and from his increasing knowledge of Scripture, which appears, together with a stronger hold on the Church's teaching, in the works just named, and even more in others of this period, such as his expositions of the Sermon on the Mount and of the Epistles to the Romans and the Galatians.

Full as the writings of this epoch are, however, of Biblical phrases and terms,-grace and the law, predestination, vocation, justification, regeneration-a reader who is thoroughly acquainted with Neoplatonism will detect Augustine's old love of it in a Christian dress in not a few places.

He has entered so far into St. Paul's teaching that humanity as a whole appears to him a massapeccati orpeccatorum, which, if left to itself, that is, without the grace of God, must inevitably perish. However much we are here reminded of the later Augustine, it is clear that he still held the belief that the free will of man could decide his own destiny. He knew some who saw in Romans ix an unconditional predestination which took away the freedom of the will; but he was still convinced that this was not the Church's teaching. His opinion on this point did not change till after he was a bishop.

WORK AS BISHOP

Election to the Bishopric

The more widely known Augustine became, the more

Valerius, the bishop of Hippo, was afraid of losing him on the first vacancy of some neighboring see, and desired to fix him permanently in Hippo by making him coadjutor-bishop,—a desire in which the people ardently concurred.

Augustine was strongly opposed to the project, though possibly neither he nor Valerius knew that it might be held to be a violation of the eighth canon of Nicaea, which forbade in its last clause "two bishops in one city" (Hefele, Conciliengeschichte, i, 407 sqq., Eng. transl., i, 409-4 10); and the primate of Numidia, Megalius of Calama, seems to have raised difficulties which sprang at least partly from a personal lack of confidence. But Valerius carried his plan through, and not long before Christmas, 395, Augustine was consecrated by Megalius. It is not known when Valerius died; but it makes little difference, since for the rest of his life he left the administration more and more in the hands of his assistant.

Possidius's View of Augustine's Services

A complete narration of Augustine's doings during the thirty-five years in which he was the glory of the little diocese would require a history of the African, almost of the whole Western, Church. Here we can do no more than briefly discuss some things which constitute his importance to later Christianity, and mention a few important biographical facts. Further details will be found in the articles Donatism, Pelagius, Semipelagianism, Monasticism, North African Church.

The life of Augustine by his friend Possidius shows that its author was possessed by the desire to erect a suitable memorial to a man who was destined to have a lasting importance in the history of the Church; it is much more than a mere product of hagiography. He considers Augustine first as an author who has left so many works in refutation of heresy and encouragement of piety that few even of diligent students can master them all; and he feels himself therefore bound to include a brief account of his subject's literary activity.

Then he deals with the services which Augustine rendered to the peace and unity of the Church by his labors against the Donatists; and finally he attributes to Augustine's encouragement of monasticism much of its growth, together with an actual regeneration of the clerical life.

His view on the two latter points, if colored a little by the local point of view, is still the respectable opinion of a contemporary; but it does not altogether agree with the deliberate historical judgment of posterity. The Vandal invasion, which came like a spring frost upon the young life of the African Church, and the Mohammedan conquests, both prevented Augustine's labors from having their full effect in Africa. Leaving aside for the moment the influence of his writings, one may really say that the condemnation of Pelagianism was the only permanant result of his work.

Doctrinal Importance of Augustine

But his writings have continued to exert such an influence, by no means confined to the time of the early Church nor to African soil, as no other Father before or since has ever attained. If we look to the posthumous effects they have had, we may agree with the verdict of Possidius, and carry it further than was possible to a contemporary. Augustine is practically the father of all western Christianity after his time.

It is true that Catholicism has never officially accepted his doctrine of grace in its entirety; but this fact is of relatively slight importance when we think of the colossal influence which his writings have had upon the gradual shaping of the Church's doctrine as a whole-there is scarcely a single Roman Catholic dogma which is historically intelligible without reference to his teaching. And it is not only the dogmas of the Western Church over which he has exerted an unparalleled influence; its hierarchical and its scientific development both derive from him.

The great struggle between the rival chiefs of medieval Christendom, the pope and the emperor, is explicable in its deepest meaning, intelligible in its course, only from his De civitate Dei; when medieval theology was most active, then it was most under his influence, and the scholastic movement was determined, not only in its speculations but in its very method, by him. From him, again, medieval mysticism, in both its authorized and its heretical forms, received its most decisive impulse; Augustinian influences must be taken into account in the study of all the so-called precursors of the Reformation. When, however, we have called him the father of medieval Catholicism, we have not yet said all. The effect of his teaching in the East has been, to be sure, slight and indirect; but the Reformers made an ally of him. The characteristic notes of what are specifically called the Reformed Churches, in contradistinction to the Lutheran, are especially founded upon Augustinian tradition. In the history of philosophy, too, he has been a force far beyond the Middle Ages; in both Descartes and Spinoza his voice may be distinctly heard.

Events of His Episcopate

Space forbids any attempt to trace all the causes of these abiding effects; and in what remains to be said, biographical interest must be largely our guide. We know a considerable number of events in Augustine's episcopal life which can be surely placed the so-called third and eighth synods of Carthage in 397 and 403, at which, as at those still to be mentioned, he was certainly present; the disputation with the Manichean Felix at Hippo in 404; the eleventh synod of Carthage in 407; the conference with the Donatists in Carthage, 411; the synod of Mileve, 416; the African general council at Carthage, 418; the journey to C~esarea in Mauretania and the disputation with the Donatist bishop there, 418; another general council in Carthage, 419; and finally the consecration of Eraclius as his assistant in 426.

None of these events, however, marks a decisive epoch in his life, which flowed on quietly and evenly during the whole time of his episcopate, e.xcept the last few months. Thus it will require careful study to determine the epochs in his intellectual development during this period.

THEOLOGY

His Anti-Manicheanism

His special and direct opposition to Manicheanism did

not last a great while after his consecration. About 397 he wrote a tractate Contra epistolam [Manichcei] quam vocant-fundamenti; in the De agone christiano, written about the same time, and in the Confessiones, a little later, numerous anti-Manichean expressions occur.

After this, however, he only attacked the Manicheans on some special occasion, as when, about 400, on the request of his "brethren," he wrote a detailed rejoinder to Faustus, a Manichean bishop, or made the treatise De natura boni out of his discussions with Felix; a little later, also, the letter of the Manichean Secundinus gave him occasion to write Contra Secundinum, which, in spite of its comparative brevity, he regarded as the best of his writings on this subject.

In the succeeding period, he was much more occupied with anti-Donatist polemics, which in their turn were forced to take second place by the emergence of the Pelagian controversy.

His Anti-Pelagianism

It has been thought that Augustine's anti-Pelagian teaching grew out of his conception of the Church and its sacraments as a means of salvation; and attention was called to the fact that before the Pelagian controversy this aspect of the Church had, through the struggle with the Donatists, assumed special importance in his mind. But this conception should be denied.

It is quite true that in 395 Augustine's views on sin and grace, freedom and predestination, were not what they afterward came to be. But the new trend was given to them before the time of his anti-Donatist activity, and so before he could have heard anything of Pelagius. What we call Augustinianism was not a reaction against Pelagianism; it would be much truer to say that the latter was a reaction against Augustine's views.

He himself names the beginning of his episcopate as the turning-point. Accordingly, in the first thing which he wrote after his consecration, the De diversis qucestionibus ad Simplicianum (396 or 397), we come already upon the new conception. In no other of his writings do we see as plainly the gradual attainment of conviction on any point; as he himself says in the Retractiones, he was laboring for the free choice of the will of man, but the grace of God won the day. So completely was it won, that we might set forth the specifically Augustinian teaching on grace, as against the Pelagians and the Massilians, by a series of quotations taken wholly from this treatise.

It is true that much of his later teaching is still undeveloped here; the question of Predestination (though the word is used) does not really come up; he is not clear as to the term" election"; and nothing is said of the "gift of perseverance." But what we get on these points later is nothing but the logical consequence of that which is expressed here, and so we have the actual genesis of Augustine's predestinarian teaching under our eyes.

It is determined by no reference to the question of infant baptism-still less by any considerations connected with the conception of the Church. The impulse comes directly from Scripture, with the help, it is true, of those exegetical thoughts which he mentioned earlier as those of others and not his own. To be sure, Paul alone can not explain this doctrine of grace; this is evident from the fact that the very definition of grace is non-Pauline. Grace is for Augustine, both now and later, not the misericordiapeccata condonans of the Reformers, as justification is not the alteration of the relation to God accomplished by means of the accipere remissionem.

Grace is rather the misericordia which displays itself in the divine inspiratio, and justification is justum or pium fleri as a result of this. We may even say that this grace is an interna illuminatio such as a study of Augustine's Neoplatonism enables us easily to understand, which restores the connection with the divine bonum esse.

He had long been convinced that " not only the greatest but also the smallest good things can not be, except from him from whom are all good things, that is, from God;" and it might well seem to him to follow from this that faith, which is certainly a good thing, could proceed from the operation of

God alone. This explains the idea that grace works like a law of nature, drawing the human will to God with a divine omnipotence.

Of course this Neoplatonic coloring must not be exaggerated; it is more consistent with itself in his earlier writings than in the later, and he would never have arrived at his predestinarian teaching without the New Testament.

With this knowledge, we are in a position to estimate the force of a difficulty which now confronted Augustine for the first time, but never afterward left him, and which has been present in the Roman Catholic teaching even down to the Councils of Trent and the Vatican.

If faith depends upon an action of our own, solicited but not caused by vocation, it can only save a man when, per JIdem gratiam accipiens, he becomes one who not merely believes in God but loves him also. But if faith has been already inspired by grace, and if, while the Scripture speaks of justification by faith, it is held (in accordance with the definition of grace) that justification follows upon the infusio caritatis,-then either the conception of the faith which is God-inspired must pass its fluctuating boundaries and approach nearer to that of caritas, or the conception of faith which is unconnected with caritas will render the fact of its inspiration unintelligible and justification by faith impossible.

Augustine's anti-Pelagian writings set forth this doctrine of grace more clearly in some points, such as the terms " election," predestination," "the gift of perseverance," and also more logically; but space forbids us to show this here, as the part taken in this controversy by Augustine is so fully detailed elsewhere.

IBNKHALDUN

IBN KHALDUN, Wali al-Din 'Abd al-Rahman b. Muhammad b. Muhammad b. Abi Bakr Muhammad b. al-Hasan (732-84/1332-82), one of the strongest personalities of Arabo-Muslim culture in the period of its decline. He is generally regarded as a historian, sociologist and philosopher. Thus his life and work have already formed the subject of innumerable studies and given rise to the most varied and even the most contradictory interpretations.

LIFE

Ibn khaldun's life may be divided into three parts, the first of which (20 years) was occupied by his childhood and education, the second (23 years) by the continuation of his studies and by political adventures, and the third (31 years) by his life as a scholar, teacher and magistrate. The first two periods were spent in the Muslim West and the third was divided between the Maghrib and Egypt.

At Tunis

Ibn khaldun was born in Tunis, on 1 Ramadan, in an Arab family which came originally from the Hadramawt and had been settled at Seville since the beginning of the Muslim conquest, playing there an important political role. The family then left Seville for Ceuta immediately before the Reconquista. From there they went to Ifriqiya and settled in Tunis during the reign of the Hafsid Abu Zakariyya'.

Ibn khaldun's great-grandfather, Abu Bakr Muhammad b. al-Hasan, who wrote a treatise on Adab al-katib. The usurper Ibn Abi 'Umara (681-2/1283-4) put an end to his career and to his life, having him strangled after confiscating his possessions and subjecting him to torture.

His son, Muhammad, also occupied various official positions, both at Bougie and Tunis, and died in, after renouncing political life upon the fall of Ibn al-Lihyani. The latter's son, the father of our Ibn khaldun, wisely avoided politics, leading the life of a faqih and man of letters.

He was thus able to ensure that his son 'Abd al-Rahman received a very thorough education. The latter also attended courses given by the most famous teachers of Tunis, to whom he devotes lengthy sections in his autobiography. He thus received a classical education, based essentially on the study of the qur'an, of hadith, of the Arabic language and of fiqh. The Marinid invasion resulted in the arrival in Tunis, with the sultan Abu 'l-Hasan, of a large number of theological and literary scholars. This widened the horizons of the young Ibn khaldun, who was thus enabled, particularly under the supervision of al-Abili, to learn about the philosophy and the main problems of Arabo-Muslim thought.

He was however to undergo much suffering. The Marinid occupation ended in disorder and bloodshed, and in addition the terrible Black Death which ravaged the world in the middle of the century, coming from the East, claimed many victims in the country, among them Ibn khaldun's parents.

He was at this time 17 years of age and was to retain all his life a memory of the horror of this event, which is reflected in many passages in his Ta'rif and his Muqaddima. This was the first traumatic experience of his life, which was later to have an undoubted influence on the direction of his thought.

In addition, the departure of the Marinid scholars left a great intellectual vacuum at Tunis, and it seems that at this time the sole aim of the young Ibn khaldun was to leave Tunis for Fez, then the most brilliant capital of the Muslim West. He states that he had a great thirst for learning. His elder brother, Muhammad, dissuaded him from his project, but not for long.

At the court of Fez

He was not yet t0 when, towards the end of , the powerful chamberlain Ibn Tafragin appointed him to the office of writer of the 'alama (the ruler's official signature) on behalf of the sultan Abu Ishaq. He accepted, without, it seems, the intention of remaining long in the post. The invasion of Ifriqiya by the amir of Constantine, Abu Yazid, provided him with the desired opportunity. Under cover of the defeat, he parted company with his master, took refuge for a time at Ebba, then reached Tebessa, then Gafsa, before arriving at Biskra, where he spent the winter with his friends the Banu Muzni.

Thus the second period of his life, which was both scholarly and adventurous, began with one of those changes of direction which were to recur on later occasions and which have been severely criticized by the majority of those who have made a study of his life and work. But it was in fact probably not a bad thing: intuitively, Ibn khaldun was refusing to be engulfed in an Ifriqiya which was then in the process of disintegration and whose court furthermore was far from providing an example of loyalty and good behaviour.

Meanwhile, the Marinid Abu 'l-Hasan, after an unfortunate adventure, had been killed, leaving the western territories of the Maghrib to his son Abu 'Inan, who in any case had not waited for his death before supplanting him in Fez. Once again the Marinid hegemony seemed to be consolidating itself. Abu 'Inan seized Tlemcen and reduced Bougie again to submission. From Biskra, Ibn khaldun offered him his services. On his journey he met the Marinid chamberlain Ibn Abi 'Amr, appointed governor of Bougie, who invited him to his new residence, where he lived for some time, before being summoned to the court at Fez.

He was officially part of the sultan's literary circle (madhlisuh al-'ilmi) and soon afterwards also formed part of his secretariat, though without much enthusiasm it seems, for such a post 'was not in the family tradition'—that is to say it was beneath their dignity.

This remark reveals a far-reaching ambition in a young man of barely 23 years. Somewhat disappointed, he therefore continued to occupy himself mainly with his studies. 'I devoted myself', he writes, 'to reflection and to study, and to sitting at the feet of the great teachers, those of the Maghrib as well as those of Spain who were residing temporarily in Fez, and I benefited greatly from their teaching'. In brief, his desire for learning still took precedence over his political interests.

Nevertheless, it may be that, taking advantage of the sultan's illness, he took part in a plot aiming to liberate the former amir of Bougie, Abu 'Abd Allah, and to re-install him in his former kingdom. He himself denies this and refers to intrigues, jealousy and malice; he was certainly thrown into prison however, remaining there for two years until the death of Abu 'Inan. This was followed by disturbances, by clashes between the claimants to the throne, and by treachery and bloodshed. Ibn khaldun, now set free, took part in all this according to the custom of the time. Changes of loyalty were common and he was no exception and found himself appointed, in Sha'ban, to the office of Secretary of the Chancellery for the new sultan, Abu Salim. In order the better to perform his role and consolidate his position, he even made the effort of becoming court-poet, and he quotes long extracts from his work as a panegyrist. But this was all wasted effort, since his fortune declined. Two years later he left the chancellery for a judicial post, the mazalim.

Then further disturbances resulted in the accession of a new sultan. Ibn khaldun changed his allegiance in time, and considered that he was unjustly deprived of any fruits of the victory. He did not hide his ill-humour, made enemies and, after many difficulties, he obtained permission to withdraw to Granada.

At the court of Granada

In Ramadan, a palace revolt had driven Muhammad b. al-Ahmar from the throne, so that, in Muharram, he had taken refuge in Fez with his famous vizier Ibn al-khatib. There was formed at this time, between the latter and the young Ibn khaldun, a real friendship which, apart from inevitable spells of unpleasantness, was to withstand the test of time. In Jumada, Muhammad b. al-Ahmar regained his throne and Ibn al-khatib his former rank.

The friendship established at Fez ensured that Ibn khaldun, forced in his turn to flee to the other side of the Mediterranean, was received in Granada with the highest honours. At the end of, he was even sent to Seville, charged with a delicate peace mission to Pedro the Cruel. This contact with the Christian world, then in the midst of a period of change, had an important influence on him. On his return, the Nasrid amir showered favours on him. Ibn khaldun then sent for his wife and children to come to Constantine. But Ibn al-khatib felt some resentment at the success of his young friend and Ibn khaldun preferred not to take full advantage of his favoured position.

At the court of Bougie

It is true that at this time there arose a unique opportunity for him to satisfy his ambition. His friend, Abu 'Abd Allah Muhammad, with whom he had already been in a conspiracy at Fez, had in fact regained his kingdom of Bougie, and offered him the office of hadhib (chamberlain), which was at that time the most important office in the state, and appointed to the vizierate his younger brother Yahya [see next article]. Ibn khaldun held at the same time posts as teacher of fiqh and as preacher. But this success was short-lived.

In the following year, the amir of Constantine, Abu 'l-'Abbas, took the offensive and inflicted a crushing defeat on his cousin Abu 'Abd Allah Muhammad, who was killed in the battle. Ibn khaldun, refusing suggestions that he should continue the struggle in support of one of the younger sons of the dead ruler, handed over the town to the conqueror and himself entered his service.

This was not to be for long, however. Ibn khaldun saw which way the wind was blowing: he resigned in time, and took refuge at first with the Dawawida Arabs, then with his friends the Banu Muzni at Biskra, whereas his brother Yahya was arrested. To the offer by the sultan Abu Hammu of the office of hadhib at Tlemcen, he replied with a courteous refusal, sending him instead his brother Yahya, who had in the meantime been set free.

He explains his motives thus: 'I was in fact cured of the temptation of office (ghiwayat al-rutab). Furthermore I had for too long neglected scholarly matters. I therefore ceased to involve myself in the affairs of kings and devoted all my energies to study (al-qira'a) and teaching'.

Thus at Biskra he attempted to lead the life of a man of letters. He carried on a long correspondence, much ornamented by rhetorical flourishes, with his friend Ibn al-khatib. However he could not resist intrigue. He gave his support, against Abu 'l-'Abbas, to the alliance between the Hafsid of Tunis and the 'Abd al-Wadid Abu Hammu of Tlemcen. He next took it upon himself to raise support for the Marinid Abu Faris. He was constantly on the move, attempting to form from the small tribal units a force capable of supporting a really great power. But on each occasion events upset his calculations. The claimants were simply too numerous, and this resulted in a new series of changes of front which were basically perhaps only his unsuccessful attempts to back the winner. But in the Muslim West of the 8th/14th century no winner existed. Furthermore his friends the Banu Muzni were beginning to object to the suspicious activities of their guest. Ibn khaldun tried once again to escape the lure of politics. He took refuge in the ribat of Abu Madyan, 'preferring', he writes, 'to live in retirement and devote myself exclusively to learning, if only I might be left inpeace'.

He was not left in peace, nor was he of a temperament to remain so for long. Thus, after some new setbacks in the central Maghrib, he met with failure in Fez. Welcomed at first, he was later arrested, then released, and finally permitted to withdraw to Muslim Spain, where he wished 'to settle permanently, withdraw from the world, and devote my life to learning. Yet again he was disappointed. He had become a political personality with a reputation which could not fail to arouse mistrust.

He was henceforward condemned to offer his services for hire, and to be regarded with mixed feelings never entirely free from suspicion, whereas apparently his only ambition now was to be left in peace to work out the conclusions to be drawn from his tumultuous experience and to put his ideas in order.

At the Castle of Ibn Salama

Practically ordered to leave the kingdom of Granada, Ibn khaldun returned to the Maghrib and, after some difficulties, settled with his family at Tlemcen. In the meantime his friend, the vizier Ibn al-khatib, whom he had tried in vain to save-and this is what had earned him the enmity of the amir of Granada—had been strangled in prison at Fez. Ibn khaldun may have seen this as a warning; he certainly seems after this to have made a firm decision to restrict himself to study and teaching. But the sultan of Tlemcen was willing to forget the past—Ibn khaldun had after all been in turn for him and against him—with the ulterior motive of making use of him once again.

He entrusted him with a mission to the Dawawida. Ibn khaldun pretended to accept, but as soon as he had left Tlemcen, he took refuge with the Awlad 'Arif; they gave him a warm welcome and interceded on his behalf with the sultan of Tlemcen, who gave permission for his family to join him. For the next four years Ibn khaldun lived in the castle of Ibn Salama, 6 km. south-west of the present-day Frenda, in the department of Oran.

This was a decisive turning-point in his life; really enclosed for the first time in his ivory tower, he informs us that he worked out the Muqaddima 'according to that original plan (al-nahw al-gharib) for which he received inspiration during his retirement'.

Again in Tunis

After this, to enable him to continue his work, a vast amount of documentation became more and more necessary. Ibn khaldun was at this time 47 years of age. He dreamed of returning to Tunis, which he had left at the age of 20-Tunis, where 'my ancestors lived and where there still exist their houses, their remains and their tombs'.

He wrote for, and obtained, the permission of Abu 'l-'Abbas the architect of the Hafsid restoration, with whom he had had connexions more than ten years earlier at Bougie. And thus, in Sha'ban 780/November-December, 'he abandoned his traveller's staff' in his native town.

There he followed his new career as a teacher and a scholar and completed a first redaction of his 'Ibar, the first copy of which, accompanied by a long panegyric, he presented to the sultan. But the success of his teaching—which some considered subversive—and the favours which he received from the ruler, earned him many enemies.

The formation of a cabal against him, the moving spirit in which was the famous Ibn 'Arafa, made him fear the worst. He decided to leave the Muslim West, where his awkward past followed him wherever he went.

He made the pretext for this the Pilgrimage. The sultan granted him permission for this; there was a boat on the point of leaving for Alexandria; and Ibn khaldun embarked on 15 Sha'ban 784/24 October 1382.

In Cairo

On his arrival in the Mamluk capital, Ibn khaldun was truly dazzled. Students flocked to his courses at al-Azhar, and soon he was appointed teacher of Maliki fiqh at the al-qamhiyya madrasa. Some time afterwards he was also appointed Maliki chief qadi. There then began for him a period of suffering: his family, finally given permission to join him through the intervention of the sultan al-Zahir Barquq, was shipwrecked off Alexandria.

At the same time his intransigeance and the intrigues of his enemies, who were furious at seeing one of the most important offices of the state entrusted to a 'foreigner', caused him to be dismissed from his office as qadi. In 789/1387, he was appointed to the newly built al-Zahiriyya madrasa, and then, on his return from the Pilgrimage, he was appointed teacher of hadith at the madrasa of 'arghatmish.

Ibn khaldun preserved in its entirety his inaugural course of lectures (Muharram 791/January 1389), devoted to the Muwatta' of Malik. At the same time, he was placed at the head of the khanqah of Baybars, the most important 'ufi convent in Egypt. Then, after fourteen years devoted exclusively to teaching, he was once again appointed to the office of qadi (15 Ramadan 801/t1 May 1399).

He was again dismissed (Muharram 803/August-September 1400), and some months later he was obliged to accompany al-Nasir on his expedition to relieve Damascus, which was being threatened by Timurlane, already master of Aleppo. Left in the besieged town—and abandoned without warning by al-Nasir, who suspected that a plot was being hatched in Cairo during his absence—he played a certain part in the surrender of the town under a false promise of aman, and has provided a detailed account of his interviews with the Mongol leader. He may in fact have thought that he saw in Timurlane the man of the century who possessed enough 'asabiyya to re-unite the Muslim world and to give a new direction to history. Finally, after writing for Timurlane a description of the Maghrib and having witnessed the horrors of the burning and sacking of Damascus, he returned to Cairo, having been stripped and robbed by brigands on the way. In spite of his compromising attitude towards Timurlane, he was well received at the court. Four times more he was appointed qadi and then dismissed. His last, and sixth, appointment to this office was in Sha'ban 808/January-February 1406, a few weeks before his death on 26 Ramadan.

During his stay in Cairo, Ibn khaldun did not sever relations with the Muslim West. He retained his Maghribi dress, a dark burnous. He also attempted to encourage the exchange of gifts between the sultans of Egypt and those of the Maghrib and to produce a climate of co-operation. He sent a copy of his 'Ibar to the Marinid Abu Faris, continued to correspond with his friends, and preserved in particular long passages, in prose and in verse, from the letters sent to him by the famous poet of Granada, Ibn Zamrak.

Ibn khaldun's life has been judged variously, and in general rather severely. There is certainly no doubt that he behaved in a detached, self-interested, haughty, ambitious and equivocal manner. He himself does not attempt to hide this, and openly describes in his Ta'rif his successive changes of allegiance. He has been accused of fickleness and a lack of patriotism. But for such judgements to be strictly applicable presupposes the existence of the idea of 'allegiance' to a country, which was not the case.

The very concept scarcely existed and was not to appear in Muslim thinking until it was affected by contact with Europe. The only treason was apostasy, nor was loyalty understood except in the context of relations between one man and another, and examples of felony were provided daily by those of the highest rank. Ibn khaldun was, moreover, readily pardoned by those who wished to use his services—he was in turn the enemy and the servant, now of one and now of another, in the same way that men were treacherously killed, with or without good reason, simply as a precaution. The struggles which rent the Muslim West in Ibn khaldun's time were merely a series of minor and abortive coups. He should therefore be judged according to the standards of his own time and not according to ours.

Furthermore, Ibn khaldun, as he proves in his Muqaddima, was an astonishingly clear thinker. It is true that his behaviour was dictated by ambition, the desire of power, a taste for adventure and even a complete ruthlessness in political matters; but it is unlikely that this was all. It would be strange if the theoretician of 'asabiyya did not envisage a plan, perhaps rather vague, for the restoration of Arabo-Muslim civilization which he saw—and he states this clearly—to be in its death-throes.

His adventures could thus be seen as only the unfruitful and calculated search for an 'asabiyya powerful enough to save Islam from ruin. Certain facts support this hypothesis, but Ibn khaldun states nothing explicity and his Ta'rif (on which moreover opinions vary) provides no assistance. As has already been mentioned, it gives us no insight into the inner thought of the author himself and presents only his external character. There is thus no way of knowing what his real intentions were.

WORKS

Ibn khaldun is known primarily forqhis Muqaddima and his 'Ibar, but he wrote other works which have not all survived.

In about his twentieth year, he attempted, under the influence of al-Abili, to make a resume of the theologico-philosophical 'summa' of al-Razi entitled Kitab Muhassal afqar al-mutaqaddimin wa 'l-muta'-akhkhirin min al-'ulama' wa 'l-hukama' wa 'l-muta-kallimin, an outline which is a condensation of all the Arabo-Muslim cultural tradition concerning the problems of dogma and its philosophical repercussions. This resume, entitled Lubab al-Muhassal fi usul al-din, shows a direction of thought which Ibn khaldun was never to lose completely.

It should also be remembered that Ibn khaldun had stressed in his Ta'rif the studious nature of his period at Fez and at Granada. During this period, that is between 752-65/

1351-64, the date at which Ibn al-khatib's Ihata was finished (to which we owe the following information), he wrote five works: (1) a commentary on the Burda [q.v.] of al-Busiri; (2) an outline of logic; (3) a treatise on arithmetic; (4) several resumes of works by Ibn Rushd, though unfortunately it is not known which ones; and (5) a commentary on a poem by Ibn al-khatib on the usul al-fiqh. All these works are now lost, and indeed seem to have been quickly forgotten even during the author's lifetime. Ibn khaldun does not even mention them in his Ta'rif, and his Egyptian biographers do not appear to have heard of them.

They seem moreover to have been of a traditional theologico-philosophical type, including the arithmetic which a faqih had to know. Nothing up to this time indicated that Ibn khaldun would go down to posterity as the brilliant founder of the science of history and of other disciplines. The flowering of his genius took place at the castle of Ibn Salama, as the result of the fusion of the traditional disciplines in which he had been educated with the rich harvest of political experience which, through a bitter series of failures and impasses, had made him aware of the meaning and deep significance ('ibar) of history.

There then began, in the calm of the castle of Ibn Salama, the work of analysing the passionate and disturbing human adventure, which certainly has its grandeurs but of which he had experienced mainly the miseries. Ibn khaldun really changed as a thinker: the pedestrian faqih which he might after all have been had become a historian of genius, and even the founder of a number of disciplines which were to become some of the most productive of the modern humanities. The first draft of his Introduction (Muqaddima)—which contains the essence of his thought—to his universal history (Kitab al-'Ibar), as well as large sections of this history itself, were written between during his retirement. He later continued without ceasing, until the end of his life, to re-write this basic work, and especially the Muqaddima. The Ta'rif, an autobiography which stops in Dhu 'l-qa'da and the Shifa' al-sa'il, a treatise on mysticism written towards the end of his life, are minor works compared with his masterpiece, and their main interest is in the light they throw on it. It should be mentioned that the problem of the authenticity of the Shifa' al-sa'il, so important for the history of Ibn khaldun's thought, has not yet been definitively solved.

The Ottoman historian Na'ima praises Ibn khaldun in the introduction to his work and gives a summary of his ideas. (The first translation into Turkish, of part of the Muqaddima, was made by the Shaykh al-Islam Piri-zade Mehmed Ef. in 1143/1749; the most recent, complete, translation is by Zakir Kadiri Ugan Yet it was in Europe that Ibn khaldun was discovered and the importance of his Muqaddima realized: by d'Herbelot, by Silvestre de Sacy (Chrestomatie arabe, 1806), by von Hammer-Purgstall and especially by Quatremere, who, in 1858, produced the first complete edition of the Muqaddima—another edition of it was published in the same year in Cairo by Nasr al-Hurini, based on another manuscript containing in particular the dedication to the sultan Abu Faris of Fez and by de Slane, who, some years afterwards, produced the first French translation of it .

Since then there has been a continual series of editions and studies on it, in both the East and the West, a proof of the increasing interest in Ibn khaldun's thought, and there have recently been so many of them that bibliographical works on them became necessary. The most recent translation, by F. Rosenthal, has the advantage of having been made from the Istanbul manuscript, which contains a note in Ibn khaldun's writing stating that it had been 'scientifically revised' by the author.

The 'Ibar, the Universal History itself, naturally aroused less interest. The first to produce an edition and translation of extensive passages from the 'Ibar was Noeel Desvergers, under the title Histoire de l'Afrique sous la dynastie des Aghlabites et de la Sicile sous la domination musulmane, Paris 1841. Another partial translation was published some years later by de Slane under the title Histoire des Berberes et des dynasties musulmanes de l'Afrique Septentrionale, followed by an edition of the passages translated. Next there appeared the complete Bulaq edition, and since then there have followed also some partial translations. There has not yet appeared, however, a truly critical edition of either the Muqaddima or the 'Ibar. The latest edition, that of Beirut from which our references are taken—is a commercial one, which is however provided with useful indexes.

The criticism generally made of the 'Ibar is that it did not fulfil the promises made in the Muqaddima. This is obvious, but it could not have been otherwise. No one man could write alone a universal history according to the demands of the Muqaddima. But it has more serious shortcomings: Ibn khaldun at times demonstrates a surprising lack of learning, for example, concerning the Almohads and their doctrine: 'In addition, precise dates are rarely given; the chronological details throughout the work are too often contradictory, and one is obliged to prefer on many occasions those provided in other more humble and much more succinct works'.

Nevertheless, the Kitab al-'Ibar, through its intelligent arrangement of facts and the detail and scope of the account, remains, in the opinion of the specialist who has made most use of it, an incomparable tool, particularly 'for the two centuries nearest to our author, the 13th and the14th' . It should also be added that this work, often disappointing on the history of the East, is generally valuable especially for the Muslim West, and in particular for the Berbers.

But Ibn khaldun's main work, of universal value, is the Muqaddima. In the author's intention, and as the title indicates, it is an Introduction to the historian's craft. Thus it is presented as an encyclopaedic synthesis of the methodological and cultural knowledge necessary to enable the historian to produce a truly scientific work. Initially, in fact, Ibn khaldun was preoccupied with epistemology. Then gradually, meditating on the method and the matter of history, he was led, in full consciousness of what he was doing, to create what he refers to as his 'new science', which itself turned out to contain more or less implicitly the starting points of several avenues of research leading to the philosophy of history, sociology, economics and yet other disciplines.

In his preface to the Introduction proper, Ibn khaldun begins by defining history—which he expands to include the study of the whole of the human past, including its social, economic and cultural aspects—defining its interest, denouncing the lack of curiosity and of method in his predecessors, and setting out the rules of good and sound criticism.

This criticism is based essentially, apart from the examination of evidence, on the criterion of conformity with reality, that is of the probability of the facts reported and their conformity to the nature of things, which is the same as the current of history and of its evolution. Hence the necessity of bringing to light the laws which determine the direction of this current. The science capable of throwing light on this phenomenon is, he says, that of 'umran, 'a science which may be described as independent ('ilm mustaqill bi-nafsih), which is defined by its object: human civilization (al-'umran al-bashari) and social facts as a whole'.

All that follows, that is the main part of the Muqaddima itself, is only the detailed exposition of this new and independent science which the author had perceived. In it he develops his argument, contrary to some opinions, according to a strict plan, the broad lines of which he states and clearly explains (68) before beginning his exposition. This exposition is divided into six long chapters which in turn are subdivided into many paragraphs of varying lengths and often mathematically arranged.

In it Ibn khaldun makes an outline study of the influence of environment on human nature, an ethnological and an anthropological study. Chapter t: on the societies of rural and, generally speaking, fairly primitive, civilization ('umran badawi). Chapter 3: on the different forms of government, on states and institutions. Chapter 4: on the societies of urban civilization, that is of the most developed and sophisticated forms of civilization.

This plan clearly shows that Ibn khaldun in his Muqaddima was inclined to concentrate on social phenomena in general. The central point around which his observations are built and to which his researches are directed is the study of the aetiology of decline, that is to say the symptoms and the nature of the ills from which civilizations die. Henceqthe Muqaddima is very closely linked with the political experiences of its author, who had been in fact very vividly aware that he was witnessing a tremendous change in the course of history, which is why he thought it necessary to write a summary of the past of humanity and to draw lessons ('ibar) from it.

He remarks that at certain exceptional moments in history the upheavals are such that one has the impression of being present 'at a new creation (ka'annahu khalqdhadid), at an actual renaissance (nash'a mustahdatha), and at [the emergence of] a new world (wa 'alam muhdath). It is so at present (li-hadha 'l-'ahd). Thus the need is felt for someone to make a record of the situation of humanity and of the world'. This 'new world', as Ibn khaldun knew (866), was coming to birth in other lands; he also realized that the civilization to which he belonged was nearing its end. Although unable to avert the catastrophe, he was anxious at least to understand what was taking place, and therefore felt it necessary to analyse the processes of history.

His main tool in this work of analysis is observation. Fairly recently there has been stressed the realistic aspect of his thought. Ibn khaldun, who has a thorough knowledge of the sources on logic and makes use of it, particular of induction, greatly mistrusts speculative reasoning. He admits that reason is a marvellous tool, but only within the framework of its natural limits, which are those of the investigation and the interpretation of what is real. He was much concerned about the problem of knowledge and it led him finally, after a radical criticism, to a refutation of philosophy.

'In casting doubts on the adequacy of universal rationality and of individual reality, Ibn khaldun at the same time casts doubts on the whole structure of speculative philosophy as it then existed'. Having thus calmly dismissed Arabo-Muslim philosophy, he chose, in order to explore reality and arrive at its meaning, a type of empiricism which has no hesitation in 'having recourse to the categories of rational explanation which derive from philosophy'. In short, Ibn khaldun rejects the traditional speculation of the philosophers, which gets bogged down in fruitless argument and controversy, only to replace it by another type of speculation, the steps of which are more certain and the results more fruitful since it is directly related to concrete facts.

This new positive speculation which he suggests and of which he provides an example in the Muqaddima is operated through a dialectical process which has been referred to in several studies. He could not in fact penetrate to the heart of reality, describe the struggles and conflicts, the tensions and the successive failures of states and civilizations produced by their internal dissensions without encountering, and calling attention to, the process of dialectic, especially since he had encountered logic in his earlier years and since the ideas of contradiction, antithesis, opposition, the complementariness of opposites, of ambiguity, of complexity and of confusion had long been familiar to the Muslim thinking in which he had been educated.

They are thus often evoked as operative concepts permitting understanding and explanation. In surmounting the contradictions dialectically, and in attempting to explain them and hence to resolve them, Ibn khaldun thus arrives at a dynamic conception of the dialectic development of the destiny of man, and at a system of history which is retrospectively intelligible, rational and necessary. His famous cyclic schema of historical interpretation, which in itself is not particularly original, must be included, in order for its true meaning to be seen, in this general view.

The wealth of the ideas provided in the Muqaddima has enabled several specialists to find in it the early beginnings of a number of disciplines which have become independent sciences only very recently. There is of course no argument about Ibn khaldun's quality as a historian. Y. Lacoste writes: 'If Thucydides is the inventor of history, Ibn khaldun introduces history as a science'. But he has been regarded also as a philosopher, and it is surprising in particular to discover in his Muqaddima a very elaborate system of sociology. His 'new science', his 'ilm al-'umran, the discovery of which dazzled even himself, is basically, strictly speaking, nothing but a system of sociology,—conceived it is true as an auxiliary science to history.

He considers that the basic causes of historical evolution are in fact to be sought in the economic and social structures. He therefore set himself to analyse them, elaborating as he did so a certain number of new operative concepts, the most pregnant of which is incontestably that of 'asabiyya [q.v.]. It should be mentioned that this concept of 'asabiyya, and that of 'umran, have given rise in modern times to many discussions—which cannot be enumerated here—regarding their interpretation.

He was interested particularly in the influence of the way of life and of methods of production on the evolution of social groups. In a famous sentence, he states: 'The differences which are seen between the generations (adhyal) in their behaviour are only the expression of the differences which separate them in their economic way of life' (210). This sentence is often compared with an equally famous one of Marx: 'The method of production in the material matters of life determines in general the social, political and intellectual processes of life'. The similarity is indeed striking, and it is not the only one between them.

Thus Ibn khaldun's thought is often interpreted, particularly in recent years, in the spirit of dialectical materialism. But, in spite of the undoubted similarities, it would be difficult to regard Ibn khaldun as a forerunner of materialism. Moreover the explanation he gives is not exclusively a socio-economic one but also psychological. 'The Prolegomena do not contain only a general sociology but also a very detailed and subtle social psychology which may be divided into political psychology, economic psychology, ethical psychology and general psychology. The intermingled and closely linked elements of this social psychology and this general sociology form a whole complex which it is difficult to disentangle'.

There have been identified also, in this complex, economic doctrines sufficiently detailed to justify a study devoted to them, and a philosophy of history to which M. Mahdi has devoted an important work. It also provides ethnographic, anthropological and demographic information of real value.

Thus the atypical figure of Ibn khaldun in Arabo-Muslim culture has been unanimously considered, since his discovery in Europe, as that of an authentic genius, 'un penseur genial et aberrant', whose Muqaddima represents 'one of the solemn moments of human thought' (Bouthoul). Certainly a 'solitary genius', he does not belong to any definite current of Arabo-Muslimqthought, since his works are in fact the product of a multitude of agonizing enquiries.

His thinking represents a radical change, which unfortunately remained as unproductive as his political misadventures. 'Just as he had no forerunners among Arabic writers, so he had no successors or emulators in this idiom until the contemporary period.

Although he had a certain influence in Egypt on some writers of the end of the Middle Ages, it can be stated that, in his native Barbary, neither his Muqaddima nor his personal teaching left any permanent mark. And indeed the systematic lack of comprehension and the resolute hostility which this nonconformist thinker of genius encountered among his own people forms one of the most moving dramas, one of the saddest and most significant pages in the history of Muslim culture'.

Unit II

Historiography

RENAISSANCE – MACHIAVALLI

Niccolo Machiavelli, 1469-1527

The father of modern political theory, Niccolo di Bernardo dei Machiavelli, was born at Florence, May 3, 1469, saw the troubles of the French invasion (1493), when the Medici fled, and in 1498 became secretary of the Ten, a post he held until the fall of the republic in 1512.

He was employed in a great variety of missions, including one to the Emperor Maximilian, and four to France. His dispatches during these journeys, and his treatises on the *Affairs of France and Germany*, are full of far-reaching insight. On the restoration of the Medici, Machiavelli was involved in the downfall of his patron, Gonfaloniere Soderini.

Arrested on a charge of conspiracy in 1513, and put to the torture, he disclaimed all knowledge of the alleged conspiracy. Although pardoned, he was obliged to retire from public life and devoted himself to literature.

It was not until 1519 that he was commissioned by Leo X to draw up his report on a reform of the state of Florence. In 1521-25 he was employed in diplomatic services and as historiographer.

After the defeat of the French at Pavia (1525), Italy was helpless before the advancing forces of the Emperor Charles V and Machiavelli strove to avert from Florence the invading army on its way to Rome. In May 1527 the Florentines again drove out the Medici and proclaimed the republic — but Machiavelli, bitterly disappointed that he was to be allowed no part in the movement for liberty, and already in declining health, died on June 22.

Through misrepresentation and misunderstanding his writings were spoken of as almost diabolical, his most violent assailants being the clergy. The first great edition of his works was not issued until 1782. From that period his fame as the founder of political science has steadily increased.

Besides his letters and state papers, Machiavelli's historical writings comprise *Florentine Histories, Discourses on the First Decade of Titus Livius* (commonly known as *The Discourses*), a *Life of Castruccio Castrancani* (unfinished) and *History of the Affairs of Lucca.* His literary works comprise an imitation of the *Golden Ass* of Apuleius, an essay on the Italian language, the play *Mandragola,* and several minor compositions. He also wrote *Seven Books on the Art of War.*

The greatest source of Machiavelli's reputation is, of course, *The Prince* (1532). The main theme of this short book is that all means may be resorted to for the establishment and preservation of authority — the end justifies the means — and that the worst and most treacherous acts of the ruler are justified by the wickedness and treachery of the governed.

BOOK OF MACHIAVELLI'S *DISCOURSES ON TITUS LIVIUS*

Although the envious nature of men, so prompt to blame and so slow to praise, makes the discovery and introduction of any new principles and systems as dangerous almost as the exploration of unknown seas and continents, yet, animated by that desire which impels me to do what may prove for the common benefit of all, he have resolved to open a new route, which is not yet been followed by any one, and may prove difficult and troublesome, but may also bring me some reward in the approbation of those who will kindly appreciate my efforts.

And if his talents and experience of the present and insufficient study of the past, should make the result of my labors defective and of little utility, he shall at least have shown the way to others, who will carry out my views with greater ability, eloquence, and judgment, so that if he do not merit praise, he ought at least not to incur censure.

When we consider the general respect for antiquity, and how often — to say nothing of other examples — a great price is paid for some fragments of an antique statue, which we are anxious to possess to ornament our houses with, or to give to artists who strive to imitate them in their own works; and when we see, on the other hand, the wonderful examples which the history of ancient kingdoms and republics present to us, the prodigies of virtue and of wisdom displayed by the kings, captains, citizens, and legislators who have sacrificed themselves for their country, — when we see these, he said, more admired than imitated, or so much neglected that not the least trace of this ancient virtue remains, we cannot but be at the same time as much surprised as afflicted.

Though more so as in the differences which arise between citizens, or in the maladies to which they are subjected, we see the same people have recourse to the judgments and remedies prescribed by the ancients. The civil laws are in fact nothing but decisions given by their jurisconsults, and which, reduced to a system, direct our modern jurists in their decisions. And what is the science of medicine, but the experience of ancient physicians, which their successors have taken for their guide? And yet to found a republic, maintain states, to govern a kingdom, organize an army, conduct a war, dispense justice, and extend empires, you'll find neither prince, nor republic, nor captain, nor citizen, who has recourse to the examples of antiquity!

This neglect, as he is persuaded, due less to the weakness to which the vices of our education have reduced the world, than to the evils caused by the proud indolence which prevails in most of the Christian states, and to the lack of real knowledge of history, the true sense of which is not known, or the spirit of which they do not comprehend. Thus the majority of those who read it take pleasure only in a variety of the events which history relates, without ever thinking of imitating the noble actions, deeming that not only difficult, but impossible; as though heaven, the sun, the elements, and then had changed the order of emotions and power, and were different from what they were in ancient times.

Wishing, therefore, so far as in me lies, to draw mankind from this error, I have thought it proper to write upon those books of Titus Livius that have come to us entire despite the malice of time; touching upon all those matters which, after a comparison between the ancient and modern events, may seem to me necessary to facilitate their proper understanding.

ERASMUS

THE EARLY LIFE OF ERASMUS

Information as to his family and early life comes from a few meager accounts written or suggested by himself at a somewhat advanced age and from many but vague references in his writings at all periods of his life. He was doubtless born out of wedlock, well cared for by his parents till their early death, and then given the best education open to a young man of his day in a series of monastic or semi-monastic schools. All this early education is made by him in the light of later experience to appear like one long conspiracy to force him into the monastic life. He was admitted to the priesthood and took the monastic vows at about the age of twenty-five, but there is no record that he ever exercised the priestly functions, and monasticism was one of the chief objects of his attack in his lifelong assault upon the evils of the Church.

STUDIES AND TRAVELS OF ERASMUS

Almost immediately after his consecration the way was opened to him for study at the University of Paris, then the chief seat of the later scholastic learning, but already beginning to feel the influence of the revived classic culture of Italy. From this time on Erasmus led the life of an independent scholar, independent of country, of academic ties, of religious allegiance, of everything that could interfere with the free development of his intellect and the freedom of his literary expression. The chief centers of his activity were Paris, Louvain, England, and Basel; yet it could never be said that he was identified with any one of these. His residences in England were fruitful in the making of lifelong friendships with the leaders of English thought in the stirring days of Henry VIII.—John Colet, Thomas More, Thomas Linacre, and William Grocyn. He held at Cambridge an honorable position as Lady Margaret professor of divinity, and there seems to have been no reason except his unconquerable aversion to a routine life, why he should not have spent his days as an English professor. He stayed at Queens' College, Cambridge and may have been an alumnus.

He was offered many positions of honor and profit in the academic world, but declined them all on one or another pretext, preferring the uncertain, but as it proved sufficient rewards of independent literary activity. In Italy he spent three years (1506-09), part of the time in connection with the publishing house of Aldus Manutius at Venice.

The residence at Louvain exposed Erasmus to the petty criticism of men nearer to him in blood and political connections, but hostile to all the principles of literary and religious progress to which he was devoting his life. From this lack of sympathy, which he always represented as persecution, he sought refuge in the more congenial atmosphere of Basel, where under the shelter of Swiss hospitality he could express himself with freedom and where he was always surrounded by devoted friends. Here he was associated for many years with the great publisher Froben, and hither came the multitude of his admirers from all quarters of Europe.

ERASMUS'S LITERARY ACTIVITY

Erasmus's literary productivity began comparatively late in his life. It was not until he had made himself master of a telling Latin style that he undertook to express himself on all current subjects of literature and religion. His revolt against the forms of Church life did not proceed from any questionings as to the truth of the traditional doctrine, nor from any hostility to the organization of the Church itself. Rather, he felt called upon to use his learning in a purification of the doctrine and in a liberalizing of the institutions of Christianity (at a point in time where "liberalization" actually meant the opposite of what it means today!) He began as a scholar, trying to free the methods of scholarship from the rigidity and formalism of medieval traditions; but he was not satisfied with this. He conceived of himself as, above all else, a preacher of righteousness. It was his lifelong conviction that what was needed to regenerate Europe was sound learning applied frankly and fearlessly to the administration of public affairs in Church and State.

It is this conviction that gives unity and consistency to a life which at first eight seems to have been full of fatal contradictions. Erasmus was a marked individual, holding himself aloof from all entangling obligations; yet he was in a singularly true sense the centre of the literary movement of his time. In his correspondence he put himself in touch with more than five hundred men of the highest importance in the world of politics and of thought, and his advice on all kinds of subjects was eagerly sought, if none too readily followed.

WRITINGS OF ERASMUS

His more serious writings begin early with the *Enchiridion Militis Christiani*, the "Manual (or Dagger) of the Christian Gentleman" (1503). In this little volume Erasmus outlines the views of the normal Christian life which he was to spend the rest of his days in elaborating. The key-note of it all is sincerity. The chief evil of the day, he says, is formalism, a respect for traditions, a regard for what other people think essential, but never a thought of what the true teaching of Christ may be. Another of Erasmus's books worthy of mention was, *Praise of Folly*, dedicated to his friend Sir Thomas More.

While in England Erasmus began the systematic examination of manuscripts of the New Testament to prepare for a new edition and Latin translation. This edition was published by Froben of Basel in 1516 and was the basis of most of the scientific study of the Bible during the Reformation period. It was the first attempt on the part of a competent and liberal-minded scholar to ascertain what the writers of the New Testament had actually said. The Greek text produced by

Erasmus is known as textus receptus and was the basis for the King James Version of the New Testament. Erasmus dedicated his work ironically, to Pope Leo X., and he justly regarded this work as his chief service to the cause of a sound Christianity. Immediately after he began the publication of his Paraphrases of the New Testament, a popular presentation of the contents of the several books. These, like all the writings of Erasmus, were in Latin, but they were at once translated into the common languages of the European peoples, a process which received the hearty approval of Erasmus himself.

ERASMUS ON THE REFORMATION

The most significant contribution of Erasmus to the Protestant Reformation was undoubtedly his publication of his 1516 Greek-Latin New Testament. It was this book that was used as the primary source-text for Martin Luther to translate the New Testament into German for the first time in 1522. It was this book that was used as the primary source-text for William Tyndale to translate the New Testament into English for the first time in 1526.

The outbreak of the Lutheran movement in the year following the publication of Erasmus's Greek-Latin New Testament brought the severest test of Erasmus's personal and scholarly character. It made the issue between European society and the Roman Church system so clear that no man could quite escape the summons to range himself on one side or the other of the great debate. Erasmus, at the height of his literary fame, was inevitably called upon to take sides, but partisanship in any issue which he was not at liberty himself to define was foreign equally to his nature and his habits.

In all his criticism of clerical follies and abuses he had always carefully hedged himself about with protests that he was not attacking church institutions themselves and had no enmity toward the persons of churchmen. The world had laughed at his satire, but only a few obstinate reactionaries had seriously interfered with his activities. He had a right to believe that his work so far had commended itself to the best minds and also to the dominant powers in the religious world.

There can be no doubt that Erasmus was in sympathy with the main points in the Lutheran criticism of the Church. For Luther personally he had and expressed the greatest respect, and Luther always spoke with admiration of his superior learning. Luther would have gone to great lengths in securing his cooperation in a work which seemed only the natural outcome of his own. When Erasmus hesitated or refused this seemed to the upright and downright Luther a mean avoidance of responsibility explicable only as cowardice or unsteadiness of purpose, and this has generally been the Protestant judgment of later days.

On the other hand the Roman Catholic party was equally desirous of holding on to the services of a man who had so often declared his loyalty to the principles it was trying to maintain, and his half-heartedness in declaring himself now brought upon him the suspicion of disloyalty from this side.When Erasmus was charged—and very justly—with having *"laid the egg that Luther hatched"* he half admitted the truth of the charge, but said he *"had expected quite another kind of a bird!"*

RELATIONSHIP WITH LUTHER

In their early correspondence Luther expressed in unmeasured terms his admiration for all Erasmus had done in the cause of a sound and reasonable Christianity, and exhorted with him now to put the seal upon his work by definitely casting in his lot with the Lutheran party. Erasmus replied with many expressions of regard, but declined to commit himself to any party attitude.

His argument was that to do so would endanger his position as a leader in the movement for pure scholarship which be regarded as his real work in life. Only through that position as an independent scholar could he hope to influence the reform of religion. The constructive value of Luther's work was mainly in furnishing a new doctrinal basis for the previously scattered attempts at reform.

In reviving the half forgotten principle of the Augustinian theology Luther had furnished the needed impulse to that personal interest in religion which is the essence of Protestantism. This was precisely what Erasmus could not approve. He dreaded any change in the doctrine of the Church and believed that there was room enough within existing formulas for the kind of reform he valued most. Twice in the course of the great discussion he allowed himself to enter the field of doctrinal controversy, a field foreign alike to his nature and his previous practise.

One of the topics formally treated by him was the freedom of the will, the crucial point in the whole Augustinian system. In his De libero arbitrio diatribe sive collatio (1524), he analyzes with great cleverness and in perfect good temper the Lutheran exaggeration, as it seemed to him, of the obvious limitations upon human freedom. As his habit was, he lays down both sides of the argument and shows that each had its element of truth. His position was that Man was bound to sin, but that after all he had a right to the forgiving mercy of God, if only he would seek this through the means offered him by the Church itself.

It was an easy-going Semi-Pelagianism, humane in its practise, but opening the way to those very laxities and perversions which Erasmus and the Reformers alike were combating. The "Diatribe," clever as it was, could not lead men to any definite action, and this was precisely its offense to the Lutherans.

THE FINAL YEARS OF ERASMUS

Thus, as the visible outcome of his reformatory activities Erasmus found himself at the close of his life at odds with both the great parties. His last years were embittered by controversies with men toward whom he was drawn by many ties of taste and sympathy.

Notable among these was his passage at arms with Ulrich von Hutten, a brilliant, but erratic genius, who had thrown himself with all his heart into the Lutheran cause and had declared that Erasmus, if he had a spark of honesty about him, would do the same. In his reply, Spongia adversus aspergines Hutteni (1523), he displays, better than almost anywhere else, his skill in twisting words and phrases to suit the purpose of the moment. He accuses Hutten of having misinterpreted his utterances about reform and reiterates his determination never to take sides in the division of parties.

When the city of Basel was definitely and officially "reformed" in 1529, Erasmus gave up his residence there and settled in the imperial town of Freiburg-im-Breisgau. It would seem as if he found it easier to maintain his neutrality under Roman Catholic than under Protestant conditions. His literary activity continued with out much abatement, chiefly on the lines of religious and didactic composition.

The most important work of this last period is the Ecclesiastes or "Gospel Preacher" (Basel, 1535), in which he brings out the function of preaching as the most important office of the Christian priest, an emphasis which shows how essentially Protestant his inner thought of Christianity was. The same impression comes from his little tract of 1533 on "Preparation for Death," in which the emphasis throughout is on the importance of a good life as the essential condition of a happy death.

For unknown reasons Erasmus found himself drawn once more to the happiest of his homes, at Basel, where he returned in 1535 after an absence of six years. Here, in the midst of the group of Protestant scholars who had long been his truest friends, and, so far as is known, without relations of any sort with the Roman Catholic Church, he died.

THOMAS MORE

Thomas More was born in London on February 7, 1478, the son of Sir John More, a prominent judge. His education took place at St Anthony School in London. In his youth he served as a page in the household of John Morton, Bishop of Ely who had served Edward IV while remaining at heart a Lancastrian, who predicted he would be a "marvellous man." More's studies took him to Oxford to study under Thomas Linacre and William Grocyn. While at Oxford, he studied Greek and Latin literature and wrote comedies.

Around 1494 More returned to London to study law, was

admitted to Lincoln's Inn in 1496, and became a barrister in 1501. However, More did not yet seem to have made the law his permanent career choice. He was undecided as to whether to follow a monastic calling or seek a position in the civil service. While at Lincoln's Inn, he made a decision to become a monk and to live at a nearby monastery. The monastic lifestyle of prayer, fasting, and penance habits stayed with him for the rest of his life. More's sense of duty to serve his country, by entering politics, put an end to his desire for the monastery. He entered Parliament in 1504, and in 1504 or 1505 he married for the first time.

One of More's first acts in Parliament had been to argue for a decrease in a proposed appropriation for King Henry VII. Henry VII imprisoned More's father in revenge and kept him until a fine was paid and More himself retired from public life. After the death of the king in 1509, More once more became active in politics. In 1510, he was appointed one of the two under-sheriffs of London. In 1511, More's first wife died in childbirth, but he was soon re-married to Dame Alice.

Over the next ten years, More came to the attention of King Henry VIII. In 1515 he was part of a delegation sent to Flanders to help clear disputes about the wool trade. His work *Utopia* opens with a reference to this delegation. More also play an instrumental role in helping to quell a 1571 London uprising against foreigners. More was part of the king's entourage at the Field of the Cloth of Gold. In 1518 he became a member of the Privy Council, and was knighted in 1521.

Henry VIII's *Defence of the Seven Sacraments*, a repudiation of Luther, may have been co-written by More who, writing under another name, also sent an answer to Luther's reply. In further proof of Henry's favour, More was made Speaker of the House of Commons in 1523 and Chancellor of the Duchy of Lancaster in 1525. A turn of events came about when he refused to endorse King Henry VIII's plan to divorce his first wife, Katherine of Aragón in 1527. Still, More became Lord Chancellor after Thomas Wolsey fell in 1529, becoming the first layman to hold the post.

More continued to succeed, but in the end his fall came

quickly. He resigned in 1532, claiming ill health. At this time Henry VIII was breaking with Rome and More could not countenance that. His refusal to attend the coronation of Anne Boleyn in June 1533 did not escape the king's attention. In 1534 Elizabeth Barton, a nun of Kent publicly opposed Henry's break with Rome.

Thomas More was implicated in the plot but was not attainted due to protection from the Lords who refused to pass the bill until More's name was taken off the list of those charged with complicity. In April 1534, More refused to swear to the Act of Succession, and the Oath of Supremacy, and was sent to the Tower of London on April 17. He was found guilty of treason and was beheaded on July 6, 1535.

More's unfinished work, *The History of Richard III,* was found after his death and was subsequently published by his son-in-law, Rastell in 1557. The following foreword was part of this publication:

The History of Richard III (unfinished) written by Master Thomas More, then one of the under-Sheriffs of London about the year 1513 Which work hath been before this time printed in Hardyng's Chronicle and in Hall's Chronicle, but very much corrupt in many places sometime having less and sometime having more and altered in words and whole sentences, much varying from the copy in his own hand, by which this is printed.

Since More was only a child of seven at the time of the Battle of Bosworth it stands to reason that he must have received the information from John Morton, in whose home More has spent time as a youth. Morton had served in Edward IV's government but always remained steadfastly for the Lancastrian cause. He would prove to be a formidable enemy to the last Plantagenet king.

There is some suggestion that Morton was himself the author of *The History* and that More had only set out to copy it out, never finishing the task. In the seventeenth century George Buck supported this theory stating that *"Doctor Morton made the book and Master More...set it forth, amplifying it and glossing it."* The level of detail presented about certain events at which Morton was known to be present, i.e., the deathbed scene of Edward IV, supports this theory.

Whether or not Morton wrote the manuscript, we can be almost certain that he provided the source of information for More. Given the implacable enmity that Morton bore Richard III that source must always be viewed upon as being besmirched. Thomas More had a reputation for integrity and may have believed what he had been told by his former mentor. The fact that the manuscript was left unfinished could also be an indication that More had stumbled upon facts that did not jive with the story Morton had given him.

More's account of events basically follow the same outline as Polydore Vergil but is more richly detailed, further supporting the idea that an eye-witness had supplied More with his information.

More's *History* makes the following claims:

Richard III began plotting to claim the throne long before the death of his brother, Edward IV.The fact that this would have meant removing not only Edward's sons, but also Clarence and his two children only gives More the opportunity to accuse Richard of being responsible for the death of Clarence.

More is the first historian to make this accusation against Richard. Yet even in doing so he couches it in such a way as to show Richard as being evil and scheming, while still claiming that all is hearsay:

Some wise men also ween that his drift covertly conveyed lacked not in helping forth his brother Clarence to his death; which he resisted openly howbeit somewhat (as men deemed) more faintly than he that were heartily minded to his weal.

And they that thus deem think that he long time in King Edward's life forethought to be King in case that the King his brother (whose life he looked that evil diet should shorten) should happen to decease (as indeed he did) while his children were still young; and they deem that for this intent he was glad of his brother's death the Duke of Clarence, whose life must needs have hindered him so intending whether the same Duke of Clarence had kept him true to his nephew the young King or enterprised to be King himself. But of all this point there is no certainty, and who divineth upon conjectures may as well shoot too far as too short.

Next, More has Richard plotting to prevent the new young king, Edward, from entering London with a large escort. At the time Richard was in the North and an unaware as yet of the happening down South. More cites that he has the evidence of certain people, but does not substantiate who they are – more hearsay.

More continues his narrative with the incidents leading up to the removal of the Duke of York from his mother. While the sequence of events appear to be factual it is the spin that More puts on them that is damaging to Richard. More emphasizes a motive whereby Richard is trying to get both young princes in his clutches. This is unsubstantiated evidence and it would be just as easy to spin it another way and say that Richard wanted the younger prince to keep his older brother company in the Tower while awaiting his coronation.

The infamous council chamber meeting in the Tower, which ended with the execution of Lord Hastings is another example of how More twisted actual events to point up a darker version. Again the actual events are probably set down correctly. Richard, after arriving in good spirits suddenly turned and accused Morton, Rotherham, Stanley, Hastings and the Woodvilles of plotting against him. Hastings was executed soon after, although the actual date is still in question.

More's account leads the reader to believe that Richard had fully planned out the events before the meeting and killed off Hastings quickly because he believed Hastings would oppose his plan of seizing the throne for himself. V.B. Lamb in The Betrayal of Richard III put another interpretation forth. Lamb puts forth that Richard, being faced by Bishop Stillington's revelation of the illegitimacy of Edward IV's children, had to find out who his allies were.

He would have sent Catesby to determine if Hastings could be relied upon. Catesby, discovering the scope of the plot against Richard, interrupts the council meeting, calling Richard out of the room to inform him of his findings. Richard, upon returning is, by even More's account, deeply shocked and fighting for self-control. Lamb's view is that this would not have been the case if Richard had already fully planned out the events of that day. Lamb further points out that the quick execution of Hastings (whether it occurred that day or a week later) is another indication of the suddenness of the plot with which Richard was faced. Richard was well known to be a stickler for all forms of justice and to have proceeded as he did indicates how deeply shaken he was.[1]

The point being made here is that More's version of the council meeting events have been twisted to show Richard as being evilly manipulative, ruthless in eliminating those who stand in his way. Since John Morton was one of those involved in the plot and present at the council meeting it is most conceivable that More would have gotten his information from him. Again, given that Morton was instrumental in Richard's downfall, not much credence should be given to his relation of the story.

There are a few blatant errors in More's *History*. He places the executions of Rivers, Vaughn and Grey on the same day as Hastings thereby giving the impression that they were all part of the same plot. The actual date was not for ten days later, as can be substantiated by the date on River's will, June 23rd. Another error is the name given by More as the woman to whom Edward IV was pre-contracted.

More states the name is Elizabeth Lucy. The subsequent finding of *Titulus Regius* indicates that Lady Eleanor Butler was in fact the correct name. There is no good reason why More used Elizabeth Lucy instead, unless Morton, providing the details to More, decided to muddy the waters further with a false name.

The question of the fate of the two princes is most vague in More's account. His telling of the story is close to Vergil's version and is based upon the confession of John Tyrrel. What is most intriguing is More's statement concerning the supposed murder of the two princes. He states:

"whose death and final infortune hath natheless so far come in question that some yet remain in doubt whether they were in his (Richard's) days destroyed or no"

More was obviously very unsure of what really happened.

The portion of More's *The History of Richard III* written in his own hand-writing breaks off at the point where Morton, under captivity by the Duke of Buckingham in Wales, is successfully attempting to get the Duke to turn on Richard and back Henry Tudor. Hardyng, who brings it up to Richard's death, then continues the narrative.

It is Hardying who gives a physical description of Richard, almost identical to Vergil's. More he made no mention of any physical deformities, which Morton, as his source, would undoubtedly have mentioned.

Shakespeare would have had access to More's *History* and very likely relied upon it for his play. However, just by the fact alone that Morton was a primary source for Thomas More calls the whole version into question. The account would have been biased and self-serving. As one of Henry Tudor's staunch supporters, Morton saw More's work as a propagandist tool to discredit the former regime.

SIR FRANCIS BACON

Francis Bacon was the son of Nicolas Bacon, the Lord Keeper of the Seal of Elisabeth I. He entered Trinity College Cambridge at age 12. Bacon later described his tutors as "Men of sharp wits, shut up in their cells of a few authors, chiefly Aristotle, their Dictator." This is likely the beginning of Bacon's rejection of Aristotelianism and Scholasticism and the new Renaissance Humanism.

His father died when he was 18, and being the youngest son this left him virtually penniless. He turned to the law and at 23 he was already in the House of Commons. His rich relatives did little to advance his career and Elisabeth apparently distrusted him. It was not until James I became King that Bacon's career advanced. He rose to become Baron Verulam, Viscount St. Albans and Lord Chancellor of England. His fall came about in the course of a struggle between King and Parliament. He was accused of having taken a bribe while a judge, tried and found guilty. He thus lost his personal honour, his fortune and his place at court.

Loren Eiseley in his beautifully written book about Bacon *The Man Who Saw Through Time* remarks that Bacon: "...more fully than any man of his time, entertained the idea of the universe as a problem to be solved, examined, meditated upon, rather than as an eternally fixed stage, upon which man walked."

This is the title page from Bacon's *Instauratio Magna* which contains his *Novum Organum* which is a new method to replace that of Aristotle. The image is of a ship passing through the pillars of Hercules, which symbolized for the ancients the limits of man's possible explorations. The image represents the analogy between the great voyages of discovery and the explorations leading to the advancement of learning. In *The Advancement of Learning* Bacon makes this analogy explicit.

Speaking to James I, to whom the book is dedicated, he writes: "For why should a few received authors stand up like Hercules columns, beyond which there should be no sailing or discovering, since we have so bright and benign a star as your Majesty to conduct and prosper us." The image also forcefully suggests that using Bacon's new method, the boundaries of ancient learning will be passed. The Latin phrase at the bottom from the Book of Daniel means: "Many will pass through and knowledge will be increased."

Bacon saw himself as the inventor of a method which would kindle a light in nature - "a light that would eventually disclose and bring into sight all that is most hidden and secret in the universe." This method involved the collection of data, their judicious interpretation, the carrying out of experiments, thus to learn the secrets of nature by organized observation of its regularities.

. Bacon's proposals had a powerful influence on the development of science in seventeenth century Europe. Thomas Hobbes served as Bacon's last *amunensis* or secretary. Many members of the British Royal Society saw Bacon as advocating the kind of enquiry conducted by that society.

MODERN HISTRIOGRAPHY – MACAULAY

Thomas Babington Macaulay, eldest child of Zachary

Macaulay, was born in Leicestershire on 25th October, 1800. Zachary Macaulay, who had worked in Jamaica as a young man and had witnessed at first-hand the way slaves were treated, became active in the attempts to make the trade illegal. He became editor of the *Christian Observer* and in 1823 joined with others to form the Anti-Slavery Society.

Thomas was an extremely intelligent child he began writing poems about historical characters at the age of eight. Thomas Macaulay went to Trinity College, Cambridge in October 1818. Macaulay became friends with other students who held progressive political views including Lord Grey and Charles Austin. Macaulay became very interested in utilitarianism and was influenced by the ideas of Jeremy Bentham and Joseph Priestley. One of Macaulay's campaigns at university was to bring an end to the rule that forbade a discussion of public affairs at the Student Union later than those of the last century.

Macaulay became a lawyer after he left university. He continued to be interested in politics and in 1824 received publicity for an impressive speech at a meeting of the Anti-Slavery Society. Macaulay also became a regular contributor to the *Edinburgh Review*, a journal formed by Whig politician, Henry Brougham. Lord Lansdowne was impressed by Macaulay's articles and in 1830 offered him the seat of Calne, a pocket borough under his control.

On 2nd March 1831, Macaulay made a speech in support of the parliamentary reform measures being proposed by Lord John Russell. It was claimed that Macaulay's speech was one of the most impressive heard in the House of Commons. Even Sir Robert Peel who was leading the campaign against the Reform Act, praised Macaulay's contribution to the debate. In June 1832 Earl Grey appointed Macaulay as a commissioner of the board of control.

In the general election that followed the passing of the 1832 Reform Act, Macaulay was the Whig candidate for the newly established parliamentary constituency of Leeds. His rival for the seat was the Radical Tory, Michael Sadler, who had been involved in the campaign against child labour.

Macaulay was elected with 2,012 votes with Sadler only obtaining 1,596.

Macaulay pleased his father with his role in abolishing the British slave-trade in the West Indies. Zachary Macaulay had been involved in several bad business deals and was now deeply in debt. In an attempt to help his father pay off his creditors, Thomas Macaulay accepted a lucrative post on the Supreme Council of India. During his stay in office Macaulay received £50,000 and was able to pay off his father's debts.

In 1839 Macaulay was elected to represent Edinburgh. Soon after arriving back in the House of Commons, Lord Melbourne appointed Macaulay as his Secretary of War. He held the post until the fall of the Melbourne government in 1841.

Out of office, Macaulay now had the time to write. As well as producing articles for the *Edinburgh Review,* Macaulay began work on his *History of England.* In 1846 Macaulay became postmaster-general in the government led by Lord John Russell. Macaulay rarely spoke in the House of Commons but he did play an active role in support of John Fielden and his campaign for the Ten Hour Act.

After his defeat in the 1847 general election, Macaulay once again returned to writing his *History of England.* The first two volumes were published to great acclaim in 1848. Over 13,000 copies were sold in four months. Only Sir Water Scott and Charles Dickens could compete with Macaulay's popularity as a writer.

In July 1852 Thomas Macaulay was once again returned as MP for Edinburgh. However, he rarely attended the House of Commons and spent most of his time trying to finish his *History of England.* The third and four volumes were published in December 1855. Although criticised for its pro-Whig sympathies, the *History of England* sold over 26,000 copies in ten weeks. The work was also translated into German, Polish, Danish, Swedish, Italian, French, Dutch, Spanish, Hungarian, Russian, Bohemian and Persian.

In August 1857 Lord Palmerston granted Macaulay the title Baron Macaulay of Rothley. He attended the House of

Lords for debates but refused the offer of a post in the government. Thomas Macaulay died on 28th December 1859.

ENLIGHTMENT HISTORIOGRAPHY - MONTESQUIEU

Montesquieu (1689-1755)

In The Spirit of the Laws, Charles de Secondat, Baron de Montesquieu, sought to analyse government, laws, and political culture from a wholistic and comparative perspective. He examined the relationship between the laws, history, climate, culture, political institutions, and mores of nations, drawing upon examples from the ancient and modern world.

While Montesquieu sought to develop theories that were empirical and objective, following the model of Newtonian science, it is clear with hindsight that his theories were also conditioned by his political ideological commitments, and especially by the principle of "liberty" as it was embodied (he believed) in the English constitution.

POLITICAL LIBERTY

In every government there are three sorts of power; the legislative; the executive, in respect to things dependent on the law of nations; and the executive, in regard to things that depend on the civil law.

DANGERS TO LIBERTY

By virtue of the first, the prince or magistrate enacts temporary or perpetual laws, and amends or abrogates those that have been already enacted. By the second, he makes peace or war, sends or receives embassies; establishes the public security, and provides against invasions. By the third, he punishes criminals, or determines the disputes that arise between individuals. The latter we shall call the judiciary power, and the other simply the executive power of the state.

PRESERVING THE DANGERS

The political liberty of the subject is a tranquility of mind, arising from the opinion each person has of his safety. In order to have this liberty, it is requisite the government be so constituted as one man need not be afraid of another.

APPROACH AND THEORY

When the legislative and executive powers are united in the same person, or in the same body of magistrates, there can be no liberty; because apprehensions may anse, lest the same monarch or senate should enact tyrannical laws, to execute them in a tyrannical manner.

Again, there is no liberty, if the power of judging be not separated from the legislative and executive powers. Were it joined with the legislative, the life and liberty of the subject would be exposed to arbitrary control, for the judge would then be the legislator. Were it joined to the executive power, the judge might behave with all the violence of an oppressor.

There would be an end of every thing were the same man, or the same body, whether of the nobles or of the people to exercise those three powers that of enacting laws, that of executing the public resolutions, and that of judging the crimes or differences of individuals .

Hence it is that many of the princes of Europe, whose aim has been levelled at arbitrary power, have constantly set out with uniting in their own persons, all the branches of magistracy, and all the great offices of state.

It is not my business to examine whether the English actually enjoy this liberty, or not. It is sufficient for my purpose to observe, that their laws establish it; and he inquire no further.

Neither he pretended by this to undervalue other governments, not to say that this extreme political liberty ought to give uneasiness to those who have only a moderate share of it nor should he have any such design. According to him even the excess of reason is not always desirable, and that mankind generally find their account better in mediums than in extremes?

VOLTAIRE

French writer, satirist, the embodiment of the 18th-century

Enlightenment. Voltaire is remembered as a crusader against tyranny and bigotry. Compared to Rousseau's (1712-1778) rebelliousness and idealism, Voltaire's world view was more skeptical, but both of their ideas influenced deeply the French Revolution. Voltaire disliked Rousseau and wrote to him in 1761: "One feels like crawling on all fours after reading your work."

"Liberty of thought is the life of the soul."

François-Marie Arouet de Voltaire was born in Paris into a middle-class family. His father was a minor treasury official. Voltaire was educated by the Jesuits at the Collège Louis-le-Grand (1704-11). He learned Latin and Greek and later in life he became fluent in Italian, Spanish and English.

From 1711 to 1713 he studied law. Before devoting himself entirely to writing, Voltaire worked as a secretary to the French ambassador in Holland. From the beginning, Voltaire had troubles with the authorities, but he energetically attacked the government and the Catholic church. These activities led to numerous imprisonments and exiles. In his early twenties he spent eleven months in the Bastille for writing satiric verses about the aristocracy.

Voltaire did not support the dogmatic theology of institutional religions, his religiosity was anticlerical. With his brother Armand, who was a fundamentalist Catholic, Voltaire did not get on as well as with his sister. Atheism Voltaire considered not as baleful as fanaticism, but nearly always fatal to virtue. The doctrines about the Trinity or the Incarnation he dismissed as nonsense.

As a humanist, Voltaire advocated religious and social tolerance, but not necessarily in a direct way. Well known is Voltaire's hostility toward the Jews. His play LE FANATISME, OU MAHOMET LE PROPHÈTE (1741), which portrayed the founder of Islam as an intriguer and greedy for power, was denounced by Catholic clergymen. They had no doubts that the true target was Christian fanaticism. However, Pope Benedict XIV, whom Voltaire dedicated the work, replied by saying that he read it with great pleasure.

In 1716 Voltaire was arrested and exiled from Paris for

five months. From 1717 to 1718 he was imprisoned in the Bastille for lampoons of the Regency. During this time he wrote the tragedy ŒDIPE, and started to use the name Voltaire. The play brought him fame which did not lessen the number of his enemies at court.

At his 1726 stay at the Bastille, Voltaire was visited by a flow of admirers. Between 1726 and 1729 he lived in exile mainly in England. There he avoided trouble for three years and wrote in English his first essays, ESSAY UPON EPIC POETRY and ESSAY UPON THE CIVIL WARS IN FRANCE, which were published in 1727. After returning to France Voltaire wrote plays, poetry, historical and scientific treatises and became royal historiographer. HISTOIRE DE CHARLES XII (1731) used novelistic technique and rejected the idea that divine intervention guides history.

In 1734 appeared Voltaire's *Philosophical Letters* in which he compared the French system of government with the system he had seen in England. Voltaire stated that he had perceived fewer barriers between occupations in England than in his own country. The book was banned, and Voltaire was forced to flee Paris. The English edition became a bestseller outside France.

"In general, the art of government consists in taking as much money as possible from one class of citizens to give to the other."

Voltaire's economic situation improved substantially, when he joined a syndicate, which made a large profit with the state lottery. In addition, with lucky speculation in the Compagnie des Indes he became so wealthy, that he lent money to dukes and princes.

At the age of thirty-nine, Voltraire started his famous sixteen-year liaison with Mme du Châtelet. She was twenty-seven, married, and the mother of three children. "I found, in 1733, a young woman who thought as I did," Voltaire wrote in his memoirs, "and who decided to spend several years in the country, cultivating her mind." The Marquis du Châtelet was well aware of the affair. With madame du Châtelet Voltare lived at the Château de Cirey in 1734-36 and 1737-40. Between the years Voltaire took a refuge in Holland (1736-37). Mme du Châtelet, who was a mathematician and scientist, translated Newton's *Principia Mathematica* and Voltaire wrote ELÉMENTS DE LA PHILOSOPHIE DE NEWTON. Voltaire nicknamed her "Mme Neuton Pompom."

In 1740 Voltaire was an ambassador-spy in Prussia, then in Brussels (1742-43), and in 1748 he was at the court of King Stanislas in Lunéville. From 1745 to 1750 he was a historiographer to Louis XV and in 1746 he was elected to the French Academy. In Paris, Voltaire had a new mistress, Marie-Louise Denis, his eldest niece.

At the invitation of Fredrick the Great, Voltaire moved in 1750 to Berlin, realizing eventually that the ruler was more enlightened in theory than in practice. Voltaire settled in 1755 in 1755 in Switzerland, where he lived the rest of his life, apart from trips to France.

He had his own château, Les Delices, outside Geneva, and later at nearby Ferney, in France. Anybody of note, from Boswell to Casanova, wanted to visit the place; Voltaire's conversations with visitors were recorded and published and he was flattered by kings and nobility. "Common sense is not so common," Voltaire wrote.

Voltaire's official publishers were Gabriel and Philibert Cramer from Geneve. They operated from Stockholm to Naples, and from Venice to Lisbon and Paris, spreading the ideas of Enlightenment. As an essayist Voltaire defended freedom of speech and religious tolerance. In his DICTIONNAIRE PHILOSOPHIQUE (1764) he defined the ideal religion – it would teach very little dogma but much morality. Voltaire's thoughts were condemned in Paris, Geneva, and Amsterdam. For safety reasons Voltaire denied his authorship.

In his late years Voltaire produced several anti-religious writing. In Ferney he built a chapel with the inscription 'Deo Erexit Voltaire' inscribed on the lintel. He also led campaign to open up a trial, in which the Huguenot merchant Jean Calas was found guilty of murdering his eldest son and executed. The parliament at Paris declared afterwards in 1765 Calas and all his family innocent.

Voltaire died in Paris on May 30, 1778, as the undisputed leader of the Age of Enlightenment. He had suffered throughout his life from poor health, but at the time of his death he was eighty-four. Voltaire left behind him over fourteen thousand known letters and over two thousand books and pamphlets. Among his best-known works is the satirical short story CANDIDE (1759), which reflected the nihilism of Jonathan Swift. In the story the young and innocent hero, Candide, experiences a long series of misfortunes and disastrous adventures.

He is kicked out of the castle of Thunder-Ten-Tronckh for making love to the baron's daughter, Cunégonde, in the army he is beaten nearly to death, in Lisbon he experiences the famous earthquake, he is hunted by the Inquisition and Jesuits, and threatened with imprisonment in Paris. Meanwhile Cunégonde's father, mother and brother are hacked to pieces by invaders, and she is raped repeatedly. Eventually Candide marries Cunégonde, who has become an ugly gummy-eyed, flat-chested washerwoman, with wrinkled cheeks."If this is the best of possible worlds," Voltaire wrote, "what then are the others." Finally Candide finds the pleasures of cultivating one's garden - "Il faut cultiver notre jardin."

Candide's world is full of liars, traitors, ingrates, thieves, misers, killers, fanatics, hypocrites, fools and so on. However, Voltaire's outrage is not based on social criticism but on his ironic view of human nature. When Candide asks his friend Martin, does he believe that men have always massacred one another, Martin points out that hawks eat pigeons. " – Well, said Martin, if hawks have always had the same character, why do you suppose that men have changed?" Candide rejects the philosophy of his tutor, the unsuccessfully hanged Doctor Pangloss, who claims that "all is for the best in this best of all possible worlds".

Candide was partly inspired by the devastating Lisbon earthquake of 1755, Dr. Pangloss was allegedly a caricature of Leibniz, but it is possible that the real model was Pierre-Louis Moreau de Maupertuis (1698-1759), a French philosopher and scientist. The prolific writer produced a number of studies from the physics of Venus to the proof of the existence of God. Voltaire's L'HISTOIRE DU DOCTOEUR AKAKIA ET DU NATIF DE SAINT-MALO (1753) openly ridiculed Maupertuis' ideas. *Candide's* narrative frame, the education of a young man, was again utilized among others in Stendhal's *The Red and the Black* and Thomas Mann's *The Magic Mountain*. Leonard Bernstein made *Candide* a musical comedy in 1957.

In addition to *Candide*, Voltaire treated the problem of evil in his classic tale ZADIG (1747), set in the ancient Babylon, and in 'Poem of the Lisbon' Earthquake'. "But how conceive a God supremely good," Voltaire asked in the poem, "Who heaps his favours on the sons he loves, / Yet scatters evil with as large a hand?" MICROMÉGAS (1752) was an early science-fiction story, in which two ambassadors from the outer space visit Earth, and witness follies of human thought and behaviour. Voltaire possibly wrote the *conte* already in 1738-39. It has similarities with 'Voyage du Baron Gangan', which he sent to Fredrick the Great.

Voltaire's *Dictionnaire Philosophique* was burned with the young Chevalier de la Barre, who had neglected to take of his hat while passing a bridge, where a sacred statue was exposed. Later Voltaire introduced his *Dictionary* as a dialogical book: its short, polemical articles were more useful when "the readers produce the other half". In *Essay on the Manner and Spirit of Nations*, Voltaire presented the first modern comparative history of civilizations, including Asia. Later he returned to the Chinese philosophy is his *Dictionary*, praising the teachings of Confucius: "What more beautiful rule of conduct has ever been given man since the world began? Let us admit that there has been no legislator more useful to the human race."

SELECTED WORKS

- ŒDIPE, 1718 (tragedy).
- ARTÉMISE, 1720 (drama).
- LA HENRIADE, 1723 - The Henriad: a Poem (tr. Charles L. S. Jones, 1834) / The Henriade; with the Battle of Fontenoy, Dissertations on Man, Law of

Nature, Destruction of Lisbon, Temple of Taste, and Temple of Friendship.

- Essay on Epic Poetry, 1727 (tr. by Florence D. White) / Critical Essays on Dramatic Poetry - L'ESSAI SUR LA POÉSIE ÉPIQUE, 1765.
- HÉRODE ET MARIAMNE, 1725 (tragedy).
- L'INDISCRET, 1725 (comedy).
- LA FÊTE DE BÉLÉBAT, 1725 (divertissement).
- Essay upon the Civil Wars in France, 1727 (tr. anonymously) - ESSAY SUR LES GUERRES CIVILES DE FRANCE, 1729.
- LA HENRIADE, 1728 - The Henriad; a Poem; with the Notes and Variations (tr. Charles L. S. Jones).
- LE POUR ET LE CONTRE, 1728.
- BRUTUS, 1730 (tragedy, publ. 1731).
- HISTOIRE DE CHARLES XII, 1731 - The History of Charles the XIIth, King of Sweden.
- LES ORIGINAUX, OU MONSIEUR DU CAP-VERT, 1732 (tragedy, publ. 1820)
- ÉRYPHILE, 1732
- ZAÏRE, 1732 (tragedy, publ. 1733) - Zaire: a Tragedy in Verse in Five Acts, by Voltare (ed.by Charles W. Cabeen, 1910) / Zaïre (ed. by Eva Jacobs, 1975)
- SAMSON, 1733 (opera, publ. 1750)
- TANIS ET ZÉLIDE, OU LES ROIS PASTEURS, 1733 (tragedy).
- LA MORT DE CÉSAR, 1733 (tragedy, publ. 1735)
- Letters Concerning the English Nation, 1733 (tr. John Lockman) - LETTRES PHILOSOPHIQUES SUR LES ANGLAIS, 1734 (Voltaire's satirical attack among others on Descates' theory of vortices)- Philosophical Letters: Letters Regarding the English Nation (tr. Prudence L. Steiner, 2007)
- LE TEMPLE DU GOÛT, 1733 - The Temple of Taste (tr. 1734).
- ADÉLAÏDE DU GUESCLIN, 1734 (play).
- ALZIRE, 1736 (tragedy) - Alzira: a Tragedy.
- L'ENFANT PRODIGUE, 1736 (drama).

- ELÉMENTS DE LA PHILOSOPHIE DE NEUTON, 1738 (with Emilie du Châtelet) - The Elements of Sir Isaac Newton's Philosophy (tr. by John Hanna, 1738)
- ESSAI SUR LA NATURE DU FEU, 1739
- VIE DE MOLIÈRE, 1739
- ZULIME, 1740 (tragedy, publ. 1761)
- PANDORE, 1740 (opera, publ. 1748)
- LA PRUDE, 1740 (comedy, based on William Wycherley's The Plain Dealer, 1676, publ. 1747)
- LE FANATISME, OU MAHOMET LE PROPHÈTE, 1741

EDWARD GIBBON

EDWARD GIBBON, the historian of The Decline and Fall of the Roman Empire, was born at Putney on the 27th of April, 1737, and was the first child of Edward Gibbon and Judith Porten, and the only one of seven children that survived infancy. He spent a sickly childhood in occasional lessons, and desultory reading and discussion with his mother's sister, a lady of a srtong understanding and a warm heart, whom he calls "the mother of his mind," and to whose kindness he ascribes not only the bringing out of his intellectual faculties, but the preservation of his life in these "critical early years. One of his temporary masters, was the Rev. Philip Francis, the translator of Horace.

His father had him entered at Magdalen College, Oxford, at the age of 15. Here he became a convert to the Church of Rome, and found himself shut out of Oxford. To effect his cure from Catholicism, he was sent to Lausanne, in Switzerland, to board in the house of M. Pavillard, a Calvinist minister, a poor, but sensible and intelligent man, who judiciously suggested books and arguments to his young charge and had the satisfaction of seeing him reconverted to Protestantism, in witness of which conversion he received the sacrament in the church of Lausanne on Christmas Day, 1754, his belief in the Roman Church having lasted not quite 18 months.

He lived nearly five years in this house, and it was here that he began and carried out steadily and joyously those private studies, which, aided by his enormous memory, made him master of erudition without a superior, and with hardly an equal. After his return to England and his father's house, he persevered in these studies as best he could.

He entered parliament for the borough of Liskeard at the beginning of the struggle with America. He sat eight years, but never had the courage to speak; "the great speakers filled him with despair, the poor ones with terror." In 1776, the first volume of The Decline and Fall was published, and its success was prodigious. The reputation of the author was established before the religious world had had time to consider and attack the last chapters of the work - the 15th and 16th - in which, while admitting, or at least not denying the "convincing evidence of the doctrine itself, and the ruling providence of its great author," he proceeds to account for the rapid growth of the early Christian church, by "secondary," or human causes. He finished this great work on the 27th of June 1787, at Lausanne, to which he had retired for quiet and economy, after leaving parliament, and holding office under government for a short time. He died on the 16th of January, 1794, in St. James Street, London.

It is not easy to characterize a man of so gigantic and cultivated an intellect in few or many phases. He was a faithful friend, pleasant and hardly rivalled in conversation, not disliked by any who came near him. His Decline and Fall is probably the greatest achievement of human thought and erudition in the department of history. It is virtually a history of the civilized world for thirteen centuries, during which paganism was breaking down and Christianity was superseding it: and thus bridges over the chasm between the old world and the new.

THOMAS CARLYLE

Thomas Carlyle, Scottish historian, critic, and sociological writer. was born in the village of Ecclefechan, Dumfriesshire, eldest child of James Carlyle, stonemason, and Margaret (Aitken) Carlyle. The father was stern, irascible, a puritan of the puritans, but withal a man of rigid probity and strength of character. The mother, too, was of the Scottish earth, and both the parents began Thomas' education at home. From the age of five to nine he was at the village school; from nine to fourteen at Annan Grammar School. Where he showed proficiency in mathematics and was well grounded in French and Latin. In November 1809 he walked to Edinburgh, and attended courses at the University till 1814, with the ultimate aim of becoming a minister. He left without a degree, became a mathematical tutor at Annan Academy in 1814, and three years later abandoned all thoughts of entering the Kirk, having reached a theological position incompatible with its teachings.

He had begun to learn German in Edinburgh, and had done much independent reading outside the regular curriculum. Late in 1816 he moved to a school in Kirkcaldy, where he became the intimate associate of Edward Irving, an old boy of Annan School, and now also a schoolmaster. This contact was Carlyle's first experience of true intellectual companionship, and the two men became lifelong friends. He remained there two years, was attracted by Margaret Gordon, a lady of good family (whose friends vetoed an engagement), and in October 1818 gave up schoolmastering and went to Edinburgh, where he took mathematical pupils and made some show of reading law.

During this period in the Scottish capital he began to suffer agonies from a gastric complaint which continued to torment him all his life, and may well have played a large part in shaping the rugged, rude fabric of his philosophy. In literature he had at first little success, a series of articles for the Edinburgh Encyclopaedia bringing in little money and no special credit. In 1820 and 1821 he visited Irving in Glasgow and made long stays at his father's new farm, Mainhill; and in June 1821, in Leith Walk, Edinburgh, he experienced a striking spiritual rebirth, which is related in Sartor Resartus.

Put briefly and prosaically, it consisted in a sudden clearing away of doubts as to the beneficent organization of the universe; a semi-mystical conviction that he was free to think and what would not thwart work, and that honest effort and striving he called the "Everlasting No."

For about a year, from the spring of 1823, Carlyle was tutor to Charles and Arthur Buller, young men of substance, first in Edinburgh and later at Dunkeld. Now likewise appeared the first fruits of his deep studies in German, the Life of Schiller, which was published serially in the London Magazine in 1823-24 and issued as a separate volume in 1825. A second garner from the same field was his version of Goethe's Wilhelm Meister, which earned the praise of Blackwood's and was at once recognized as a very masterly rendering.

In 1821 Irving had gone to London, and in June 1821 Carlyle followed, in the train of his employers, the Bullers. But he soon resigned his tutorship, and, after a few weeks at Birmingham, trying a dyspepsia cure, he lived with Irving at Pentonville, London, and paid a short visit to Paris. March 1825 saw him back; in Scotland, on his brother's farm, Hoddam Hill, near the Solway. Here for a year he worked hard at German translations, perhaps more serenely than before or after and free from that noise which was always a curse to his sensitive ear and which later caused him to build a sound-proof room in his Chelsea home.

Before leaving for London Irving had introduced Carlyle to Jane Baillie Welsh daughter of the surgeon, John Welsh, and descended from John Knox. She was beautiful, precociously learned, talented, and a brilliant mistress of cynical satire. Among her numerous suitors, the rough, uncouth Carlyle at first made an ill impression; but a literary correspondence was begun, and on October 17, 1826, after a courtship that was in some sort a battle of strong wills, the two were married and went to live at Comely Bank, Edinburgh starting with a capital of £200. Francis Jeffrey, editor of the Edinburgh Review, was a cousin of the Welshes. He accepted Carlyle as a contributor, and during 1827 printed two important articles — on "Richter" and "The State of German Literature."

The Foreign Review published two penetrating essays on Goethe; and in 1827 a cordial correspondence was begun with the great German writer, who backed Carlyle (unsuccessfully) for the vacant Chair of Moral Philosophy at St. Andrews.

Another application for a university chair, this time at the new University of London, failed equally. An attempt at a novel was destroyed.

In May 1828 the Carlyles moved to Craigenputtock, an isolated farm belonging to the Welsh family, which was their permanent home until 1834. Carlyle lived the life of a recluse and scholar, and his clever wife, immersed in household duties and immured in solitude, led a dull and empty existence. Jeffrey, who paid visits in 1828 and 1830, said: "Bring your blooming Eve out of your blasted Paradise, and seek shelter in the lower world," but Carlyle was lacking in consideration for his partner, and would not. Jeffrey even thought of Carlyle as his successor in the editorship of the Edinburgh, when he gave it up in 1829, but the matter could not be arranged. A memorable visit, in August 1833, was that of the young Ralph Waldo Emerson, who was kindly received and became a fast friend.

At Craigenputtock was written the first of Carlyle's great commentaries on life in general, Sartor Resartus, which appeared in Fraser's Magazine between November 1833 and August 1834. The idea of a philosophy of clothes was not new; there are debts to Swift, Jean Paul Richter, and others; but what were new were the amazing, humorous energy, the moral force, the resourceful (if eccentric) command over English. It was damned by the press, and was not issued in book-form until 1838; but it is now numbered among his most significant works. Other notable writings of this time were essays on Voltaire, Novalis, and Richter (a new paper) in the Foreign Review.

After visits to Edinburgh and London, and an unsuccessful application for a professorship of astronomy at Edinburgh in January 1834, Carlyle decided to set up house in London, settling at 5, Cheyne Row, Chelsea. His struggle to live was made more severe by his refusal to engage in journalism: even an offer of work on The Times was rejected; and instead a grandiose history of the French Revolution was begun. In the spring of 1835 occurred one of the great heroisms of literature. The manuscript of the first volume of the new work had been lent to the philosopher, J. S. Mill, who in his turn had lent it to a Mrs. Taylor. An illiterate housekeeper took it for waste paper, and it was burnt. Mill was inconsolable; Carlyle behaved with the utmost stoicism and nobility, and was only with difficulty induced to accept £ 100 as a slight pecuniary compensation.

The French Revolution was re-written, and its publication in January 1837 brought the praise of Thackeray, Southey, Hallam, and others of weight, and consolidated Carlyle's reputation as one of the foremost men of letters of the day. Even so, it sold slowly, and he had to resort to public lecturing (arranged by Harriet Martineau) to raise funds; and it was only in 1842, when Mrs. Welsh died and left them an annuity, that the Carlyles were able to rid them of financial worry.

Of outward event Carlyle's life contains little. From his establishment in London his history was one of enormous work and the gradual building up of a literary fame that became worldwide. In the 'forties and onward he became more and more sought after by men of letters, statesmen and the aristocracy, and his friends included such names as Monckton Milnes, Tyndall, Peel, Froude, Grote, Browning, and Ruskin. One friendship, with the clergyman, John Sterling, was close and warm, and left its record in the Life published in 1851. Another, with Lady Harriet Ashburton, caused grave dissension in the Carlyle home, being strongly disapproved by Mrs. Carlyle, though there was no suggestion of anything more than high mutual regard.

ROMANTICIST HISTORIOGRAPHY – ROUSSAEU

Jean Jacques Rousseau, born at Geneva, was deserted by his family at age 10. As a young man he ran away from his caretakers and was to be referred, by a charitable agency, to the care of Madame de Warens a person with connections who saw to Rousseau's conversion to Catholicism. During his years, it would seem, Rousseau had no problem launching and maintaining love affairs, and had no qualms in bedding married women with absent or distracted husbands. In time, Rousseau was to return to Madame de Warens and was to become her general factotum and lover. After deserting her he took up with a maid at the hostelry in which he was staying; Thérèse Le Vasser and Rousseau were to continue to have a life time relationship which brought into the world five children; whom, Rousseau — this man who wrote of man's natural goodness and the corrupting forces of institutions — assigned to a foundling hospital. In time, Rousseau had the good fortunate to meet Voltaire and Diderot. The Parisian crowd were soon to place Rousseau among *Le Siècle des Lumières*, and, like the rest, was lionized. Rousseau was the author of *Discours* (1755), and, of course, his masterpiece

As a brilliant, undisciplined, and unconventional thinker, Jean-Jacques Rousseau spent most of his life being driven by controversy back and forth between Paris and his native Geneva. Orphaned at an early age, he left home at sixteen, working as a tutor and musician before undertaking a literary career while in his forties. Rousseau sired but refused to support several illegitimate children and frequently initiated bitter quarrels with even the most supportive of his colleagues. His autobiographical *Les Confessions* (1783) offer a thorough (if somewhat self-serving) account of his turbulent life.

Man is born free; and everywhere he is in chains" — Man must "be forced to be free." These were the notions of Rousseau and those who followed him. With the cry of "Liberty, Equality, Fraternity," the French mobs hit the bloody barricades. The French Revolution, in addition to the immediate blood and damage, left a train of tattered notions in its long comet like tail in which we still exist. First there was Napoleon and years of war. There then followed, down through the centuries, power hungry men who forced people, often with violent acts, to do their bidding, pronouncing that it was to the advantage of the people.

Rousseau's concept of a social contract (that there existed unstated reciprocal obligations between the people and government) is not near as upsetting as his view that the existing social conventions should be immediately upset like a barrow of apples at the Saturday morning market, every apple all at once to be bruised and kicked. What Rousseau failed to observe or appreciate is that the state evolved over a very long time and runs (and can only run) on culture, on custom and on tradition. It would take more than long years of repeated war to change the fundamental beliefs of a people. Time and generations will have had to pass, with wise men in power applying gentle non-hurting pressure, simple and steady pressure — like so many orthodontists at work.

However, let me say that my principal conclusion as to Rousseau, is that he judged all men in reference to himself. And while there is little doubt that Rousseau had "a pure and overwhelming desire for knowledge," the question is — Can that be said of mankind in general? Here are some classic criticisms of Rousseauian theory, first Edmund Burke:

KANT

Immanuel Kant was born on April 22, 1724, the son of Johann Georg Kant, a herness maker. He grew up and never traveled more than seventy miles form the captial city of East Prussia, called Königsberg.

In 1732, at the age of eight, Kant was sent to the Collegium Fredericianum, a Pietist school directed by Franz Albert Schultz, the Kant family's pastor. When Kant was thirteen, his mother caught rheumatic fever and died.

When he was sixteen years old, Kant entered the Albertus University of Königsberg. Here Kant enrolled as a student of philosophy. He studied for a while, until 1746, when his father died. Kant was now without financial support and without employment. He left Königsberg to take up a position as family tutor. After a while, and a couple of different families, Kant became tutor for Count Kayserling, and his family.

In 1755, Kant was qualified to start his life work, and he taught as a Privatdozent (a lecturer that receives no payment for his lectures, except that of which the attendees pay) between 1755 and 1770. Kant was a marvelous speaker, and may times the students would arrive early just to get a good seat. In 1766, he was appointed second librarian of the Royal Library, a government position with a salary. Three years later, he considered accepting a professorship in logic and metaphysics at Erlangen. Meanwhile, a mathematics chair in Königsberg became open, and Dr. Buck took over that chair, which left open the logic and metaphysics chair, which was given to Kant.

In the August of 1770, Kant read his dissertation in Latin. Most thought it was pivotal work, the best written yet. Kant then wrote out what he called, "the proper procedure for metaphysics." And in 1781 his rivoting book was published, it was called *Critique of Pure Reason.* It was widely accepted, but it took some time to catch on because it was longwinded (about seven-hundred pages), as well as hard to read. However, in the next ten year, he wrote nothing that was substantial, and historians called this time, his silent decade.

The next several decades were hard for Kant. The enlightened king Fredrick the Great died, and is illiberal nephwe, Fredrick William the second took the throne. King William the second took it upon himself to censor all writings which made it tough on Kant. But, Kant survived and published his four book series called *Religion* as well as some other pieces. Fredrick sent Kant a letter that told him that he was "distorting and depreciating many of the basic teaching of the Holy scrpture" and he was to produce a "conscientious vindication" of his actions. Kant wrote a letter back to the king telling the king that not to fall under suspicion, he would not lecture or write about anything religious. And until the king's death in 1797, Kant kept his promise, publishing only non-religious pieces.

In late 1803, it was no longer safe for Kant to be alone, and his youngest sister came to live with him. On February 12 ,1804 he died, and his final words were "It is good."

HEGAL

Hegel was born in Stuttgart on August 27, 1770, the son of Georg Ludwig Hegel, a revenue officer with the Duchy of Wurttemburg. Eldest of three children (his younger brother, Georg Ludwig, died young as an officer with Napoleon during the Russian campaign), he was brought up in an atmosphere of Protestant pietism. His mother was teaching nim Latin before he began school, but died when he was 11. He was very attached to his sister, Christiane, who later developed a manic jealousy of Hegel's wife when he married at age 40 and committed suicide three months after his death. Hegel was deeply concerned by his sister's psychosis and developed ideas of psychiatry based on concepts of dialectics.

Hegel soon became thoroughly acquainted with the Greek and Roman classics while studying at the Stuttgart Gymnasium (preparatory school) and was familiar with German literature and science. Encouraged by his father to become a clergyman, Hegel entered the seminary at the University of Tübingen in 1788. There he developed friendships with the poet Friedrich Hölderlin and the philosopher Friedrich Wilhelm Joseph von Schelling.

From Hölderlin in particular, Hegel developed a profound interest in Greek literature and philosophy. Early on and throughout his life, Hegel recorded and committed to memory everything he read – and he read profusely! Hegel worshipped Goethe and long regarded himself as inferior to his brilliant contemporaries Schelling and Hölderlin.

The Germany of Hegel's time was extremely backward from an economic point of view. Germany was a myriad of tiny, backward states, relatively insulated from the turmoils of Europe. He was an avid reader of Schiller and Rousseau. Hegel was 18 when the Bastille was stormed and the Republic declared in France and Hegel was an enthusiastic supporter of the Revolution, and participated in a support group formed in Tübingen.

Hegel finished his first great work, *The Phenomenology of Mind* on the very eve of the decisive Battle of Jena, in which Napoleon broke the Prussian armies and dismembered the kingdom. French soldiers entered Hegel's house and set it afire just after he stuffed the last pages of the *Phenomenology* into his pocket and took refuge in the house of a high official of the town. In the *Phenomenology* he attempts to understand the revolutionary terror of the Jacobins in terms of their interpretation of Freedom. Hegel celebrated Bastille Day throughout his life.

Having completed a course of study in philosophy and theology and having decided not to enter the ministry, Hegel became (1793) a private tutor in Berne, Switzerland. In about 1794, at the suggestion of his friend Hölderlin, Hegel began a study of Immanuel Kant and Johann Fichte but his first writings at this time were *Life of Jesus* and *The Positivity of Christian Religion*.

In 1796, Hegel wrote *The First Programme for a System of German Idealism* jointly with Schelling. This work included the line: "... the state is something purely mechanical – and there is no [spiritual] idea of a machine. Only what is an object of freedom may be called 'Idea'. Therefore we must transcend the state! For every state must treat free men as cogs in a machine. And this is precisely what should not happen; hence the state must perish". In 1797, Hölderlin found Hegel a position in Frankfurt, but two years later his father died, leaving him enough to free him from tutoring.

In 1801, Hegel went to the University of Jena. Fichte had left Jena in 1799, and Schiller had left in 1793, but Schelling remained at Jena until 1803 and Schelling and Hegel collaborated during that time.

Hegel studied, wrote and lectured, although he did not receive a salary until the end of 1806, just before completing the first draft of *The Phenomenology of Mind* – the first work to present his own unique philosophical contribution – part of which was taken through the French lines by a courier to his friend Niethammer in Bamburg, Bavaria, before Jena was taken by Napoleon's army and Hegel was forced to flee – the remaining pages in his pocket.

Having exhausted the legacy left him by his father, Hegel became editor of the Catholic daily *Bamberger Zeitung*. He disliked journalism, however, and moved to Nuremberg, where he served for eight years as headmaster of a Gymnasium. He continued to work on the *Phenomenology*. Almost everything that Hegel was to develop systematically over the rest of his life is prefigured in the *Phenomenology*, but this book is far from systematic and extremely difficult to read. The *Phenomenology* attempts to present human history, with all its revolutions, wars and scientific discoveries, as an idealistic self-development of an objective Spirit or Mind.

During the Nuremberg years, Hegel met and married Marie von Tucher (1791-1855). They had three children – a daughter who died soon after birth, and two sons, Karl (1813-1901) and Immanuel (1814-91). Hegel had also fathered an illegitimate son, Ludwig, to the wife of his former landlord in Jena. Ludwig was born soon after Hegel had left Jena but eventually came to live with the Hegels, too.

While at Nuremberg, Hegel published over a period of several years *The Science of Logic* (1812, 1813, 1816). In 1816, Hegel accepted a professorship in philosophy at the University of Heidelberg. Soon after, he published in summary form a systematic statement of his entire philosophy entitled *Encyclopaedia of the Philosophical Sciences* which was first translated into English in 1959 and includes *The Shorter Logic*, as Part I. The *Encyclopaedia* was continually revised up till 1827, and the final version was published in 1830.

In 1818, Hegel was invited to teach at the University of Berlin, where he was to remain. He died in Berlin on November 14, 1831, during a cholera epidemic.

The last full-length work published by Hegel was *The Philosophy of Right* (1821), although several sets of his lecture notes, supplemented by students' notes, were published after his death.

UTILITRIANISM HISTORIOGRAPHY BENTHAM

British gentleman, political activist, legal scholar, social philosopher, linguist, Jeremy Bentham is best known as the founder of British "utilitarianism" or "philosophical radicalism".

Born into a wealthy Tory family, Jeremy Bentham was educated at Westminster school and Queen's College, Oxford. He trained as a lawyer and was called to the bar in 1769. His independent wealth permitted him to set himself up as a writer in London. According to his contemporary William Hazlitt, "Bentham has lived for the last forty years in a house in Westminster...like an anchorite in a cell, reducing law to a system, and the mind of man to a machine." In 1768 that Bentham came across a political tract by Joseph Priestley in which the the phrase "the greatest happiness for the greatest number" was invoked. Intrigued, Bentham followed this up by reading Hume, Helvetius and Beccaria and slowly began forming his utilitarian ideas.

Bentham's first book (1776) was an attack on Blackstone's immensely popular *Commentaries on the Laws of England.* For Bentham, Blackstone's obsession with the "rule of law" made a fetish out of ancient laws that were long outdated and prevented the passing of new legislation more appropriate for changing circumstances. Bentham claimed that all laws, ancient and modern, should be evaluated according to the single ethical principle of "utility". A law is good or bad depending upon whether or not it increased general happiness of the population.

From 1785 to 1788, Bentham traveled to Russia to visit his brother. Upon his return, he published his most famous work, *Introduction to the Principles of Morals* (1789), which has been widely regarded as the founding document of British utilitarianism. In 1791-94, Bentham actively campaigned for his "model prison" – the "Panopticon". Bentham's first disciple, Étienne Dumont, published French translations of several of Bentham's works, giving him a good deal of popularity abroad. Despite his adamant opposition to the "natural law" language and principles of the 1776 *Declaration of Independence* and the 1789 *Declaration of the Rights of Man,* Bentham welcomed both the American and French Revolutions. He was made an honorary citizen of the French Republic in 1792.

expounding tract after tract on utilitarian philosophy, legal theory and social reform. He struck up important friendships with the politicians Earl of Shelburne and William Pitt and the economist David Ricardo.

HIS FIRST BOOK (1776)

Bentham introduced the distinction between individual "hedonic calculation" (maximizing individual utility) as a basis of a *positive* theory of behaviour, and social calculation (maximizing aggregate utility) as a *normative* theory of social organization.

"Nature has placed mankind under the governance of two sovereign masters, pain and pleasure. It is for them alone to point out what we ought to do as well as to determine what we shall do. On the one hand, the standard of right and wrong, on the other the chain of causes and effects, are fastened to their throne."

Bentham argued that virtually all humans seek to maximize their "happiness", defined as the surplus of pleasures over pains. He also posited that *all* human actions arise from the hedonic calculus. Altruism, asceticism, love, duty, a desire for freedom, obedience to the law, faith, etc. are reducible to individual pleasure and pain calculations. By applying his utility hypothesis so widely, Bentham made it empirically unverifiable. No piece of evidence could conceivably be brought up to disprove it.

Bentham also correlated happiness with the means to happiness. The wealthier a person is, the greater the happiness he can attain. However, he recognized the principle of diminishing marginal utility, i.e. that the greater the amount of utility a person already has, the smaller will be the utility gain of any extra increment of wealth.

The critical question Bentham puzzled over was whether the unhindered pursuit of individual happiness could be reconciled with morality. The only ethical principle he accepted was that increasing general happiness is "good", while decreasing it is "bad". From the outset, then, Bentham dismissed all "ipsedixitisms", i.e. moral judgments based on criteria such as "sympathy" or "intentions". Similarly, all abstract notions of social ethics like "natural rights", "social justice", etc. were hogwash. For Bentham, only consequences mattered. Actions are to be judged strictly on the basis of how their *outcomes* affect general utility.

But what is general utility of a society? Bentham argued it was no more and no less than the sum total of individual utilities of all members of a society. Whom we include in our definition of "society" depends on our sphere of consideration. It may be a nation, it may be all of humanity. It may be confined to living adult voters, or it may embrace all people and generations yet unborn.

WHAT IS UTILITY?

He emphasized the need for equal weights in this summation: no person's utility counted more than another's (it somehow slipped Bentham's notice that this presumption implicitly introduces elements of some "natural law" doctrines, but so be it). "equal capacity for pleasure" was a natural law notion slipped through.

Insisting that individuals are the best judges of their own happiness, Bentham had an automatic tendency to default to non-interference by government. However, he recognized that individual actions of one individual often implicated the happiness of others and that individuals may not have the incentive or ability to coordinate concerted actions that improve aggregate utility.

As such, Bentham laid some responsibilities in the hands of the State. The first obligation is to not let people suffer needlessly. This means guaranteeing a minimal subsistence level of income to ensure survival for all citizens and the provision of security of individuals (as well as their property) against the violence of other citizens or foreign nations.

The second obligation is to encourage abundance, both of wealth and of population. This was a tricky issue. If wealth is constant, then a greater population will reduce wealth *per capita*. However, Bentham believed that a plentiful population is necessary for defence. At any rate, as argued by Paley (1785), by the principle of diminishing marginal utility and direct summation of utility, a large but poor population might have a higher "aggregate utility" than a small and rich population.

The third obligation was equality of means. By the principle of diminishing marginal utility, an extra £1 contributes less utility to a rich man than it does to a poor one. Consequently, reallocation of income to complete equality is desirable as the utility loss of the rich is more than compensated by the utility gain of the poor. However, he recognized that radical redistribution can also thwart incentives and productivity, and thus decrease general abundance. Bentham argued that some amount of redistributive taxation is warranted, but it must be carefully balanced against these other considerations.

JAMES MILL

Born a son of a cobbler in Montrose, Scotland, James Mill (*née* Milne) was destined for greater things. Encouraged by his mother, Mill attended to his studies and eventually, in 1790, enrolled at the University of Edinburgh with the help of a local gentleman, Sir John Stuart (after whom Mill later named his son). At Edinburgh, he came under the influence of the philosopher Dugald Stewart and imbibed the legacy of the Scottish Enlightenment.

Originally intending to become a minister of the Church of Scotland, Mill received his M.A. in 1794. Mill left Edinburgh in 1797, with a license to preach but gradually lost his faith. He worked for a while as an itinerant tutor in Scotland until 1802, when Stuart invited Mill to join him in London. He tried his hand at journalism, landing a steady job at the *Literary Journal* and feeling confident enough to marry Harriet Burrow in 1805. However, the journal folded in 1806, and soon enough Mill's only source of income was as a writer of hack articles, editorials and essays for a wide assortment of newspapers and journals.

In 1804, James Mill wrote his an essay which reviewed the history of the Corn Laws, calling for the removal of all export bounties and import duties on grains and criticizing Malthus for defending them. Soon after, he came across the tracts of Cobbett and Spence, who argued that land (rather than industry) was the source of wealth, that there were losses to foreign trade between nations, that the public debt was not a burden, that taxes were productive and that crises were caused by a general glut of goods. Mill's *Commerce Defended* (1808) attacked all of these arguments, dismantling them point by point. It was here that Mill articulated his version of Say's

Law of Markets. Mill argued that "annual purchases and sales" will "always balance" so the excess supply of any good was necessarily counterbalanced by excess demand for other goods. Or, more accurately, he argued that the overproduction of of one good had to be made from capital withdrawn from other goods, which were thus left, necessarily, underproduced:

"A nation may easily have more than enough of any one commodity, though she can never have more than enough of commodities in general. The quantity of any one commodity may easily be carried beyond its due proportion, but by that very circumstance is implied that some other commodity is not provided in sufficient proportion.

What is indeed meant by a commodity's exceeding the market? Is it not that there is a portion of it for which there is nothing that can be had in exchange. But of those other things then the proportion is too small. A part of the means of production which had been applied to the preparation of this superabundant commodity, should have been applied to the preparation of those other commodities till the balance between them has been established. Whenever this balance is properly preserved, there can be no superfluity of commodities, none for which a market will not be ready."

A partisan of the "Banking School", James Mill also participated in the Bullionist Controversies of the time.

In 1808, Mill forged long-lasting friendships with two very influential men: David Ricardo and Jeremy Bentham. Ricardo would provide him his economics; Bentham would guide his political and social philosophy. Interestingly, the two doctrines seemed to never have met each other in the mind of James Mill. With a few exceptions, it never occurred to him to bring the Benthamite concept of utility into his economics, nor to bring the utilitarian "greatest happiness" principle to bear on the analysis of fiscal policy.

In 1817, Mill produced his massive *History of India,* which he had been working on the side for many years. Its analysis was clearly inspired by the conjectural histories typical of the Scottish Enlightenment: India was deemed a nation just emerging out of its barbarian stage and saw the English role as a civilizing mission (although he would later famously claim that the British Empire was "a vast system of outdoor relief for the upper classes").

He defended the rule of the East India Company (rather than the English government). Mill recommended several reforms for India, perhaps the most interesting was his call for the elimination of taxes and the complete nationalization of land (EIC fiscal revenue would thus arise from rents — which were easier to collect and less distortionary). The success of his *History* led him to be hired by the London office of the East India Company in 1823, which provided him with financial security for the remainder of his life.

In the meantime, Mill was busy forging the Classical Ricardian School in economics. An energetic man, it was Mill who encouraged David Ricardo to publish his 1817 treatise on value and distribution and then pushed him to run for Parliament. In 1821, Mill helped found the Political Economy Club in London, which became a stomping ground for Ricardian economists and Benthamite radicals. After Ricardo's death, James Mill, Ramsey McCulloch and Thomas de Quincey became the high priests of Ricardian economics.

James Mill's *Elements of Political Economy,* (1821) quickly became the leading textbook exposition of doctrinaire Ricardian economics. As this was compiled from the lectures on political economy he had given to his young son, John Stuart Mill, there were was little that was novel in it — except for the ill-fated "Wages Fund" doctrine:

"Universally, then, we may affirm, other things remaining the same, that if the ratio which capital and population bear to one another remains the same, wages will remain the same; if the ratio which capital bears to population increases, wages will rise; if the ratio which population bears to capital increases, wages will fall."

Simultaneously, on a separate front, Mill was advancing the utilitarian doctrines of Bentham and the "Philosophical Radicals". Mill's personal relationship with Bentham was more intimate than with Ricardo, so it inevitably also had more complicated and heated moments. Nonetheless, Mill remained an uncritical admirer of Bentham's philosophy. He helped found the *Westminster Review*, the principal organ of the Philosophical Radicals. Mill was at his most radical in his 1820 article, where he defended widespread democracy and civil rights, not on the basis of any "natural law" considerations, but rather on the more pragmatic utilitarian grounds that it was the best way to ensure a good, stable and efficient government.

It must also be noted that Mill, unlike Bentham, was a great advocate of government non-intervention in the economy, and thus very much a classical liberal. He came out against any other sort of redistribution schemes, arguing that fiscal policy should be designed so as to leave the *status quo* in place (e.g. proportional rather than progressive taxation). Mill was a strict "welfarist", excluding social justice and any other such considerations from all utilitarian "greatest happiness" calculations. It was Mill who was mostly responsible for forwarding the argument that since each individual acts in his own self-interest, then any collection of people necessarily acts in the interest of the whole.

Interestingly, Mill was also a great advocate of widespread education. He believed, like Bentham, that people need to be educated so as to best be able to figure out what is their own best interest. But he added that what is in their own self-interest is often quite complicated. This includes consideration of the impact of their actions on other people, choosing the right government and pushing for the right policies. Wage claims by trade unions or protection against foreign commerce, for instance, might *seem* to be in the self-interest of workers, but a truly educated workforce would realise that their long-run interests are best served otherwise. His belief that people were myopic, in the sense that they underestimated their future utility, was one of the earliest articulations of the "time preference" idea.

In psychology, Mill is widely regarded as the father of "monism" or "association of ideas" in mental states. Mill's 1829 *Analysis* originated as an attempt to decipher the psychological foundations of utilitarianism. However, he ended up closer to the "moral sentiments" theories of Adam Smith and the Scottish philosophers than to anything Bentham would have envisioned.

JOHN STUART MILL

"Born in London in 1806, son of James Mill, philosopher, economist and senior official in the East India Company. Mill gave a vivid and moving account of his life, and especially of his extraordinary education, in the *Autobiography* 1873 that he wrote towards the end of his life. Mill led an active career as an administrator in the East India Company from which he retired only when the Company's administrative functions in India were taken over by the British government following the Mutiny of 1857. In addition, he was a Liberal MP for Westminster 1865-8, and as a young man in the 1830s edited the London and *Westminster Review*, a radical quarterly journal. He died at Aix-En-Provence in 1873.

His father, with the advice and assistance of Jeremy Bentham and Francis Place, educated Mill. He learned Greek at three, Latin a little later; by the age of 12, he was a competent logician and by 16 a well-trained economist. At 20 he suffered a nervous breakdown that persuaded him that more was needed in life than devotion to the public good and an analytically sharp intellect. Having grown up a utilitarian, he now turned to Coleridge, Wordsworth and Goethe to cultivate his aesthetic sensibilities. From 1830 to his death, he tried to persuade the British public of the necessity of a scientific approach to understanding social, political and economic change while not neglecting the insights of poets and other imaginative writers.

His *System of Logic* 1843 was an ambitious attempt to give an account not only of logic, as the title suggests, but of the methods of science and their applicability to social as well as purely natural phenomena. Mill's conception of logic was not entirely that of modern logicians; besides formal logic, what he called "the logic of consistency", he thought that there was a logic of proof, that is, a logic that would show how evidence proved or tended to prove the conclusions we draw from the evidence. That led him to the analysis of causation, and to an account of inductive reasoning that remains the starting point of most modern discussions. Mill's account of explanation in science was broadly that explanation seeks the causes of events where it is events in which we are interested; or seeks more general laws where we are concerned to explain less general laws as special cases of those laws. Mill's discussion of the possibility of finding a scientific explanation of social events has worn equally well; Mill was as unwilling to suppose that the social sciences would become omniscient about human behaviour as to suppose that there was no prospect of explaining social affairs at any deeper level than that of common sense.

Throughout the *System of Logic* Mill attacked the "intuitionist" philosophy of William Whewell and Sir William Hamilton. This was the view that explanations rested on intuitively compelling principles rather than on general, causal laws, and that ultimately the search for such intuitively compelling principles rested on understanding the universe as a divine creation governed by principles that a rational deity must choose. Mill thought that intuitionism was bad philosophy, and a comfort to political conservatism into the bargain. His *Examination of Sir William Hamilton's Philosophy* 1865 carried the war into the enemy camp with a vengeance; it provoked vigorous controversy for some twenty years or so, but is now the least readable of Mill's works.

To the public at large, Mill was better known as the author of *Principles of Political Economy* 1848, a work that tried to show that economics was not the "dismal science" that its radical and literary critics had supposed. Its philosophical interest lay in Mill's reflections on the difference between what economics measured and what human beings really valued: leading Mill to argue that we should sacrifice economic growth for the sake of the environment, and should limit population as much to give ourselves breathing space as in order to fend off the risk of starvation for the overburdened poor. Mill also allowed that conventional economic analysis could not show that socialism was unworkable, and suggested as his own ideal an economy of worker-owned cooperatives. Commentators have argued inconclusively over whether this is a form of socialism or merely "workers' capitalism". Mill remains most nearly our contemporary in the area of moral and political philosophy, however. His *Utilitarianism* 1861 remains the classic defence of the view that we ought to aim at maximizing the welfare of all sentient creatures, and that welfare consists of their happiness. Mill's defence of the view that we ought to pursue happiness because we do pursue happiness, has been the object of savage attack by, among others, F. H. Bradley in his *Ethical Studies* 1874 and G. E. Moore in *Principia Ethica* 1903. But others have argued that on this particular point, Mill was misinterpreted by his critics.

His insistence that happiness was to be assessed not merely by quantity but by quality - the doctrine that a dissatisfied Socrates is not only better than a satisfied fool, but somehow happier, too - has puzzled generations of commentators. And his attempt to show that justice can be accounted for in utilitarian terms is still important as a riposte to such writers as John Rawls

During his lifetime, it was his essay *On Liberty* 1859 that aroused the greatest controversy, and the most violent expressions of approval and disapproval. The essay was sparked by the feeling that Mill and his wife, Harriet Taylor, constantly expressed in their letters to one another: that they lived in a society where bold and adventurous individuals were becoming all too rare. Critics have sometimes thought that Mill was frightened by the prospect of a mass democracy in which working-class opinion would be oppressive and perhaps violent. The truth is that Mill was frightened by middle-class conformism much more than by anything to be looked for from an enfranchised working class. It was a fear he had picked up from reading Alexis de Tocqueville's *Democracy in America* 1836, 1840; America was a prosperous middle-class society, and Mill feared that it was also a society that cared nothing for individual liberty.

Mill lays down "one very simple principle" to govern the use of coercion in society - and by coercion he means both legal penalties and the operation of public opinion; it is that we may only coerce others in self-defence - either to defend ourselves, or to defend others from harm. Crucially, this rules out paternalistic interventions to save people from themselves, and ideal interventions to make people behave "better". It has long exercised critics to explain how a utilitarian can subscribe to such a principle of self-restraint. In essence, Mill argues that only by adopting the self-restraint principle can we seek out the truth, experience the truth as "our own", and fully develop individual selves.

Of Mill's shorter works, two others deserve mention. *The Subjection of Women* 1869 was thought to be excessively radical in Mill's time but is now seen as a classic statement of liberal feminism. Its essential case is that if freedom is a good for men, it is for women, and that every argument against this view drawn from the supposedly different "nature" of men and women has been superstitious special pleading.

If women have different natures, the only way to discover what they are is by experiment, and that requires that women should have access to everything to which men have access. Only after as many centuries of freedom as there have been centuries of oppression will we really know what our natures are. Mill published *The Subjection of Women* late in life to avoid controversies that would lessen the impact of his other work. He chose not to have his *Three Essays on Religion* 1874 published until after his death.

They argued, among other things, that it is impossible that the universe is governed by an omnipotent and loving God, but not unlikely that a less omnipotent benign force is at work in the world. They thus tended to disappoint those of Mill's admirers who looked for a tougher and more abrasive agnosticism, while doing nothing to appease critics who deplored the fact that he was any kind of agnostic.

POSITIVISTIC HISTORIOGRAPHY-AUGUSTE COMTE

Auguste Comte was born in 1798 and had a significant part in the formation of sociology. Comte was the founder of

French positivism. Comte can also be given credit for inventing or coining the term sociology.

Comte was born a Catholic, but somewhere around the age of fourteen, he apparently stopped believing in God. At the same time, he left the ideals of his royalist family behind and became a republican. Comte attended the Ecole Polytechnique, which was a leading scientific institution in France at the time. He was kicked out of this school for leading a student protest.

Comte's philosophy of positivism developed from historical studies of the human mind. This led to Comte's views of the three stages of the history of sciences. In order as follows, the stages are:

- *Theological:* Nature has a will of it's own. This stage is broken down into three stages of its own, including animism, polytheism, and monotheism.
- *Metaphysical state:* Though substituting ideas for a personal will.
- *Positive:* A search for absolute knowledge.

When Auguste Comte claimed to have invented the new science of sociology, he said that it was going to be the science that held all other sciences together. As in the course of Positive Philosophy, he said that a science must depend on the previous science to be understood. It was also in the 47th volume of the book that he changed the name of the social physics to sociology.

When Auguste Comte claimed to have invented the new science of sociology, he said that it was going to be the science that held all other sciences together. As in the course of Positive Philosophy, he said that a science must depend on the previous science to be understood. It was also in the 47th volume of the book that he changed the name of the social physics to sociology.

SCIENTIFIC SOCIALISM – KARL MARX

Karl Marx was born on May 5, 1818 , in the city of Trier in Rheinish Prussia. His family was Jewish, but converted to Protestanism in 1824. The family was petty-bourgeois; his father was a lawyer. After graduating from a Gymnasium (High School) in Trier, Marx entered the university, first at Bonn and later in Berlin, where he read law, majoring in history and philosophy.

He concluded his university course in 1841, submitting a doctoral thesis on the philosophy of Epicurus. At the time Marx was a Hegelian idealist in his views. In Berlin, he belonged to the circle of "Left Hegelians" (with Bruno Bauer and others) who sought to draw atheistic and revolutionary conclusions from Hegel's philosophy. Ludwig Feuerbach began to criticize theology, particularly after 1836, and he began his turn to materialism, which in 1841 gained ascendancy in his philosophy (The Essence of Christianity).

After graduating from university, Marx moved to Bonn, hoping to become a professor. However, the reactionary policy of the government made Marx abandon the idea of an academic career, after Ludwig Feuerbach had been deprived of his chair in 1832 (and who was not allowed to return to the university in 1836); and in 1841 the government had forbade the young Professor Bruno Bauer to lecture at Bonn.

At the begining on 1842, some radical bourgeois in the Rhineland (Cologne), who were in touch with the Left Hegelians, founded a paper in opposition to the Prussian government, called the Rheinische Zeitung. Marx and Bruno Bauer were invited to be the chief contributors, and in October 1842 Marx became editor-in-chief and moved from Bonn to Cologne.

The newspaper's revolutionary-democratic trend became more and more pronounced under Marx's editorship, and the government first imposed double and triple censorship on the paper, and then on January 1 1843 suppressed it. Marx was forced to resign the editorship before that date, but his resignation did not save the paper, which suspended publication in March 1843.

Of the major articles Marx contributed to Rheinische Zeitung, Engels notes, an article on the condition of peasant winegrowers in the Moselle Valley. Marx's journalistic activities convinced him that he was insufficiently acquainted with political economy, and he zealously set out to study it. In 1843, Marx married, at Kreuznach, a childhood friend he had become engaged to while still a student. His wife came from a bourgeois family of the Prussian nobility, her elder brother being Prussia's Minister of the Interior during an extremely reactionary period — 1850-58.

In the autumn of 1843, Marx went to Paris in order to publish a radical journal abroad, together with Arnold Ruge (1802-1880). Only one issue of this journal, Deutsch-Französische Jahrbücher, appeared. Publication was discontinued owing to the difficulty of secretly distributing it in Germany, and to disagreement with Ruge. Marx's articles in this journal showed that he was already a revolutionary who advocated "merciless criticism of everything existing", and in particular the "criticism by weapon", and appealed to the masses and to the proletariat.

Also in 1843, Feuerbach wrote his famous Principles of the Philosophy of the Future. "One must have experienced for oneself the liberating effect" of these books, Engels subsequently wrote. "We all became at once Feuerbachians."

In September 1844, Frederick Engels came to Paris for a few days, and from that time on became Marx's closest friend. Shortly after meeting, Marx and Engels worked together to produce the first mature work of Marxism — The German Ideology. In this work, largely produced in response to Feuerbach's materialism, Marx and Engels set down the foundations of Marxism with the materialistic conception of history, and broke from Left Hegelian idealism with a critique against Bruno Bauer and Max Stirner. "The philosophers have only interpreted the world in various ways;" Marx wrote in an outline for the begining of the book, " the point is to change it."

In the mid to late-1840s both Marx and Engels took a most active part in the then seething life of the revolutionary groups in Paris (of particular importance at the time was Proudhon's doctrine), which Marx broke into pieces in his Poverty of Philosophy, (1847).

At the insistent request of the Prussian government, Marx was banished from Paris in 1845, considered by both governments a dangerous revolutionary. Marx then moved to Brussels. In the spring of 1847 Marx and Engels joined a secret propaganda society called the Communist League. Marx and Engels took a prominent part in the League's Second Congress (London, November 1847), at whose request they drew up the Communist Manifesto, which appeared in February 1848. With outstanding clarity, this work outlines a new world-conception based on materialism. This document analysises the realm of social life; the theory of the class struggle; the tasks of the Communists; and the revolutionary role of the proletariat – the creators of a new, communist society.

On the outbreak of the Revolution of February 1848, Marx was banished from Belgium. He returned to Paris, whence, after the March Revolution, he went to Cologne, Germany, where Neue Rheinische Zeitung was published from June 1 1848 to May 19 1849, with Marx as editor-in-chief. The victorious counter-revolution first instigated court proceedings against Marx (he was acquitted on February 9, 1849), and then banished him from Germany (May 16, 1849). First Marx went to Paris, where he was again banished after the demonstration of June 13, 1849, and then went to London, where he lived until his death.

Marx's life as a political exile was an extremely difficult one, as the correspondence between Marx and Engels clearly reveals. Poverty weighed heavily on Marx and his family; had it not been for Engels' constant and selfless financial aid, Marx would not only have been unable to complete Capital but would have inevitably have been crushed by hunger and malnutrition.

The revival of the democratic movements in the late fifties and in the sixties thrusted Marx back into political work. In 1864 (September 28) the International Working Men's Association – the First International – was founded in London. Marx was the heart and soul of this organization, and author of its first address and of a host of resolutions, declaration and manifestos. In uniting the labor movement of various forms of non-proletarian socialism (Mazzini, Proudhon, Bakunin, liberal trade-unionism in Britain,

Lassallean deviations to the right, etc.), and in combating the theories of all these sects and schools, Marx here hammered out uniform tactics for the proletarian struggle of the working in the various countries.

Following the downfall of the Paris Commune (1871) — of which Marx gave a clear-cut materialistic analysis of these events in The Civil War In France, 1871 — and the Bakunin cleavage in the International, the organization could no longer exist in Europe. After the Hague Congress of the International (1872), the General Council of the International had played its historical part, and now made way for a period of a far greater development of the labor movement in all countries in the world, a period in which the movement grew in scope, and mass socialist working-class parties in individual national states were formed.

SCIENTIFIC HISTORIOGRAPHY – LEOPOLDVONRANKE

Leopold von Ranke was born 200 years ago. On the 21st December 1795 in Wiehe/Unstrut, Leopold was born into an old Lutheran theologian family. Having attended school in Schulpforta, studied in Leipzig and Halle, and taught in a grammar school in Frankfurt an der Oder, he was offered a professorship in history at the Berlin University in 1825, then a chair in 1834, where he taught until 1871 and had amongst his students a large number of well known historians.

This important, very effective and for that very reason controversial historian was given titles such as 'The greatest German historian', 'The father of the objective writing of history', and 'The founder of the science of history'. The authoritative criticism of sources which he mainly developed is still valid today as a method of working in history, even if he did limit himself to official documents and with this the perspective of those in power, which has since been expanded critically to include, for example, social and cultural sources and lines of questioning.

Numerous weighty publications on the 100th anniversary of his death in 1986 cover the unbroken desire for debate on the individuals' thoughts during the Romantic period, which he transferred to the world of politics, and the relative worth contained within it. As maxim for the historicism represented by him, Ranke formulated his view in an incontrovertible way: 'From the particular, one can carefully and boldly move up to the general; from general theories, there is no way of looking at the particular.' With individuality as the aim of discovery of the 'godly ideas' in the world of intellectuals, and objectivity as the task of the historian, Ranke educated his students with particular fondness on the basis of medieval sources, whilst his own writings concerned themselves exclusively with the modern period.

Even in his first work in 1824, he wrote provocatively that he did not want to judge the past, but simply wanted to show how it was, provocatively because with this he was turning against the current interests of the ideas of enlightenment, but at the same time he tried to do no less than to explain the idea of World History.

We admire Ranke's methodological and presentational achievements, which were true to their sources, but have to go along new paths without dismissing his ideas. As ever, Ranke polarizes opinions, for example Thomas Nipperdey noted in 1986 that, 'Ranke's idea of objectivity' was even today 'a strong theory'. To what extent Ranke's literary qualities continue to carry weight, as also with the Berlin ancient historian Theodor Mommsen, can be seen for example in the new editions of his German history at the time of the Reformation, his history of the Roman Popes, and his French and English histories.

Ranke aimed at world history, but his basic mood was nationalistic and conservative, the massive changes after the French Revolution are hardly discussed, and his books on Prussian history contained, with no intention for it to be used for propaganda purposes, the seeds for a Prussian national German picture of history. This legacy compels one to critical reflection, but at the same time it points to a flourishing time in historical research at the Berlin University, started by Ranke, which above all Max Lenz and Friedrich Meinecke were able to continue. Ranke himself was well aware of the dynamics of his time. In 1875 he wrote to his brother: 'With trains and telegraphic communications all empires and states are brought together into the closest and quickest contact...On the whole globe, there are no longer any total divisions.

Who still speaks of compassion? It goes without saying that this is what we demand.' The perception of time as a blissful utopia when looking back? On the 8.8.1885, the mayor of Berlin, Max von Forckenbeck visited Ranke in his flat in the Luisenstrasse, in order to make him a freeman of the city. They talked about general political and municipal affairs, but scarcely had the delegation gone, when Ranke observed: 'and now back to the empire of Otto III, with whose end I was occupied, when the mayor came.'

In the last years of his life, Ranke received numerous honours, many honorary doctorates confirmed his international reputation and he was, amongst other honours, made chancellor of the order 'pour le mérite'. From 1871, he devoted himself to the publication of his various works.

On the 23rd May 1886, von Ranke died in Berlin. His grave in the Sophien cemetery, which is still kept nowadays, was decorated with a medallion portrait of him. His personal legacy remained in Germany, his library taken to Syracuse in the state of New York. The Humboldt University remembered him on his 200th birthday as an influential and controversial founder of the modern German history of science who is kept alive by these controversies. The methodologically strict training of his classes and lectures remains even today as an obligation for research which desires quality.

SPENGLER

German philosopher of history, whose famous work, *The Decline of the West* (1918-1922) combined Nietzschean poetic argument with a pessimistic view of the permanence of humankind's achievements. According to Spengler, Western culture is doomed, as other cultures have been before it, and has already entered its degenerate last stage. The idea of decline was in fact ancient - Hesiod wrote of the lost golden age in the 8th century BC - but Spengler gave to the theme the most eloquent and prophetic interpretation.

"Is there a logic of history? Is there, beyond all the casual and incalculable elements of the separate elements of the separate events, something that we may call a metaphysical structure of historic humanity, something that is essentially independent of the outward forms - social, spiritual and political - which we see so clearly? Are not these actualities indeed secondary or derived from that something? Does world-history present to the seeing eye certain grand traits, again and again, with sufficient constancy to justify certain conclusions? And if so, what are the limits to which reasoning from such premisses may be pushed?"

Oswald Spengler was born at Blankenburg am Hars, the son of Bernhard Spengler, a post office official, and Pauline (Grantzow) Spengler. The atmosphere of his childhood home was emotionally reserved, and in his loneliness Spengler found consolation from the thoughts of giant cultural personalities: Richard Wagner, Henrik Ibsen, Ernst Haeckel, and Friendrich Nietzsche. After attending the Halle Latin School, Spengler studied at the universities of Munich, Berlin, and Halle, where his main subject was mathematics. He also studied philosophy, history and art. In 1903 Spengler failed his doctoral thesis which was a deep blow to his academic career plans.

Spengler received his Ph.D. in 1904. His thesis at Berlin was *Der metaphysische Grundgedanke der Heraklitischen Philosophie*. In 1905 he suffered a nervous breakdown. He worked as a teacher in Saarbrücken and Düsseldorf and from 1908 to 1911 he taught science, German, history, and mathematics in a high school in Hamburg. After moving to Munich he started to write the first volume of his magnum opus, *Gestalt und Wirklichkeit*. Crucial for the work was the Agadir crisis, in which the arrival of the German warship *Panther* at Agadir triggered a political struggle between France and Germany over control of Morocco. Germany was forced to back down and Spengler believed that it signalled the end of that era.

After seeing in a bookshop a volume entitled *The Decline*

of Antiquity, written by Otto Seeck, he knew what name he would give his own book.

Spengler's early years in Munich were marked by poverty and loneliness. He lived in a lugubrious room, spent his mornings at the public library, lunched in cheap cafeterias, and drank tea. He owned no books. To earn extra income he wrote to different magazines and worked as a tutor. He also became known as an outspoken opponent of the Weimar Republic. *Gestalt und Wirklichkeit* (Form and Actuality) was completed in 1914. Wartime delayed its appearance, publishers did not want to print it, and it was not published until 1917 in Vienna and in Munich the next year.

Welthistorische Perspektiven (Perspectives of World History) appeared in 1922 together with the first volume, which Spengler had revised. The work had a huge commercial success and became one of the most talked about books in post-war Germany, where defeat in the war was regarded as a national humiliation, and severe depression seemed to prove Spengler's thesis right. Spengler himself had believed in victory while writing *Form and Actuality*.

The grand vision of history in *The Decline of the West* deeply influenced Spengler's readers between the world wars. Thomas Mann compared its effect on him to that of reading Schopenhauer for the first time. The work was widely discussed in the 1920s even by those who knew it only superficially. The German artist George Grosz says in his book of memoirs, *A Small Yes and a Big No* (1982) about his friend, who confessed: "That book is my Bible, Herr Grosz, even though I don't get much time for reading these days..." In academic circles *The Decline of the West* was received with mixed feelings. Max Weber described Spengler as a "very ingenious and learned dilettante" and Karl Popper attacked Spengler's thesis as "pointless".

Spengler's obscure thoughts, intuitionalism and mysticism were easy targets for his critics. All attempts to find the meaning of history had been denounced by the positivists and neo-Kantians of the late nineteenth century as irresponsible metaphysical speculation. This attitude did not change but was perhaps even hardened after the rise of neo-positivism and analytic tradition. One of the exceptions was the Austrian/British philosopher Ludwig Wittgenstein (1889-1951), who shared Spengler's cultural pessimism, and confessed once that he felt "intensely the terrible degeneration that had come over the human spirit in the course of only a hundred years." Georg Henrik von Wright, Wittgenstein's successor at the University of Cambridge, accepted Spengler's cyclic view of history and wrote in 1951 an essay in which he compared Spengler and Toynbee.

In *Preussentum und Sozialismus* (1920) Spengler made a difference between Marxism and German socialism as first realized in 18th century Prussia, where the rule of the state over all individuals and classes had been accepted. He advocated the idea that socialism can be part of the conservative ideology, as exemplified in the Prussian tradition with its sense of duty toward the fatherland. In 1931 he published *Der Mensch und die Technik* in which he warned of the danger of technology and industrialism and their destructive impact on culture. Only dreamers, he claimed, ignored this fact. *Jahre der Entscheidung* (1934) was a bestseller; it sold 150,000 copies, but was condemned by the government.

Spengler's attacks on liberal ideas and institutions was first welcomed by the National Socialists, who wrongly believed that *The Decline of the West* glorified militarism. Although Spengler approved parts of the Nazi programme he rejected its unscientific biological doctrines and persecution of the Jews. In 1933 Spengler met Hitler, whom Spengler - a conservative humanist - found vulgar. Germany didn't want a "heroic tenor but a real hero," Spengler said. He quarrelled with one of the chief Nazi theoreticians, Albert Rosenberg, and eventually his pessimism and remarks about the Führer and his followers led to his isolation and public silence.

In 1933 Spengler became a member of the Academy of Germany. His last years Spengler spent in Munich, listening to Beethoven, reading the works of Shakespeare and Molière, buying several thousand books, and collecting primitive Persian, Turkish, and Hindu weapons. Occasionally he made trips to the Harz Mountains and to Italy. Just before his death Spengler wrote to a friend that in ten years "the German Reich will probably no longer exist." He died suddenly of a heart attack in Munich on May 8, 1936 three weeks before his fifty-sixth birthday. His sister's daughter, Hildegard Kornhardt, Ph.D. edited and published fragments from Spengler's unfinished works, *Reden und Aufsätze* (1937) and *Gedanken.*

"It is, and has always been, a matter of knowledge that the expression-forms of world-history are limited in number, and that eras, epochs, situations, persons, are ever repeating themselves true to type."

Spengler rejected traditional unilinear accounts of historical development and also causal explanations. Instead he examined history within the framework of cyclic patterns. "Each culture has its own new possibilities of self-expression which arise, ripen, decay and never return." Augustine saw in the City of God a divine plan behind history, and for Marx the driving force behind historical development was the class struggle. In Spengler's garden of cultures there is no gardener, a visible purpose or unifying meaning, except fate, which cannot be explained. Cultures spring mysteriously into being; they have morphological similarities but nothing else.

The central theme in *The Decline of the West* is that all higher cultures go through a life cycle analogous to that of an organic evolution, from birth to maturation, and to inevitable decline. Spengler also used the analogy of four seasons: the spring (birth and infancy), summer (youth), fall (maturity), and winter (old age and decay). When Toynbee had in his work *A Study of History* (1914-1961) over twenty great cultures, Spengler found eight which are self-contained and have a distinctive "soul" or "style" - the Egyptian, the Chinese, the Ancient Semitic (Babylonian), the Indian, the Magian (roughly, Arabic), the Apollonian or Greco-Roman, the Faustian or Western, and Mayan. Each of these units has an identical life cycle lasting some thousand years.

What really separated Spengler from the majority of historians was his method, the "form-language of human history", his concern to see analogies between different cultural epochs. "The means whereby to identify dead forms is Mathematical Law. The means whereby to understand living forms is Analogy," he wrote.

Thus he regarded Pythagoras, Mohammed and Cromwell as the embodiments of the one and same puritanical movement, compared modern times to late antiquity and saw similarities between the electoral campaigns of Rome and the United States, and forecast that the Western world would face the same chaos as ancient Egypt in 1800-1550 BC. Spengler acknowledged his debt to Goethe, who followed in his poem 'Die Metamorphose der Pflanze' the development of the plant-form from the leaf through a series of intermediate forms.

Goethe's poem also inspired Wittgenstein's views in *Logik, Sprache, Philosophie* where he dealt with the morphology of the use of an expression. In *Culture and Value* he wrote: "Spengler could be better understood if he said: I am *comparing* different cultural epochs with the lives of families; within a family there is a family resemblance, though you will also find a resemblance between members of different families; family resemblance differs from the other sort of resemblance in such and such ways, etc."

Spengler saw that the style of a Soul comes out in the higher Cultures, above all in art, mathematics, philosophy, sciences, music, drama, and poetry, and reflects the essence of the soul of that particular Culture. "There are several number-worlds as there are several Cultures. We find an Indian, an Arabian, a Classical as Western type of mathematical thought, and corresponding with each, a type of number - each type fundamentally peculiar and unique, an expression of a specific world-feeling..." Each of the civilizations has its special driving idea (Urphänomen) - Western culture is characterized by its restless thrust toward the infinite.

In architecture this can be seen in Gothic cathedrals and in painting in the use of depth perspective, parallel lines which meet in infinity. Spengler believed that his own era, Faustian, had reached its last stage. Signs of cultural decay were, among other things, atonal music, art produced for oversensitive connoisseurs, manipulation of the public opinion by mass media, imperialism, and Caesarism", a universal, formless will to power, which breaks the dictatorship of plutocracy and its political ally, democracy. According to Spengler, Russia did not belong to Western culture. A Faustian soul looks upward, a Russian soul toward the horizon. Thus Russian "Urphänomen" is the boundless steppe.

For a short time in the 1960s a new interest arose toward *The Decline of the West* when its abridged English version was published. It was also said that Henry Kissinger gave the work to President Nixon as a bedside book. In general, Spengler's impact was in his time immense but brief. At the turn of the millennium Spengler's prophesies received in Europe less attention than Karl Marx's predictions of worldwide revolutionary changes.

COLLINGWOOD

Collingwood was born when Hegelianism reigned supreme in British philosophy, but by the time of his death on 9 January, 1943 he was one of the last representatives of a philosophy that had gradually fallen out of fashion since the end of the First World War. Although Collingwood never fully embraced the Idealist label for his philosophy, he was widely acknowledged as one of its leading latter-day exponents.

Born on 22 February, 1889 at Gillhead, Cartmel Fell, in the Lake District of England, to Edith Mary Collingwood, formerly Isaacs (1857-1828), a talented artist and pianist, and William Gershom Collingwood (1854-1932), artist, writer, archaeologist and secretary to John Ruskin, he was educated at home till the age of thirteen by his father and became well versed in Greek, Latin, and ancient and modern history. It was in these early years that his passion for philosophy was aroused, but he was also curious about the natural sciences. Unusually for his age he read Kant's *Theory of Ethics* at the age of eight but felt ashamed of himself for not being able to understand it!

At the age of thirteen he was sent to Rugby School, which proved to be something of a disappointment because it failed to stimulate his natural inquisitiveness. In 1908 he entered University College, Oxford, where his father had studied and been tutored by Bernard Bosanquet, and it was here that Robin Collingwood for the first time was able to indulge his insatiable appetite for learning. But his untiring yearning for knowledge would also prove to be his undoing. In these early years of university Collingwood first became an insomniac which contributed to his later ill-health. He took classes in Philosophy, History and Archaeology. He was the only pupil of the famous archeologist F. J. Haverfield to survive World War I. Important influences on Collingwood in these early years were the Italian Idealists Croce, Gentile and Guido de Ruggiero, the last of whom was also a close friend.

In 1912 he was elected to a philosophy fellowship at Pembroke College, and subsequently, in 1927, became University Lecturer in Philosophy and Roman History. From 1924 to 1933, after his father became ill, Collingwood assisted him as joint editor of *Transactions of the Cumberland and Westmoreland Antiquarian and Archaeological Society*.

In 1934 he was elected a Fellow of the British Academy and in 1935, supported by Samuel Alexander, he was appointed Waynflete Professor of Metaphysical Philosophy, a position that he ultimately was forced to resign in 1941 on grounds of ill health. He returned to his late father's home, Lanehead, in Coniston with Kathleen Edwardes who had become his second wife in 1942. There he died of pneumonia a few weeks before his fifty-fourth birthday. His high blood pressure and the series of strokes he suffered from 1938 onwards impressed upon him the likelihood of an early death. He drove himself to exhaustion in order to complete his life's work and exacerbated the condition.

His *An Autobiography* (1939) is an account, not of his life, but of the work that he had been refining and was yet to complete, and of which he intended to give a brief account in case his early demise prevented him completing his work. He managed to finish *An Essay on Metaphysics* (1940) and a work on ethics, *The New Leviathan* (1941). He almost completed the revisions for *The Idea of Nature* which was published after his death. The same was his most famous book *The Idea of History* (1946), a work collated from various sources soon after his death by his pupil, T. M. Knox.

TOYNBEE

IT IS FASHIONABLE nowadays for academic historians far less learned than Arnold J. Toynbee to snip and sneer at him and the vast project to which he devoted his life: the synthesis of global history within a single framework based ostensibly on empirical scholarship rather than metaphysical or religious speculation. I recall in graduate school an eminent historian saying that Toynbee wrecked his career as a classical scholar when he embarked on his study of history. That's rather like saying that Ronald Reagan ruined himself as an actor by going into politics.

William H. McNeill's biography of the author of A Study of History is intended in part to rescue Toynbee from the derision that now generally greets references to him and his work. Mr. McNeill is well suited to the task, having made his own reputation through such works of world history as The Rise of the West. Unfortunately, his study of Toynbee does little to achieve its goal.

With a masterly touch, McNeill expounds the personal life of his subject, revealing details of a checkered family life, social and educational background, and professional career that were not previously well known. What is missing is any systematic account of what Toynbee believed and why he believed it, and nowhere in the book is there any statement of the general theory of history and civilization that he articulated. Despite brief references to the influences of Herodotus, Thucydides, and Henri Bergson, there is no detailed discussion of the intellectual currents from which Toynbee emerged.

Despite vague allusions to Toynbee's efforts to educate himself in Asian, African, and Latin American history, there is no account of what he read, why he read it, or how it influenced him. And despite hasty mentions of the criticisms of his work by H. R. Trevor-Roper and Pieter Geyl, there is no real discussion of the controversies surrounding Toynbee's work or of how well the ideas and research of A Study of History stand up today, or how they relate to current work in the discipline of comparative history. As a result there is little in McNeill's biography to justify his conclusion that "Toynbee is a real though not-toopromising candidate for the dignity of ranking as a major figure in European (and an emerging global) literary and historical culture." His comparison of Toynbee to Milton and Dante thus remains outre..

Yet depite Toynbee's intense dislike of anything that smacked of "nationalism" or "tribeworship," he was a major influence on the intellectual development of the American Right in the 1940s. McNeill demonstrates that Whittaker Chambers's sympathetic cover story on Toynbee in Time's issue of March 17, 1947, made him famous in the United States overnight. Chambers saw in the first six volumes of A Study of History an alternative and essentially Christian model of history and human destiny that could supplant Marxism.

Toynbee's book, he wrote, was "the most provocative work of historical theory written in England since Karl Marx's Capital" and offered an affirmation that "not materialist but psychic factors are the decisive forces of history." The Time story appeared five days after Harry Truman's pronouncement of the Truman Doctrine, the U.S. response to the Soviet challenge, and Toynbee was thus drafted into the cold war. Though McNeill does not mention it, another book published the same week, James Burnham's The Struggle for the World, also relied heavily on Toynbee's interpretation of history.

Whatever virtues thinkers like Burnham and Chambers found in Toynbee's schema, they were drawing on only the first part of his work. In the second part, published in four volumes in 1954, Toynbee's perspective, because of personal religious experiences, shifted radically, away from the secular patterns of human civilization and toward a more ethereal view. "Civilizations were not," writes McNeill, "as he had formerly assumed, humankind's supreme work of art. Rather, the supreme end and goal of human life was a more perfect communion with God, and this was achieved, however imperfectly, by the various higher religions."

Toynbee's more other-worldly and syncretic perspective in his later years probably accounts for the virtually antiWestern cast of his political opinions in his old age. Despite his denunciations of American "materialism" and "imperialism" on American lecture tours, however, he deliberately used these tours to get rich, often gouging his academic hosts for large fees and delivering only a small repertoire of lectures.

His (at least theoretical) preoccupation with the universal and the eternal seems to have driven him into antagonism toward the particular political and cultural institutions of his own civilization and led him to sympathize with Buddhism and other non-Western cultures and religions. In 1972 he went to Greece, where he publicly prayed to Apollo to protect the biosphere from Western materialism.

McNeill believes that in an age of "global culture" Toynbee's work may yet enjoy a renaissance. But A Study of History, for all its self-proclaimed cosmopolitanism, remains very much a Victorianbook, bubbling with English ethnocentrism, anti-American prejudices, and unexamined assumptions about man, mind, and history.

The anti-Western racism and nationalism that today mask themselves as "global culture" will have as little use for the thought of this last Victorian as they do for the rest of the Western heritage.

Unit III

Indian Historiography

ABUL FAZL

ABUL FAZL, wazir and historiographer of the great Mogul emperor, Akbar, was born in the year A.D. 1551. His career as a minister of state, brilliant though it was, would probably have been by this time forgotten but for the record he himself has left of it in his celebrated history.

The *Akbar Nameh,* or *Book of Akbar,* as Abul Fazl's chief literary work, written in Persian, is called, consists of two parts - the first being a complete history of Akbar's reign and the second, entitled *Ain-iAkbari,* or *Institutes of Akbar,* being an account of the religious and political constitution and administration of the empire.

The style is singularly elegant, and the contents of the second part possess a unique and lasting interest. An excellent translation of the *Ain* by Francis Gladwin was published in Calcutta, 1783-1786. It was reprinted in London very inaccurately, and copies of the original edition are now exceedingly rare and correspondingly valuable.

It was also translated by Professor Blockmann in 1848. Abul Fazl died by the hand of an assassin, while returning from a mission to the Deccan in 1602. The murderer was instigated by Prince Selim, afterwards Jahangir, who had become jealous of the minister's influence.

What or who is an "intellectual?" Those who mock such people call them "eggheads, boffins, highbrows" and use other such deprecatory diminishing and derogatory remarks. As we tend to favour them we shall quote Aldus Huxley in support of the intellectual being a rare, sentient and, even, on occasion, a lovable being.

"Books and a coloured skein of thoughts was mine
and magic words lay ripening in my soul
till their much whispered music turned a wine
whose subtlest power was all in my control.
These things were mine and they were real for me
As lips and darling eyes and a warm breast
For I could love a phrase, a melody
As a fair woman worshiped and possessed"

The intellectual thus can live with notions, ideas and concepts as if they were real live persons. A part of existence occurs inside the spacious, well appointed mansion which is his or her head. This is as rich and variegated as anything outside.

Those unable to access and relish this dimension look askance at the minority who can and often become the victims of negative emotions such as envy and jealousy. This breeds fear and distrust and can lead to violence. Especially if the intellectual is action oriented and successful in making a mark in the world of practical affairs.

To include Abul Fazl in the category of intellectuals we shall recount an incident from the time he was in power.

"It is said that when the Shaikh was Prime Minister and Plenipotentiary Wakeel-I-Mutluq he had many important callers. The Khan-I-Khaanaan Mirza Abdur Rahim brought the erstwhile ruler of Sind, Mirza Jani to visit the Shaikh.

In view of their standing the visitors were rapidly ushered into the study of the host. Abul Fazl was lying stretched out on his diwan perusing a copy of the court chronicle, the Akbarnama.

So engrossed was he in his reading that he did not rise up from the bed to greet his most distinguished visitors. All he could manage was to say 'Do enter . Come in Mirza Sahebs and pray be seated.' Mirza Jani Beg erstwhile ruler of Sind had not quite lost the expectations of near servile courtesy he thought due to his station. He was appalled and disgusted and left in a huff. Mirza Abdul Rahim stayed on to talk.

A few days later Rahim entreated Mirza Jani to let bygones be bygones and accompany him on a repeat visit to Shaikh Abul Fazl. After much protest, humming and hawing the erstwhile Sind king listened to his friend and accompanied him to the Shaikh's mansion.

This time round things were different from the very beginning. As soon as their names were announced the Shaikh came right out and upto the front main gate.

He was all courtesy and attention. To Mirza Jani he said 'We are from the same place (Sind) as your highness. We are your servants'.

Mirza Jani was astonished at the change in the attitude of the Shaikh and enquired of the possible reason from Rahim.

Rahim responded,

'Do you remember what Abul Fazl was doing when we entered? He was reading the chronicles of the reign of his master. He was deeply embroiled in the narrative. He was hardly aware of the world around him. In the circumstances he responded as best as he could. No offence was intended as he was just not there but in the text he was reading.'

Today he was his urbane and courtly self. Fully aware of what was happening around him. There is no mystery to the difference in his conduct on the two different occasions !"

The reader may well ask "How then was Abul Fazl a success in the practical world of men and affairs?" We can give an example of the Shaikh's practical wisdom from the arrangements he made during his most successful campaign in the Deccan.

At every halt a very large tent chahal raawati was erected wherein a deewaan/masnad of considerable magnificence and splendour was set out and spread for Shaikh Abul Fazl.

In the kitchens accompanying the army camp (Urdu) one thousand plates (portions /thhaalees) of food was prepared for distribution to all officers accompanying.

A separate nine yard marquee (Nau guzee) was also erected to cook khichhree in enormous cauldrons and throughout the day so that food could be distributed throughout the day to whoever wanted it.

WAS ABUL FAZL A SYCOPHANT?

The slave mentality ghula-amaanaa zehniyat inculcated by the British continues to bedevil Indian history. Thus, Mansura Haidar of Aligarh unthinkingly parrots the erstwhile feringhee rulers to, allege: "In Akbarnama, however, one may fail to find an objective analysis and a balanced and unbiased presentation of facts..." As the reader can see the chronicle of a great reign written by a prominent intellectual of the 16th century has been given short shrift and condemned only because Indians continue to echo distortions of Indian history caused by the British need to badmouth all "natives" to justify their own intrusion and destruction of value systems.

Dr Haider, a professor of history at the Centre for Advanced Study, Department of History in Aligarh Muslim University should have known better. She has, under the auspices of the Indian Council of Historical Research, edited selected translations of the legendary Insha or collection of prose masterpieces of Abul Fazl which have been taught as model and text for nearly 400 years as part of the Persian studies syllabus. Her history is not as pointed for accuracy as her critical faculty.

She says, "It is significant that the contemporary chronicles present Abul Fazl as the most important figure at court during the first three decades of Akbar's reign even though he did not hold any important post at that time." As readers know the Emperor came to the throne in 1556, and Abul Fazl makes his entry into the court on June 20, 1573. The translations fail to convey the power and the glory the romance and the heartbreak of what was unquestionably one of the most fascinating reigns in the history of the world. Alas!

Perhaps these points will be addressed in the second edition of Maktubat-I-Allami. To return to Abul Fazl and the great and encyclopaedic chronicle, the Akbar-nama let us see how the Allama treats the death of his rival, Mahesh Bhatt "Brahm," better known as Raja Birbal. "One of the occurrences was the sending of Rajah Birbar to Swat," Abul Fazl states that he himself was anxious for a military command and asked to be considered for the commission.

"Inasmuch as the head of this confused and ambitious one (Abul Fazl himself) was filled with thoughts of (earning glory in) battle, he represented to his majesty that although serving the presence in person and directly was the elixir of fortune, yet he wished to make an attempt at military service in a distant place as such an assignment would be the testing place of loyalty.

Abul Fazl further records his feelings thus: "I too had been raised by His Majesty from the dark recesses of the lane beneath contempt to a post of prominence and had become conspicuous in the world. By undertaking a venturesome risky commission I too could lighten the burden of gratitude on my back and shoulders... should I lose my brief life, I would acquire an eternal good name!"

His Majesty perceived in my demeanour the marks of sincerity, and accepted my earnest prayer."

At the end of the day when it was time for taking leave the Emperor said it had occurred to him that lots should be cast and drawn between the Rajah Birbar and myself to decide as to who should be given the command. This way the wishes of the two nobles wanting the command would not come into play but the divine decree or what Fate had in store could come into play"

Perhaps Akbar did not want either of his intimate friends and counsellors to feel that he had favoured the other by giving in to his wishes.

As "the little throw came out in his (Birbar's) name... I left with the broken thorn of grief in my heart, and seated myself in the caravanserai of meditation."

That man who was fitted for battle or banquet (babuzm-o-ruzm) went by Heaven's decree on 12 Bahman, January 21, 1586. Qasim Khwaja, Gadai Beg, Haji Siyunduk, Ahmad Beg, Tash Beg, Khwaja Hisamuddin and other distinguished persons went with him."

Abul Fazl informs us that the experienced commander Zain Kh-an Koka who was already in Swat had asked for reinforcements. "Zain Khan Koka had represented that by God's favour he had got through difficult defiles, and had gained possession of Bajaur and most of Swat, but the troops were exhausted by their strenuous efforts and the forced marches they had had to undertake."

The Afghans were assembled in Karaakar Pass between Swat and Buneyr. If some brave men (reinforcements) were sent to him the enemy would soon have his just desserts and the whole country come into possession in an excellent manner"

Accordingly on the 19th Bahman (a week after despatch of Rajah Birbar's force) Hakim Abul Fath was given Hasan Beg, S. Umri, Ahmad Qasim, Toofaan Beg, Mulla Ghiyuri, Mohan Das along with Cerus and shumsheerbaazaan (skilled wielders of the scimitar) to accompany his force to reinforce Zain Khan Koka. At the end of the day His Majesty visited the Hakim's tents and gave him excellent counsel." As the reader can see the reinforcements sent to Zain Khan Koka were two armies commanded by his favourites who had no experience of warfare except by hearsay.

Abul Fazl comments: "The Kokaltash (Zain Khan Koka) asked for reinforcements, and His Majesty nominated Rajah Birbar, Hakim Abul Fath and others. When they joined the dust of dissension and doublemindedness (durangey) rose up. Previously, there had been hot words between the Kokaltash (Zain Khan Koka) and the Rajah, and the latter and the Hakim were also not on good terms. By the jugglery of fortune, they in spite of their lofty natures, entered into the narrows of envy. They could not brook any partnership in the royal favour..."

The above observation of Abul Fazl applies to all career development charts military, civil or commercial. A man who could write thus in a chronicle which had to be approved by the emperor was no sycophant and modern or contemporary historians should honour him and not condemn him. The Rajah Birbal was to pay with his life for the dissensions and divided counsels. This was on February 16, 1586 and we hope to narrate details in a future column.

ELPHINSTONE

Mountstuart Elphinstone was a Scottish historian, a cofounder and Fellow of the Royal Geographical Society and a civil servant in India where he served as Governor of Bombay from 1819 until 1827. Previously, he served with distinction in the Maratha states as a British Resident.

He was especially successful with intelligence gathering. From 1808 until 1811, he was envoy to the court of the king of Afghanistan where he accumulateed information on many aspects of Afghanistan's culture and politics, later writing an account of his travels and research.

As Governor of Bombay, he took a particular interest in education, founding a College at Poona for the study of India's cultural and religious legacy. He believed that Western learning should be grafted onto India's heritage, not substituted for this.

Elphinstone saw the British task in India as equipping Indians for self-government as soon as possible. This flew in the face of the dominant view, which was Indians would not be ready for self-governance for a very long time.

In retirement, he turned down honors and offers of high office in order to write his History of India, largely to refute the work of James Mill's earlier history, which has been described as a sweeping condemnation of India and of Indians.

Elphinstone, who had mastered several Indian languages as well as Farsi, drew on a wide range of Indian sources. Aspects of his work pioneered the modern study of Indian history, remaining relevant.

Elphinstone is said to have loved India. His goal was to improve the welfare of the people; the aim of many of his peers was to advance their careers, earn as much money as they could and retire from India as soon as they could.

Although, as an administrator, Elphinstone carried out the policy of annexation, he preferred indirect to direct rule, that is, the arrangement by which princely states remained largely self-governing. Elphinstone's legacy challenges racist assumptions by demonstrating that no single civilization can claim a monopoly of what is of value, interest and benefit to the flourishing of life.

With several other administrator-scholars such as William

Jones, Elphinstone helped to inspire Western interest in the study of India, significantly advancing understanding of important contributions to the cultural patrimony of the whole human family. Elphinstone is respected and admired by many Indians, who have little positive to say about the legacies of other colonial administrators.

At this time, the East India Company was beginning to develop what became distinctive branches of service, the fiscal, the legal and the political. The latter consisted of officers who were appointed to the Indian ruled states with which the British either had or hoped to have a treaty.

In 1801, Elphinstone became assistant to the political agent in Poona, where the Maratha Empire's effective ruler, the Peshwa was based. Increasingly observant of everything he saw around him, Elphinstone recorded details of his journey in his diary, the beginning of many such accounts several of which he later published.

The British plan was to place the Marathas under their protection as part of their expansionist policy. Some of the Maratha princes were open to an alliance with the British but several opposed this; they mobilized troops. The British governor, the future Duke of Wellington, Sir Arthur Wellesley, immediately moved against the Maratha threat. Although not a soldier, Elphinstone took part in the battle of Assaye September 23, 1803 as a member of the General's staff. He also took part in an attack on Gwalior, attracting praise from the Governor. However, it was already as a political agent that his services were valued, including his intelligence skills and by 1804 Elphinstone was resident at the court of the ruler of Berar, one of the defeated Maratha princes.

Elphinstone found the posting congenial and continued to develop his understanding of Indian politics and to read works in Persian. Meanwhile, due to the Napoleonic Wars now waging in Europe, in which Wellesley himself would famously fight, suspicion that a possible French alliance with the kingdom of Afghanistan and other Indian rulers including Maharaja Ranjit Singh might threaten British India from the North East became a real concern. This led to the mission that sent Elphinstone to Afghanistan as one of the earliest British visitors to this mountainous region.

MACAULAY

English historian and author, b. Leicestershire, educated at Cambridge. After the success of his essay on Milton in the Edinburgh Review (Aug., 1825), he contributed regularly to that journal. He was called to the bar in 1826 and, elected to Parliament in 1830, distinguished himself as a Whig orator. In India, 1834—38, as a member of the supreme council of the East India Company he reformed the Indian educational system and composed a legal code for the colony. On his return to England, Macaulay devoted himself to writing history, but returned to public office as secretary of war (1839—41), paymaster of the forces (1846—47), and member of Parliament (1839—47, 1852—56). In 1857 he was raised to the peerage as Baron Macaulay of Rothley.

Macaulay''s greatest work and one of the great works of the 19th cent. was 'The History of England from the Accession of James the Second' (5 vol., 1849—61). Its brilliant narrative style and its vivid recreation of the social world of the 17th cent. made it an unprecedented success. The work has been criticized, however, for its failure to achieve objectivity, primarily because of Macaulay''s Whig and Protestant bias. He also wrote several notable short biographical essays on Bacon, Johnson, Warren Hastings, and others. His poetical work, the 'Lays of Ancient Rome' (1842), celebrated the great events of Roman history.

VINCENT SMITH

In a career that spanned half a century, painter Vincent Smith documented in brilliant colour some of the most compelling events in twentieth-century America. From the be-bop-fueled improvisation of 1940s Harlem jazz clubs, to the visceral tug of civil rights workers confronting deep-seated hate with soul-clearing hope, to the creative militancy of the Black Arts Movement, Smith was there, brush in hand, bearing witness. "A figurative painter with an often subtle, social thrust, he placed his subjects in a stylized way against geometric, textured and intricately colored backgrounds," noted the *New York Times*. "I always knew that I was either going to do something or do nothing," he told *American Visions*. "And when I thought of myself as a painter, I dreamed of myself as a great painter." He succeeded.

Vincent Dacosta Smith was born on December 12, 1929, in New York and raised in Brooklyn by his parents, Louise and Beresford Smith. As a high school student he preferred sketching to studying and at fifteen he dropped out. "I was a good student, but I got into trouble," he admitted to *American Visions*. Soon he and a friend began hanging around the Bowery district of Manhattan.

"There were hundreds of bars. There were guys sleeping all over the street, people sleeping in the back of the bars," Smith told *American Visions*. "We used to go down there and hang out and drink with those guys and sit around and talk." Many of those men worked on the railroads and filled Smith's head with visions of life on the road. "They hopped on a train, and then when they got where they're going, they hopped off. My friend and I thought that sounded exciting, so we went to the office and signed up." At the age of 16 Smith began life as a hobo. He also began to open his eyes. "My first social awareness came about in 1947 while I was working on the Lackawanna Railroad—repairing the tracks, listening to the chants, visiting bars and roadhouses, and looking into the faces of the people who lived near the tracks in rural communities," *American Visions* quoted him as writing.

After hopping off his last train, Smith signed up for a one-year stint in the Army. In 1949 he returned to Brooklyn and landed a job in the post office. He was not thrilled, however; something was missing in his life. When a friend invited him to the Museum of Modern Art to see a Cezanne retrospective, he found out what it was. "Something told me when I walked into the museum that this was where I belonged," he told *American Visions*. "I always knew that I would do art, but you know how you carry something around with you, and you know that one day it will surface, but you don't know when."

With that insight, Smith set about becoming an artist. "I came away so moved with a feeling that I had been in touch with something sacred," he was quoted in a profile on the *Afro American Newspapers* Web site. "For a year afterward I haunted the libraries reading everything I could get my hands on about art, literature, philosophy, religion, existentialism—you name it—I touched on it somewhere."

In 1953 Smith left his postal job to become a full-time artist. He took classes at the Brooklyn Museum of Art School and New York City's Art Students League. He traveled to Maine to study on scholarship at the prestigious Skowhegan School of Painting and Sculpture. He learned about technique and style, history and form. Yet some of his greatest insights came from the other black artists he met. "Most people I came in contact with never knew a black painter nor had they hardly ever heard of one," he is quoted by *Afro American Newspapers.* "We went through the hallowed halls of these museums...and we didn't see anything reflect the black experience or black contribution to American culture. We knew that we were going to be scorned and ridiculed.

We also knew that our achievements were going to have to take, not rage, but knowledge and skill and scholarship and long years of dedication." He continued: "There were no black art historians, blacks with PhD's were unheard of. Few blacks taught art in colleges in the North; there were no publications about black visual arts. There were only about four or five galleries open to us."

DOCUMENTED STRUGGLES OF BLACK AMERICA

Smith's first solo show, held at the Brooklyn Museum Art School Gallery in 1955, debuted without him. "I never even showed up...," he told *American Visions.* "It was like revealing your soul for the first time. You have to develop a tough hide to get through that early period; it is very rough." His work reflected the world he moved in—New York's avant garde music scene. "During the day I painted and at night I went to the jazz clubs," the *New York Amsterdam News* quoted Smith as saying. For a while he lived in an apartment next door to a jazz musician who introduced him to famed saxophonist Charlie "Bird" Parker. The musical legend took a look at Smith's work and told him to "stick to his vision," wrote the *New York Amsterdam News*. Smith named a 1950s series of paintings *Saturday Night in Harlem*. In the 1980s and 1990s he completed another jazz series, *Riding on a Blue Note*. One work from that group, "Rootin Tootin Blues," was given to President and Mrs. Bill Clinton during Clinton's first inauguration ceremony. Smith's work took a political turn in the mid-1950s as the civil rights movement exploded.

In 1954 the Supreme Court case "Brown vs. the Board of Education" ordered all public schools to integrate. After watching mobs of angry white adults taunting black school children, Smith made "First Day of School." The *Afro American Newspapers* Web site wrote of the black and white etching: "In this picture we see that a mob of furious people is lashing out at the seven black school-children who have arrived for their first day at school.... We see a Klansman in his Ku Klux Klan hood and a man wielding a billy club. Other men carry a knife, a gun, a Corn liquor bottle. There is no kindness in any of their faces."

R. G. BHANDERKAR

Ramakrishna Gopal Bhandarkar (also spelt Ramkrishna Gopal Bhandarkar, and known as R.G.Bhandarkar), was a scholar, Orientals and social reformer. He was born on 6th July 1837 in Malvan, Sindhudurg district of present Maharashtra. He born in a house of a small ward known as Medha, He completed his primary education in a private school of Malvan. His father was working as a clerk in Tahasildar office, Malvan.

He transferred to Ratnagiri in 1850 so Dr Bhandarkar continued his high-school education in a government school of Ratnagiri. For higher education, he secured his admission in Elphinstone College, Mumbai. While still a student, he became, a member of the Paramhansa Sabha, a secret association for the furtherance of liberal idea in 1853. It was secret in order to avoid the wrath of the powerful and orthodox elements of society. He belonged to the first batch of graduates from Bombay University in 1862 and completed his master's degree in 1863. In the course of his brilliant academic career, he won many awards and scholarships.

He served both Elphinston college and Deccan College during his distinguished teaching career. He was particularly proficient in English literature, History & Sanskrit. After working for short duration as the headmaster of Government school in Hyderabad (Sind) & Ratnagiri, He joined as an assistant professor in Elphinston College & later as a first Indian professor for Sanskrit in Deccan College, Pune.

He participated in International conferences on Oriental Studies held in London (1874) and Vienna (1886) and made invaluable contributions. In 1885, He was conferred by Ph. D. through Gotingen University in Germany. International institutes like Royal Asiatic Society (London), German Oriental Society, American Oriental society, Imperial Academy of St. Petersburg, Italian Asiatic Society etc honored him with their memberships. He became Vice Chancellor of Bombay University before he retired in 1894. In 1911, he awarded by ' K C I E ' & 'Sir'.

LANE POOLE, CHARLES EDWARD (1885 - 1970)

Born in Sussex, England, in 1885 and died in Sydney, N.S.W., on 22 November 1970. Arguably Australia's most famous forester, Charles Lane Poole introduced systematic, science-based forestry to Western Australia and made the first thorough inspection of Papua and New Guinea forests. He was the Commonwealth's first Inspector-General of Forests and trained many of Australia's professional foresters at the Australian Forestry School in Canberra.

Charles Lane Poole was born in 1885 into a well-connected English academic family. He started studying engineering in Dublin, but lost his left hand in a shooting accident when he was 19. Instead of continuing with engineering, he secured a place at the prestigious French National Forestry School, *L'École Nationale des Eaux et Forêts.* He graduated in 1906 and was sent to South Africa, where he was made a district forester in the Transvaal Province at only 22 years of age. He worked hard there to restore its depleted forests, but disagreed with the government's policies and resigned. It was not the last time he would disagree with his government employers.

The Colonial Office then sent him to Sierra Leone on Africa's ' Fever Coast'. His small field notebooks, now held in the National Library of Australia, give a picture of his work there. With little help and in spite of bouts of malaria, he drafted forest legislation, set up the first Forestry Department, laid out the first forest reserves, established nurseries, plantations and an arboretum, and collected herbarium specimens, some of which were new to science.

While on leave in 1911, Charles married Irish-born Ruth Pollexfen (who in later years designed the interiors of the Lodge and the Governor-General's residence in Canberra). She did not return with him to Sierra Leone. Charles did not believe that the tropics were 'places for white women'. The couple spent many of the early years of their marriage on opposite sides of the world. Following his stint in Africa, Charles Lane Poole came to Australia in 1916 to take up a role as Western Australia's Conservator of Forests, in which he was charged with putting forestry on a proper footing. It was a step up in his career, and it enabled him to set up home with his wife and daughter for the first time.

State archives, parliamentary papers and debates, and published reports tell of five years of intense activity. He drafted a new Forests Act and saw it passed in the face of strong opposition from the timber industry and unions. He reorganised the Forestry Department, started long-term planning for sustained timber yields, established arboretums and arranged for herbarium specimens to be collected across the state. Nationally, he argued that Australia should set up its own school to train forest officers – he never imagined that he would be called to run it – and internationally he took a prominent part in the First British Empire Forestry Conference held in London in 1920.

In 1921, Charles abruptly ended his flourishing and energetic career in Western Australia. The State Government would neither heed his advice against renewing forest concessions to a timber company, nor would it declare the state forests he wanted. He resigned in protest. Ruth returned to her home country of Ireland with their two daughters.

Charles needed new employment. Aware of his availability, the Australian timber industry pressed the Commonwealth to have the resources in Papua examined to see if they could be profitably exploited. Charles was offered the job and began 24 years of work for the Commonwealth, which left a legacy of records in the National Archives. Charles Lane Poole: forester for a nation NAA: A3087, 1 His task was to survey the forests of Papua, then an Australian territory, and later those in New Guinea. He spent an arduous three years traversing the forests from the swamps to the high mountains, surveying the country, measuring trees, and collecting herbarium specimens and timber samples.

He did not find extensive stands of timber that could be exploited economically, but took broad-ranging notes of other forest products such as resins, nuts, oils and medicinal plants. His youngest daughter was born in Ireland while Charles was in Papua. The Western Australian Senator, George Pearce, put a case to Prime Minister Stanley Bruce that the Commonwealth needed its own forester, and recommended Charles Lane Poole as the best man for the job. Charles was appointed the Commonwealth's Forestry Adviser in 1925.

He led the Commonwealth Government's involvement in forestry through the Depression of the 1930s and World War II , but never had adequate funds or staff. He also found it extremely difficult to build cooperative relationships with the states at a sensitive time in Commonwealth–state relations. Charles' insistence on universitylevel training for forest officers in the Australian Forestry School, his intolerance of state counterparts without such qualifications and, at times, his abrasive manner, polarised opinions about him. He even referred to one of his state counterparts as 'Australian forestry's enemy No. 1'. In 1928 he submitted a case to the Royal Commission on the Constitution that Australia's forests should be a national, rather than a state, responsibility. Needless to say, this did nothing to endear him to his state counterparts. Despite these difficulties, Charles energetically pursued his vision for a national approach to forest management. He was far-sighted and realised that uncontrolled grazing in the mountain catchments of the Murray River was causing erosion that might silt up the new Hume Reservoir on the river near Albury.

A reconnaissance survey was needed, but it was not until 1931 that Charles could get a research officer, Baldur Byles, to do the work on a shoestring budget, and then only on the New South Wales side, as Victoria would not agree. Charles Lane Poole retired in 1945 and died in 1970. The picture that emerges from archives in Australia, Ireland and France, and from discussions with those who knew him, is that of an energetic, committed and sometimes controversial man. His interest in forestry took him around the world and his zealous principles at times brought him into conflict with employers and colleagues. His commitment to the cause of scientific forestry and the conservation of forest resources has ensured his place in the history of Australian forestry.

R C MAJUMDAR

Born at Khandapara in Faridpur District, Ramesh passed his childhood in poverty. In 1905, he passed his Entrance Examination from Ravenshaw College, Cuttack. In 1907, he passed F.A. with first class scholarship from Ripon College and joined Presidency College, Calcutta. Graduating in B.A.(Hons.)

in 1909, he won the Premchand-Roychand studentship for his research work in 1913. He started his teaching career as a Lecturer at Dacca Government Training College. Since 1914, he spent seven years as Professor of History at Calcutta University. He got his doctorate for his thesis "Corporate Life in Ancient India". In 1921, he joined the newly established Dacca University. After spending his days there as a Professor, then Departmental Head and then Provost, he became the Vice Chancellor of that university for five years from 1937-1942.

From 1950, he was Principal of the College of Indology, Kashi University. He started his research on ancient India. After extensive travels to Southeast Asia and research, he wrote detailed histories of Champa (1927), Suvarnadvipa (1929) and

Kambuja Desa. On the initiative of Bharatiya Vidya Bhavan, he took up the mantle of editing a multi-volume tome on Indian History. Starting in 1951, he toiled for twenty six long years to describe the history of the Indian people from the Vedic Period to the present day in eleven wonderful volumes.

When the final volume of "The History and Culture of the Indian People" was published in 1977, he had turned eighty-eight. He also edited the three-volume history of Bengal published by Dacca University. His last book was "Jivaner Smritidvipe". When the Government of India set up an editorial Committee to author a history of the freedom struggle of India, he was its principal member. But, following a conflict with the then Education Minister Maulana Abul Kalam Azad on the Sepoy Mutiny, he left the government job and published his own book: "The Sepoy Mutiny & Revolt of 1857".

According to him the origins of India's freedom struggle lie in the English-educated Indian middle-class and the freedom struggle started with the Banga Bhanga movement in 1905. His views on the freedom struggle can be gone through in detail in his book "History of the Freedom Movement in India". He was also an admirer of Vivekananda and Ramakrishna. The late R.C. Majumdar, often called the dean of Indian historians, completed a three-volume work on the Indian Freedom Movement. In this he put forward two fundamental theses that few Indian historians were willing to face. First, Gandhi's role in the achievement of freedom was exaggerated by the beneficiaries of his 'legacy'.

Next, the freedom movement demonstrated that the Muslim leadership - if not the masses - was concerned more with Pan-Islamic issues than national issues, and Gandhi often acquiesced to it. As example, Majumdar cited Gandhi's defence of the Ali brothers when they invited the Amir of Afghanistan to invade India in defence of Islam. The Ali brothers actually went further. They claimed that such a jehad (holy war) would be carried out not only against the British, but also against the Hindus who refused to cooperate in the enterprise. Little of this is found in history books in use today. As Majumdar points out, all this has been whitewashed to suit the political interests of certain groups. The result is massive distortion of history.

Unit IV

Curriculum in History

RECOMMENDATIONS AFTER 1947

The twentieth century witnessed a remarkable progress in the fields of education , science, technology and media. Education is a powerful means to bring social progress. The development of science and technology led to vast changes in all our social, political and economic systems. The revolution brought by media is a land mark in the history of Tamilnadu. Thus, the state of Tamilnadu witnessed an all round progress tremendously.

EDUCATION

After independence there was a need to revamp the educational system of our country. Tosuit the changing needs and aspirations of our people, our government appointed various commissions on education.

The important educational commissions are:

- University Grants Commission.
- Secondary Education Commission.
- Kothari Commission.
- New Education Policy.
- National Policy on education.

University Grants Commission (1948)

The Government of India appointed the University Grants Commission in 1948 under the chairmanship of Dr.S.Radhakrishnan. It aimed to improve the quality in higher education.

Dr.Radhakrishnan's birthday is celebrated as "Teachers day" on 5 September every year.

The Article 45 of the Constitution of India guaranted free and compulsory education for children below the age of 14.

Secondary Education Commission (1953)

Under the chairmanship of Dr.A.Lakshmana swamy Mudaliar, the Secondary Education Commission was constituted in 1953. It insisted on the all round development of the child at the secondary level. It suggested that the secondary education should be a preparatory stage for higher education.

Kothari Commission (1964)

The Kothari commission otherwise known as National Education Commission was appointed under the Chairmanship of Dr.D.S.Kothari in 1964. It submitted its report in 1966. The report suggested the introduction of 10+2+3 pattern of education in all parts of the country. It also emphasised on vocational, technical and science education. Accordingly, in the year 1965, the three language formula was adopted in the education system of Tamilnadu.

New Education Policy (1986)

New Education Policy of 1986 gave more emphasis on human development. The policy aimed for the removal of social disparities by giving importance to education of women, scheduled castes, scheduled tribes, handicapped and minorities. Further, the policy insisted on universalisation of primary education enrolling all the children of the age 6-14 years. The policy also aimed for the protection of nature by infusing environmental consciousness in the minds.

National Policy on Education (1992)

This Educational policy introduced a programme called 'Operation Black Board' for providing basic infrastructure facilities in schools. Another programme called National Literacy Mission (NLM) under Non-Formal education was enacted to remove illiteracy among the adults. It also aims for the eradication of poverty and unemployment and there by enhancing the economy of the country.

Growth of Primary Education

In the field of primary education our state has achieved a remarkable progress. During 1949-50 the total number of elementary schools were 15,303. The number of primary schools in Tamilnadu increased from 30,844 in 1999 to 32,242 in 2003-2004 budget. In order to improve the quality of education and to avoid dropouts at the primary level the Government of India introduced a scheme called 'Sarva Sikshya Abhyan' (SSA). This scheme is being implemented in Tamilnadu successfully.

Growth of Secondary Education

The secondary education is a link between the primary education and the higher education. In the year 2003 , nearly 4859 secondary schools were functioning with 68,212 teachers in Tamilnadu. The National policy of education (1992) emphasised the need for introducing vocational education. On the basis of this policy, the Government of Tamilnadu introduced the vocational education in June 1978. At present many vocational subjects are taught on different areas like Agriculture, Home Science, Engineering etc.

Growth of Higher Education

Since Independence, the growth of higher education received considerable encouragement. Higher Education can be classified as General and Professional education. The General education consists of disciplines like Arts, Science,Commerce etc.

The Professional education is comprised of courses on Engineering, Medicine and Agriculture The needs of the students of the above two categories large number of colleges and universities were established in Tamilnadu.

In 2002-2003, there are 478 arts and science colleges and 16 universities in Tamilnadu. The Tamil language was introduced as a medium of instruction in the colleges of Tamilnadu in 1970.

Science and Technology

Tamilnadu is famous for producing very great scientists to the country. The state contributes immensely for the rapid growth of science and technology in India. Famous scientists like Ramanujam (Mathematics) Dr.Sir CV.Raman (Physics) Dr.Chandrasekar (Physics) Dr.A.P.J.Abdul Kalam (Space) belong to Tamilnadu.

Dr.Sir C.V.Raman and Dr.Chandrasekar were the noble prize winners.

Agricultural Research

Dr.M.S.Swaminathan, famous agricultural scientist of the world belonged to Tamilnadu. He reorganised the Indian Council of Agricultural Research (ICAR). He evolved new technologies for the production of rice. It is called High Yielding Variety Programme (HYVP). The Agricultural Universities in Coimbatore, Agricultural Colleges at Madurai and other places have done lot of research on agriculture.

Farmer'sday is celebrated on December 23 every year.

Industrial Research

The Council of Scientific and Industrial Research (CSIR) has established a vast network of laboratories and research institutions all over the country. Dr.G.D.Naidu was the famous Industrialist of Tamilnadu. Many industries sprang up in Coimbatore, Chennai, Trichy, Salem, Mettur, Tirunelveli etc.

Atomic Research

The Atomic Energy Commission (AEC) was established in 1948 for the development of Atomic energy. Kalpakkam near Chennai is the centre of Atomic Research in Tamilnadu.

Dr.Chidambaram who was well known as an Atomic Scientist hails from Tamilnadu. An Atomic plant at Koodangulam in Tirunelveli district is contributing a lot in the field of Atomic research

Space Research

The Indian Space Research Oraganisation was founded in 1972 to utilise the space technology for National projects.

Dr.A.P.J.Abdul Kalam, his Excellency.

Mahendra giri in Kanyakumari district, a unit of Indian Space Research Organisation (ISRO) is doing well in this field. 'Kavalur' in Vellore district has a very big 'Telescope" in South East Asia This space observatory is doing remarkable research. In Chennai the Birla Planetarium is spreading scientific knowledge among the students.

Newspapers

Mass Comunication plays an important role in creating an awareness in the minds of the people. The mass communication includes the newspaper, radio, television, telephone, etc. The newspapers are the powerful media in influencing the opinion of the masses. Besides there are number of weekly, fortnightly, monthly quarterly and annual periodicals. The above mentioned newspapers and periodicals reflect the socio-political life of the people. They also serve as a link between the government and the public. Hence they provide us literary and informative values.

Radio

Radio broadcast was started in India in 1927. The Government of India took over the transmitters and started operating the Indian Broadcasting service in 1936. The name was changed as 'All India Radio' (AIR). Further, All India Radio established broadcasting centres at Trichi, Madurai, Kovai and Tiruneveli etc. The AIR is serving as an important media in providing information and in educating the people. The Prachar Bharathi, a unit of Government of India is formulating the policies for information and broadcasting and implementing it. Apart from this, there are private music channels also broadcast their own programmes in Tamilnadu.

Television

Television is one of the wonders of science. It was

introduced in India in 1959. The television station at Madras was inaugrated in 1975.

CURRICULUM CHANGES IN HISTORY

CURRICULUM IN CONTEXT

To round off this discussion of curriculum we do need to pay further attention to the social context in which it is created. One criticism that has been made of the praxis model (especially as it is set out by Grundy) is that it does not place a strong enough emphasis upon context.

This is a criticism that can also be laid at the door of the other approaches. In this respect the work of Catherine Cornbleth (1990) is of some use. She sees curriculum as a particular type of process.

Curriculum for her is what actually happens in classrooms, that is, 'an ongoing social process comprised of the interactions of students, teachers, knowledge and milieu' (1990: 5). In contrast, Stenhouse defines curriculum as the attempt to describe what happens in classrooms rather than what actually occurs. Cornbleth further contends that curriculum as practice cannot be understood adequately or changed substantially without attention to its setting or context. Curriculum is contextually shaped. While I may quibble about the simple equation of curriculum with process, what Cornbleth does by focusing on the interaction is to bring out the significance of context.

First, by introducing the notion of milieu into the discussion of curriculum she again draws attention to the impact of some factors that we have already noted. Of especial significance here are examinations and the social relationships of the school - the nature of the teacher-student relationship, the organization of classes, streaming and so on. These elements are what are sometimes known as the hidden curriculum. This was a term credited to Philip W. Jackson (1968) but it had been present as an acknowledged element in education for some time before. For example, John Dewey in *Experience and Education* referred to the 'collateral learning' of attitudes that occur in schools, and that may well be of more long-range importance than the explicit school curriculum (1938: 48). A fairly standard (product) definition of the 'hidden curriculum' is given by Vic Kelly.

He argues it is those things which students learn, 'because of the way in which the work of the school is planned and organized but which are not in themselves overtly included in the planning or even in the consciousness of those responsible for the school arrangements (1988: 8). The learning associated with the 'hidden curriculum' is most often treated in a negative way.

It is learning that is smuggled in and serves the interests of the status quo. The emphasis on regimentation, on bells and time management, and on streaming are sometimes seen as preparing young people for the world of capitalist production.

What we do need to recognize is that such 'hidden' learning is not all negative and can be potentially liberating. 'In so far as they enable students to develop socially valued knowledge and skills... or to form their own peer groups and subcultures, they may contribute to personal and collective autonomy and to possible critique and challenge of existing norms and institutions' (Cornbleth 1990: 50). What we also need to recognize is that by treating curriculum as a contextualized social process, the notion of hidden curriculum becomes rather redundant. If we need to stay in touch with milieu as we build curriculum then it is not hidden but becomes a central part of our processes.

Second, by paying attention to milieu, we can begin to get a better grasp of the impact of structural and socio-cultural process on teachers and students. As Cornbleth argues, economic and gender relations, for example, do not simply bypass the systemic or structural context of curriculum and enter directly into classroom practice. They are mediated by intervening layers of the education system. Thus, the impact of these factors may be quite different to that expected.

Third, if curriculum theory and practice is inextricably linked to milieu then it becomes clear why there have been problems about introducing it into non-schooling contexts like youth work; and it is to this area which we will now turn.

CURRICULUM AS THE BOUNDARY BETWEEN FORMAL AND INFORMAL EDUCATION

Jeffs and Smith (1990; 1999) have argued that the notion of curriculum provides a central dividing line between formal and informal education. They contend that curriculum theory and practice was formed within the schooling context and that there are major problems when it is introduced into informal forms of pedagogy.

The adoption of curriculum theory and practice by some informal educators appears to have arisen from a desire to be clear about content. Yet there are crucial difficulties with the notion of curriculum in this context. These centre around the extent to which it is possible to have a clear idea, in advance (and even during the process), of the activities and topics that will be involved in a particular piece of work.

At any one time, outcomes may not be marked by a high degree of specificity. In a similar way, the nature of the activities used often cannot be predicted. It may be that we can say something about how the informal educator will work. However, knowing in advance about broad processes and ethos isn't the same as having a knowledge of the programme. We must, thus, conclude that approaches to the curriculum which focus on objectives and detailed programmes appear to be incompatible with informal education.

In other words, they are arguing that a product model of curriculum is not compatible with the emphasis on process and praxis within informal education.

However, process and praxis models of curriculum also present problems in the context of informal education. If you look back at at our models of process and compare them with the model of informal education presented above then it is clear that we can have a similar problem with pre-specification. One of the key feature that differentiates the two is that the curriculum model has the teacher entering the situation with a proposal for action which sets out the essential principles and features of the educational encounter. Informal educators do not have, and do not need, this element. They do not enter with a clear proposal for action. Rather, they have an idea of what makes for human well-being, and an appreciation of their overall role and strategy (strategy here being some idea about target group and broad method e.g. detached work).

They then develop their aims and interventions in interaction. And what is this element we have been discussing? It is nothing more nor less than what Stenhouse considers to be a curriculum!

The other key difference is context. Even if we were to go the whole hog and define curriculum as process there remain substantive problems. As Cornbleth (1990), and Jeffs and Smith (1990, 1999) have argued, curriculum cannot be taken out of context, and the context in which it was formed was the school. Curriculum theory and practice only makes sense when considered alongside notions like class, teacher, course, lesson and so on. You only have to look at the language that has been used by our main proponents: Tyler, Stenhouse, Cornbleth and Grundy, to see this. It is not a concept that stands on its own.

It developed in relation to teaching and within particular organizational relationships and expectations. Alter the context and the nature of the process alters . We then need different ways of describing what is going on. Thus, it is no surprise that when curriculum theory and practice are introduced into what are essentially informal forms of working such as youth work and community work, their main impact is to formalize significant aspects of the work.

One of the main outcome of curriculum experiments within youth work has been work, for example in the field of health promotion, which involve pre-specified activities, visiting workers, regular meetings and so on. Within the language of youth work these are most often called programmes or projects. Within a school they would be called a course.

What is being suggested here is that when informal

educators take on the language of curriculum they are crossing the boundary between their chosen specialism and the domain of formal education. This they need to do from time to time. There will be formal interludes in their work, appropriate times for them to mount courses and to discuss content and method in curriculum terms. But we should not fall into the trap of thinking that to be educators we have to adopt curriculum theory and practice.

The fact that so many have been misled into believing this demonstrates just how powerful the ideas of schooling are. Education is something more than schooling.

CONCLUSION

We have explored four different approaches to curriculum theory and practice:

- Curriculum as a body of knowledge to be transmitted.
- Curriculum as an attempt to achieve certain ends in students - product.
- Curriculum as process.
- Curriculum as praxis.

In a number of respects these different bodies of curriculum theory and practice link to the four main forces in North American curriculum-making in the twentieth century: the liberal educators; the scientific curriculum makers; the developmental/person-centred; and the social meliorists (those that sought more radical social change) (after Kliebart 1987).

Unit V

Theories Influencing History Materials

TASTE OF HISTORY

Less than a decade ago, every student from high school to graduate school had to know the basics of Marxism-Leninism. There was no chance one could escape studying the theory of revolution, which is one of its cornerstones. Everybody in Russia who is over thirty now should be familiar with it. But it seems that after Communist ideology was abandoned and vanished from officialdom and everyday life, Russia, with its characteristic maximalism, threw the previously idolized theory into the wastebasket of history and tried to forget all about it.

Those who wholeheartedly embraced market reforms and democracy were especially anxious to forget Marxism-Leninism. This was hardly a smart move.

Actually, the knowledge of Lenin's theory of revolution could benefit the current leaders of the country. Apparently, it does contain important aspects that are very valid for understanding what is going on in the country and, at the very least, could be used to predict what should be expected from the followers of this theory.

Lenin himself said that to succeed in a struggle with one's ideological and political enemy one should know one's enemy's ideas and theories. He said this to a professor of theology during the exam; the professor was stunned by Lenin's knowledge of the subject despite his known atheism.

Although modern Russian Communists gave up some of Lenin's ideas, including atheism, they still use Communist ideology and theory. Recent events in Russian political life made me recall Lenin's notion of a revolutionary situation. Let me explain for those who forgot or never knew it. According to Lenin, a revolutionary situation is supposed to include three components. First, "the crisis of the upper class": the authorities cannot continue ruling in the same way as they are used to. At the same time, the population does not want to live under the same political conditions any more and wants change. Second, extreme impoverishment of the masses. And, third, significant growth of political activity of masses.

What do we have today in Russia? The crisis of the political system is obvious. The entire state machine is not working. Neither the president, nor the government, nor the parliament have control over the country. The words "crisis of power" are uttered by the highest state authorities, except the president himself. This can probably be explained by his health problems, but the presidential staff says it for him. They revived negotiations with the Duma on the guarantees for the retired president and once again offered in exchange to limit the president's powers. Monday's news of the latest reshuffling in the Presidential administration looks more like agony than a recovery, both physical and political, although the presidential staff tries to create an impression of the latter.

The Primakov government, which on one hand, inherited the problem of mistrust from the population, but on the other hand, did receive some credit because it is seen as the last chance to improve the situation and bring order to the crumbling economy and state, has not yet met the expectations. Furthermore, the absence of a clear-cut economic programme and the unfulfilled promises to pay wage and pension arrears have chipped away at the initial credit of trust. Although according to many polls Primakov is considered the most influential political leader in the country, that is probably just a recognition of his potential ability to gain control over the situation rather than actual influence. And do not forget that he has no competition.

The Russian parliament has enjoyed the reputation of a corrupted "circus show" for quite a long time now. The recent Duma statements and bills, as well as newspaper items on tariffs on voting in Duma, are just more proof of this reputation. The newspaper *Komsomolskaya pravda* published a monologue of a Duma deputy, former Communist faction member Vasiliy Kobylkin, who stated that Communist deputies take bribes for each new bill. The highest bribes are paid for voting for the prime minister - $10,000 a vote.

Last week's harvest of Duma activities includes a resolution on restoration of the statue of Dzerzhinskiy, the first head of the VChK–the predecessor of the KGB–famous for the "red terror" against those who were not proletarians, poor peasants, or revolutionary soldiers. He did fight criminals as well, but he got the nickname "Iron Felix" mostly for strictly following revolutionary consciousness in the struggle with "the enemies of the people."

The Speaker of the Duma, Communist Gennadiy Seleznev, in an emotional interview with the press, went even further and suggested the revival of the institution of penal servitude. The majority of the population associates this institution with political prisoners in pre-Revolutionary Russia rather than with the fight against crime.

What else did the Duma pass last week? You would never guess. The bill on apiculture (bee-keeping). I do not want to say that apiculture is not an important issue, but it's definitely not the first on the agenda.

The second characteristic of a revolutionary situation is the significant impoverishment of the population in the country. The situation is getting scarier every day. The August 17 crisis did not have an immediate effect on the poorest. Only now, a few month later, when food supplies stored at home are gone and salaries are 2-3 times "lighter" then before (if they are ever paid!), pensioners, teachers, medical personnel at public clinics, and all others in low-paying jobs financed from the budget have to live on $20-30 a month.

The situation is worsened by continuing wage arrears. Last week one of the teachers on a hunger strike in Ulyanovsk died. Teachers in this city, which was named, incidentally, after Lenin (his real last name was Ulyanov and he was born there) went on a hunger strike in order to attract attention to their wage arrears of three months or more. Every day brings news about similar strikes from almost all regions. In the Far East and many Northern regions, the problems with wage arrears are multiplied by the lack of electricity and heat during the severe winter season, which has just begun. And it is happening in a country the greatest reserves of gas, oil, and coal in the world! Without doubt, the energy sector needs structural reforms before it can function according to market principles, but people who live where it is 10 degrees below zero do not care about structural reforms. They want heat.

The last criteria of a revolutionary situation – high political activity of the masses – is not associated with political activity in the modern meaning of this phrase, but with street protests and revolutionary readiness to fight with the regime. Fortunately, it has not yet come to that. The protest actions on October 7, the November 7 celebration of the anniversary of the October Revolution, and public opinion polls show quite a low level of public interest in armed fighting with the authorities. But it looks like Communist leaders are trying to change the situation. General Makhashov's anti-Semitic statements, the latest Duma resolution on the monument to Dzerzhinskiy, constant attempts to channel public dissatisfaction with the economic and social development of the country into a campaign for Yeltsin's resignation and against his "regime"– these actions, from my point of view, are nothing else but attempts to "revolutionize the political consciousness" of the population.

The Communists are afraid they won't be able to win the majority in the next parliamentary and presidential elections, and so they rush to use the current instability and economic crisis to return to power while they still have significant support from the electorate. Otherwise, the longer they wait, the less probability they will be able to change their status from opposition to the party of power. Russian Communists remember well another of Lenin's slogans: "the worse, the better." The worse things are for the country and its population, the better they are for the Communists, since it gives them an opportunity to claim leadership in the protests. In a situation of heated political extremism and violent mass protests, it is easier to manipulate and lead angry crowds than in a situation where the population shows little interest in revolutionary actions. Whether they will succeed in heating the political situation and then leading the protests is the most important question. There is no definite answer to it now.

The political activity of the population in the modern meaning – high voter turnout; involvement in the activities of political organizations, parties, professional associations, or trade unions; and other means of civilized interaction between the population and the government – is not yet an integral part of Russian society. The high interest and participation in elections in the early 1990s are gone and have been replaced by widespread mistrust in political leaders and authorities as well as in politics in general. As a result, people do not trust the institution of elections.

Recent local elections show a generally very low turnout. A turnout of slightly more than 40%, significant by Russian standards, was registered at the St. Petersburg city legislature elections last Sunday. The results of the poll was a surprise as well. "Yabloko" is one of the leaders in the competition for the second round. Was it Galina Starovoytova's murder or rejection of new dirty campaign techniques that brought people to the polls? Or is it the generally higher educational and intellectual level of the city's residents that made them stand up and show their political preferences? Or will we always need something extraordinary to happen before we start using common sense?

Anyway, we need to keep that third component of Lenin's revolutionary situation in mind and stay away from political extremism and "revolutionization of public consciousness." Otherwise, there is no guarantee that we will have the opportunity to vote and show our preferences in the future. Russian history has proven many times over that "a Russian riot is senseless and merciless," as our famous poet Alexander

Pushkin wrote. Let us learn from our history, including the history of political thought.

CULTURE EPOCH THEORY

The fundamental ideas of this theory is that there is a general parallelism between the development of the human race and of the individual and also this parallelism is of fundamental importance for the selection and arrangement of the materials of the course of study.

This theory says that the appropriate basis of the content of study at each period of child growth is the culture products (literature especially) of the corresponding period of race development. The general idea has never been better stated than by Goethe in the following words: "The youth must always begin anew at the beginning, and as an individual traverse the epochs of the world's culture."

The theory has been independently reached from a number of different points of view.

MODES OF THEORY

Three of these modes of approach may be especially signalized.

- *The philosophic-historic:* The reaction against the rationalism and the individualism of the French and German enlightenment of the eighteenth century led many German thinkers to a vivid appreciation of the part played by the social institutions and traditions of the past in bringing individuals to their present status, and of the necessary role of past culture in the further development of a well-founded personality. Against the "Return to Nature" of Rousseau the necessity of nurture by culture was insisted upon. Formal rationalism in its zeal for reform and progress would make a *tabula rasa* of the past, and regarding government and religion as mainly conscious inventions to keep the masses in subjection to the interests of a few, would start afresh on the basis of an equality and liberty of individuals demonstrated by pure reason. Against this Herder, Lessing, Goethe, and Hegel emphasized the continuity of institutional life, and the fact that history contained implicitly a deeper rationality than that of the isolated self-consciousness of individuals. Moreover these writers upheld the application of the idea of evolution in one form or another to the history of humanity, and thus elaborated the notion of a developing series of stages through which mankind has progressively passed in traversing its course to the full unfolding of its corporate destiny. From these conceptions they drew, with varying degrees of explicitness, the conclusion that individuals go through the same general course of development and attain their fullest and most harmonious development in the degree in which they repeat the progressive stages of the race.

- Other writers (again mostly German) approached the matter from the educational side. The aim of education is to elevate the child to the perfect cultural plane of present civilization. Because of the contrast between the immaturity and narrowness of the child's experience and the complexity and richness of present civilization, this problem of elevation must be attacked indirectly and gradually. The child cannot directly assimilate or appreciate the highest and best in the life about him. He can rise progressively to it by living through the significant and valuable factors of the past stages out of which the present has evolved; the earlier being the simpler are better adapted to the child psychology — to his apperceptive masses and his interests. Herbart and his followers presented this point of view.
- The discovery (in embryology) that the individual growth (the ontogenetic series) recapitulates the evolution of animal life (the phylogenetic series) has been employed to give the doctrine a scientific biological foundation, or at least a support by analogy.

Before considering the doctrine critically we may note some of the attempts which have been made to apply the theory to educational practice. Some pedagogical writers have laid stress upon the complete and almost unconscious absorption of the individual in the group as the characteristic mark of the earlier stage of development of the race and the child; have selected individualistic reaction and protest as the sign of the second period, and voluntary and conscious loyal reattachment of the individual to the interests and well-being of the social group as the key to the final stage. Others have fixed upon three stages of intellectual development as the common element: first, the predominance of emotional imagination, — the mythical, animistic phase of mind; second, the development of a matter-of-fact interest, expressed in tendency to observe, to collect, to make utilitarian constructions; third, the emerging of conscious reflection, characterized by interest in abstraction and generalization. Still others have fixed upon typical industrial periods in the evolution of humanity, carrying with them a great knowledge of natural energy and law and increased ability to utilize them: e.g.

- Hunting and fishing,
- Nomadic and shepherd life,
- Agriculture,
- Use of metals and beginnings of manufacture,
- Universal commerce and intercourse.

They have then sought for corresponding psychological traits in the development of the child during the years of school age.

The curricula based upon these various methods of interpretation have agreed more closely than the diversity of the point would perhaps have led us to anticipate. Myths and fairy tales afford the appropriate nurture for the earliest period. Robinson Crusoe and stories of the Biblical patriarchs make a transition to the study of tribal and national heroes and founders of states; modern history and literature (especially the development of the particular state to which the child belongs) of the later years. The German schemes are also complicated by the necessity of exerting the scheme on the side of instruction in religion and in the Old and New Testaments.

Regarding the theory in general, it must first be heartily acknowledged that it makes practically the first attempt to treat the curriculum, especially in its sequence, upon other than conventional, or formal and logical grounds. Educational theory is indebted to the doctrine for the first systematic attempts to base a course of study upon the actual unfolding of the psychology of child nature, and at the same time to connect this psychological growth with indispensable sociological considerations.

FACTS

The fact in this Theory is that it is being cordially recognized, certain important qualifications need to be introduced regarding the use of the doctrine to determine the appropriate materials and best sequence of the studies in the curriculum.

- The primacy of the contemporary social life and relations of the child must be mentioned. Even if the parallelism of child growth and social development could be made out in a general way, it would still remain true that educationally the existence of certain types of culture in the past is no reason for emphasizing the materials of those periods in present education. The child at best has only a short time to pass through what the race has taken long ages to traverse; and it may well be that certain psychological tendencies in the child (supposing that they do correspond roughly to the dominant traits of some past historic period) need to be slurred over, or at least short-circuited, rather than emphasized or brought to consciousness. Hence (a) no past period should be selected except as it serves to increase the child's insight and appreciation of significant and valuable features of present civilization. The criterion of selection and emphasis is in contemporary, not in past civilization. (b) Moreover, the starting point, the ground of departure, must always be sought in activities and materials with which the pupil is already directly familiar in his present social environment. The motive and the "apperceptive masses" of dealing with the past must be found in problems and materials with which children are confronted in their ordinary social life. Finally (e) when excursions are made from the present to the past, pains should be taken to see that the knowledge of the past does not remain isolated, but is promptly reapplied to insure a better appreciation of the present social environment. In short, the child is not, educationally speaking, to be led *through* the epochs of the past, but is to be led *by* them to resolve present complex culture into simpler factors, and to understand the *forces* which have produced the present.

- The present psychological structure and tendencies of children must be used as criteria for estimating the educational bearing of the past periods, not vice versa. That is to say, we must not assume that because certain activities and interests are presented in the history of the race, they are therefore now presented and significant in child experience. We must make an independent examination of the structure and growth, physical and mental, of children, and having ascertained the operation of certain needs and capacities look to the history of the race to find out appropriate material for supplying the needs and nurturing the capacities. (3) The doctrine, as usually expounded, underestimates the value of the processes which have marked the development of the race, and exaggerates the importance of products. Ziller, for example, stated that the culture history of the race is deposited chiefly in the literary masterpieces in which the various epochs have manifested themselves; and in general the more ardent devotees of the culture-epoch doctrine have tended to make literature and history the centers of the course of study. Two fundamental exceptions must be taken to this conception. In the first place, literary products cannot be adequately understood except with reference to the activities which have manifested themselves in artistic expressions. To isolate the literature of Greece and Rome from the social, the economic, political, and scientific, activities which lie behind that art is to deprive the latter of much of its vitality and significance. In the second place, emphasis upon past products at the expense of processes is defective in promoting an understanding of the present. The method tends toward a static conception of society; it fails to present the forces which have made society progressive and which render it still a moving, changing, dynamic process. If the activities shown in industrial struggles, of invention and scientific discovery, in the conquest of nature and in changes of social organization require primary emphasis, the literary products, while precious documents of education, should be treated as consummations of these active processes, not as the primary and essential educative material.

Unit VI

Instructional Methods for Individual

APTITUDE TREATMENT INTERACTION

OVERVIEW OF THE PROJECT

This paper describes the conceptual background for a three year aptitude-treatment interaction (ATI) study being conducted by the authors at the Human Resources Research Organization (HumRRO) and the Human Resource Directorate of the Armstrong Laboratory, and presents a brief review of the general status of ATI research. Before presenting the observations on and critique of ATI research, the project entitled, *Using the Differential Classification Research Paradigm to Study Aptitude-Treatment Interactions in Training* will be discussed.

We are presently at the end of the first year of a three-year project designed to examine the relationship between learner characteristics (e.g., cognitive aptitudes, affective factors, and conative factors) and the training environment (e.g., instructional methods and course content) using the differential prediction paradigm adopted from personnel classification. The importance of ATI research to instructional design and training evaluation is captured in the following statement by Snow and Lohman.

Educational treatment comparisons, including the programme evaluations, must at least incorporate tests of plausible ATI hypotheses in order to interpret their intended main effect conclusions properly. Any treatment environment can serve some learners well and others poorly. Research on treatment design should thus always use what is known about individual differences to determine for whom any particular instructional method is appropriate and for whom it is not appropriate.

The idea for applying the classification paradigm to ATI research comes from Cronbach and Snow (1977), who observed that the personnel classification problem is directly analogous to ATI phenomenon in training. The personnel classification problem is based on the assumption that an interaction between worker characteristics (e.g., aptitudes, interests, motivation), and job characteristics (e.g., technical content) exists. The operational classification process involves the assessment of a group of applicants simultaneously for several different jobs or occupations.

Each individual is placed in (i.e., differentially assigned or classified to) the job for which he or she has the highest estimated performance. Differential classification capitalizes on the match between each individual's aptitude and interest profile and the unique requirements of the job, thus enhancing individual performance and overall organizational productivity.

By applying the classification paradigm to ATI research, advances in the fields of training design and evaluation, especially for Adaptive Tutors, which attempt to capitalize on ATIs through student interaction with the tutor, may be made more possible. Use of the classification paradigm will make it possible to simulate the benefits (if any) of capitalizing on ATIs through student-course matching and provide an index of training effectiveness. Neither of these capabilities are possible with the traditional ATI design. Further, the classification paradigm provides a psychometric foundation for expanding our knowledge and understanding of individual characteristics and training variables that interact to enhance or degrade student performance in a particular instructional setting.

In this study the classification paradigm is applied to

examine whether learner characteristics and training environments interact to produce intra-individual differences in final course grades across Air Force technical courses. Using student-course assignment simulations, the average training performance in a sample of courses after optimal placement of students in the course that best matches their aptitude profiles will be measured. These results will be compared to random (and possible actual) assignments. It is hypothesized that training performance averages across 20 to 30 courses will be better with optimal placement than with random or actual assignments.

The project will be conducted in three Phases. The major tasks of Phase I are the design of the research method, the selection of individual difference variables to describe learner characteristics, and the development of a training characteristics inventory. Approximately 30 Air Force courses, which will vary across occupations, will be sampled. The major consideration in selecting the course sample is to obtain differentiation in the instructional methods and course content.

Phase II will entail data collection. Phase III will consist of two main tasks: the development of course prediction models and the classification cross-validation study. The classification procedure will be based on the Zeidner and Johnson (1994) method, which has received a good deal of attention within the past several years. The approach uses a Monte Carlo procedure to supplement sample data. Training effectiveness will be measured by conducting computer-based course placement simulations.

The study is being conducted over a 36 month period. The outcome of the project will be a series of reports describing the research design, variables, methodology, and results. The reports will also discuss the implications for the advancement of psychological theory in the study of ATIs, instructional theory development, and the design and evaluation of adaptive and conventional training programs.

CURRENT RESEARCH FINDINGS

As part of the preparation for this study, the literatures

in ATI, instructional design, and training evaluation were reviewed. The goal was to explore trends in the results and to identify possible course characteristics that may account for ATIs. Currently, these findings are being used to select the sample of Air Force technical courses and to develop a questionnaire on the training environment. The following is a brief synopsis of the ATI research and some general conclusions derived from the review.

The review showed that most of the studies examined cognitive aptitudes. More specifically, 48 data points from the studies could be attributed to the investigation of cognitive factors, 16 to affective factors, and 5 to conative factors. The majority of the studies examined 6 types of cognitive aptitudes, including verbal/crystallized aptitudes (14), quantitative aptitudes (7), general knowledge (7), spatial aptitudes (6), field dependence independence (5), and fluid/analytical (5). Conative factors were examined primarily using locus of control (4). The remaining 6 of the data points were divided equally among motivation, achievement via independence, and achievement via conformity. Finally, 11 data points were associated with affective factors. These factors included anxiety (6), attitudes/preferences (3) and self-efficacy (2).

The review also indicated that a variety of different treatments were used. The most frequently manipulated treatment variables were structure (26%) and elaboration (23%). The typical manipulation for structure involved providing one group with a more self-directed course of study and providing the control group with lecture in a more controlled atmosphere. Elaboration was typically manipulated by providing the experimental group with analogies or some other means of clarifying the material while the control group typically received only text.

Other experimental manipulations included either providing one group with deductive training while the other received inductive training, providing one group with cognitive modeling and comparing that group to a control group, or comparing a group that participated primarily in small groups to a group that participated in a large group.

Table 1 presents study outcomes for the cognitive factors examined by treatment. Study outcomes had to have at least two data points to be considered. The results indicated that most studies did not find an aptitude treatment interaction by manipulating structure (67%), the elaboration of the text (65%), or mapping (88%). On the other hand, the majority of data points (75%) in studies in which deductive and inductive training were manipulated indicated that subjects low in cognitive ability performed better when given deductive training and subjects high in cognitive ability performed better when given inductive training. Also, it should be noted that no apparent trend could be detected by manipulating either cognitive modeling or the group size.

Finally, although the data indicated that manipulating the elaboration of the text was not likely to result in an ATI, some trends should be noted. For example, subjects high in verbal ability tended to benefit from verbal elaboration while those low in verbal ability tended to benefit more from visual elaboration or analogies as did subjects high in spatial ability.

Table 2, presents the frequency of study outcomes for conative and affective factors by treatment. In general, there were too few data points to detect any patterns within a given treatment manipulation for conative factors. One data point indicated that subjects with an internal locus of control performed better with low structure.

The other data point indicated that there was no ATI for locus of control and deductive vs. inductive training. Finally, there were also too few data points to detect any patterns between treatment and affective factors. Although, one finding is particularly interesting and may not be clear from the table. The outcome of manipulating the group size was that students who had a preference for large groups actually performed better in small groups while students who had a preference for small groups performed better in large groups.

CRITIQUE OF ATI RESEARCH

In general, we join with most other researchers before us in concluding that there are no consistent findings of ATIs in the training and education literatures. There are some possible methodological explanations for this. First, the most obvious, and possibly the most damaging, is the small sample sizes in ATI studies. For example, in the 37 studies reviewed in this paper, the overall N ranged from 35 to 297 and the sample size within treatment ranged from 16 to 94 .

And related to sample size, the review revealed a surprising diversity in the study populations used to examine ATIs. More specifically, study populations ranged from lower and upper elementary students to high school and college students to managers, administrators, and Air Force trainees.

Second, many of the studies reviewed had compounded problems because not only did they have small sample sizes but they also used a large number of variables and analyzed every main effect and interaction possible. For example, one study examined 11 different cognitive abilities in a sample of 147 . Another study conducted 240 F tests and found that 15 of the aptitude-treatment interactions were significant.

They, not surprisingly, had to conclude that the significant interactions were not meaningful, and therefore, did not contribute to knowledge about differential educational programming. Cohen (1990) pleasantly reminds researchers that too many variables and indiscriminant analyses increase the probability of making a Type I error, thereby, reducing the likelihood of finding significant results.

Third, there was very little consistency across studies in aptitude constructs and the measures used to examine these constructs. In fact, it may be more logical to refer to aptitudes as person characteristics due to the variety of possible variables. For example, Shute, Lajoie, and Gluck (in press) discuss three categories of person characteristics that may interact with the treatment: cognitive, conative, and affective. Cognitive factors refer to the mental processes that make knowledge and skill acquisition possible. Conative factors refer to the stable traits unique to a person, such as motivation. And affective factors refer to the less stable personality traits and mood, such as neuroticism and fatigue. An examination of the ATI studies reviewed indicated that the range of cognitive factors investigated was the most diverse of the three types of person characteristics. Cognitive ability was defined as verbal/ crystallized ability, quantitative ability, general knowledge, spatial ability, field dependence independence, fluid/analytical ability, motor skills, working memory, natural science, and operation learning. In addition, the measures used to assess these aptitudes ranged from standardized tests such as the California Achievement Test and the Group Embedded Figures Test to measures developed by the researcher to other types of measures such as GPA.

In addition to the discrepancies found among the person characteristics, a lack of consistency for the type of treatment was also observed. For example, although the majority of data points from studies were associated with either the structure of the course or the elaboration of the text, there were also 13 other types of treatments examined in the studies. Nine of these treatments only contributed one data point. The diversity of the treatments used coupled with the relative lack of data points for many of the treatments made it difficult to draw conclusions about possible interactions with person characteristics.

Finally, the literature review revealed a surprising diversity of outcome measures. For example, preestablished measures included achievement tests, and reading and math tests. Measures developed by the researcher took the form of multiple choice, essay, or open ended questions and generally tested the subject's learning of the course material. Other types of measures included accuracy, number of errors, number of appropriate links, and number of concept words.

CONCLUSIONS

There is a great deal of room for improvement in ATI research. We choose to view this state of affairs as our cup being half full. Our ATI/classification study is designed to address several of the important areas, i.e., the need for: 1) large sample sizes within treatments, 2) well-established measures of person characteristics (we are using the ASVAB subtests), and 3) a research paradigm that provides a foundation for theory development and the measurement of training effectiveness.

PROGRAMMED LEARNING

OVERVIEW

Operant conditioning has been used in developing *programmed learning*. According to B. F. Skinner (1958), the purpose of programmed learning is to manage human learning under controlled conditions. Typically, a textbook or computer presents the material to be learned in a series of very small steps, called frames. Each frame contains some information and a statement with a blank that the student fills in. The student then uncovers the correct answer before going on to the next frame. Each frame introduces a new idea or reviews material covered earlier.

The agreement between the uncovered answer and the student's own response reinforces correct responses, making it likely that they will occur again. Moreover, shaping is employed, in that the frames start from the student's initial knowledge and in small steps proceed to the final knowledge. The student is therefore usually correct and continues to be reinforced, which keeps him or her at the task until completion.

The principles of programmed learning have been incorporated into a method of instruction that is usually called *Personalized System of Instruction (PSI)*. PSI is a self-paced instruction format where each student works his or her way through the course material, which is broken down into small steps. Each student must "master" the material in one unit through a quiz before moving on to the next unit. Because of active student participation, small steps, immediate feedback, and reinforcement, PSI can be very effective.

Currently, the principles of programmed learning are being applied to a form of education called computer assisted instruction (CAI). The computer can be used to present learning material and help students learn through a variety of techniques such as quizzes, simulations, explorations, and tests. Computer assisted instruction is effective in part ecause of the availability of immediate feedback. Computer and Internet sites provide the opportunity for students to actively participate in research (Brothen, 1995). There are currently a number of research opportunities on the Internet. A recent meta-analysis of the efficacy of computer assisted instruction showed it to be an effective educational technique. Programmed learning continues to be an effective way to implement in the classroom some of the basic principles of operant conditioning.

INTRODUCTION

Originally introduced in the mid-1950s by behaviorist B.F. Skinner, programmed instruction is a system whereby the learner uses specially prepared books or equipment to learn without a teacher.

It was intended to free teachers from burdensome drills and repetitive problem-solving inherent in teaching basic academic subjects like spelling, arithmetic, and reading. Skinner based his ideas on the principle of operant conditioning, which theorized that learning takes place when a reinforcing stimulus is presented to reward a correct response.

In early programmed instruction, students punched answers to simple math problems into a type of keyboard. If the answer was correct, the machine would advance to another problem. Incorrect answers would not advance.

Skinner believed such learning could, in fact, be superior to traditional teacher-based instruction because children were rewarded immediately and individually for correct answers rather than waiting for a teacher to correct written answers or respond verbally.

Programmed instruction quickly became popular and spawned much educational research and commercial enterprise in the production of programmed instructional materials. It is considered the antecedent of modern computer-assisted learning.

Two types of programmed learning can be compared. Linear programming involves a simple step-by-step procedure. There is a single set of materials and students work from one problem to the next until the end of the programme. Branching programming is more complex. Students choose from multiple-choice answers and then are prompted to proceed to another page of the book depending on their answer.

If a correct answer is given, students move on to another page with more information to learn and more questions to answer. An incorrect answer leads to comments on why the answer is incorrect and a direction to return to the original question to make another selection.

Just as the programming developed more complexity over the years, so did the teaching machines themselves. Early, simple machines were little more than electronic workbooks. Later machines allowed students to be instructed on more complex material that required more than one-word or one-number responses.

In some, students could write their responses and move ahead by comparing their answers to acceptable answers. Programmed-learning books differ from traditional workbooks because they actually teach new information through this step-by-step stimulus-response method rather than simply offering practice material for already-learned skills.

Research has shown that programmed learning often is as successful, and sometimes more successful, than traditional teacher-based learning because it recognizes the different abilities and needs of individual children. Students who have mastered the material can move ahead more quickly, while those who need more practice are repeatedly exposed to the problems.

Programmed learning also allows teachers more time to concentrate on more complex tasks. One criticism of programmed learning centers on the lack of student-teacher interaction.

Unit VII

Models of Teaching

CONCEPT ATTAINMENT MODEL

BACKGROUND

Concept Attainment is an indirect instructional strategy that uses a structured inquiry process. It is based on the work of Jerome Bruner. In concept attainment, students figure out the attributes of a group or category that has already been formed by the teacher. To do so, students compare and contrast examples that contain the attributes of the concept with examples that do not contain those attributes.

They then separate them into two groups. Concept attainment, then, is the search for and identification of attributes that can be used to distinguish examples of a given group or category from non-examples.

It seems that most of what we do in science is categorize or classify objects or events for the purpose of generalizing. To do this, scientists must observe carefully. Although scientists are certainly not the only people who classify, scientists often classify in different ways than the rest of us do. Note that there is nothing about the ways in which scientists classify that is better than the ways others classify. It is a different way, not better.

However, in science class, we want the students to learn to classify in similar ways to scientists. We want them to be familiar with science categories so they can follow a scientific conversation – at least a little bit. We want them to be able to read a newspaper science article and understand what they have read. Better yet, they would be able to guess at some of the mistakes the journalist has made in interpreting what the scientists have learned. Even better, they might also be able to critique the conclusions that scientists themselves have made. A concept attainment method involves students learning to classify a set of objects or events in a way that scientists classify. The students will be using the categories that scientists use, and will be attempting to determine the rationale behind the categories.

The Concept Attainment Method has a high tolerance for ambiguity. This means that the students might seem to be following the wrong path, but eventually, they will come up with the expected answer. You would use this method when the concept the students are expected to learn is fairly clear. You would use this method instead of just telling the students or having them read, because students will learn the material much better when they figure it out for themselves.

As your students learn more about the classification, you will also learn more about it. As well as learning the material better, and remembering it longer, the students will learn how to learn by using this model. We want students to become independent learners and critical thinkers. This method will help them with both these goals.

This method encourages certain of the Common Essential Learnings. The most obvious are critical and creative thinking, communication, and of course, independent learning. Personal and social values and skills might be included if you help your students work in a positive way with their peers. As well, if the particular concept involves mathematical relationships, the students could use their numeracy. If the particular concept involves understanding a technology, technological literacy might also be addressed. Of course, as the students classify in the ways that scientists do, they will be learning a technique of science, and understanding techniques can be part of technological literacy.

Education is the most cogent instrument in the progress of any nation, hence, the quality of education has to be improved for faster all-round development. It is universally acknowledged that any attempt at the improvement in the quality of education ultimately depends on the quality of instruction imparted in the classrooms. The purpose of education is to manage students' learning and the value of any technology used in education must, therefore, be measured by its capacity to affect learning.

In a wider perspective, technology today seems to hold out more benefits than ever before. Educational technology has exhibited a great amount of promise and potential in facilitating teaching and learning. it can help further in the development of need based courses, organisation of content units, development of educational programmes and procedure of their monitoring and feedback.

Large scale experimentation spread over the whole world has changed the face of teaching-learning process and has put forth a number of teaching strategies, radio, television, video cassettes, tape recorder, computer- assisted learning (electric and electronic media) etc., along with various models of teaching. These are being increasingly used in the field of education. Models of teaching are designed to impart repertories while helping students learn information, ideas, academic skills, developing social skills, values and understand themselves and their environments (Joyce and Weil, 1972). A teaching model includes patterns for designing educational environment through specified ways of teaching and learning, to achieve specific goals.

The scope of research in this field is very vast because the concept of models of teaching is multidimensional. There is not one but many models and these models are at different stages of development.

The process of learning begins with the birth of the child and continues till his death. As soon as he comes in contact with the environment, he starts reacting and in the process of interaction of the individual and his environment, the foundation of learning is laid down. The learning of concepts is of greater importance for human beings as they think, learn and communicate with the help of concepts. The present age is the age of computerised industry and research. The exploding population in some areas of the globe along with shrinking resources compel us to produce and grow more under high economic conditions and also compels to explore space to find additional place and resources and also information to predict weather and other natural changes. The scenario has increased the importance of physics manifold. So teaching/learning of physics at all stages of life has assumed increased importance.

This process of teaching/learning can be made efficient and economic if suitable and convenient methods of teaching-learning are employed. hence, the study in hand endeavours to measure comparatively the efficacy of two recent models of teaching, namely, Bruner's Concept Attainment Model and Ausubel's Advance Organiser model.

Here an attempt has been made to evaluate the comparative effectiveness of Bruner's Concept Attainment Model, Ausubel's Advance Organiser Model and conventional method in teaching of physics in relation to intelligence and achievement motivation of ninth class students.

WHAT IS ITS PURPOSE?

Concept attainment is designed to clarify ideas and to introduce aspects of content. It engages students into formulating a concept through the use of illustrations, word cards or specimens called examples. Students who catch onto the idea before others are able to resolve the concept and then are invited to suggest their own examples, while other students are still trying to form the concept. For this reason, concept attainment is well suited to classroom use because all thinking abilities can be challenged throughout the activity. With experience, children become skilled at identifying relationships in the word cards or specimens. With carefully chosen examples, it is possible to use concept attainment to teach almost any concept in all subjects.

ADVANTAGES

- Helps make connections between what students Know and what they will be learning.

- Learn how to examine a concept from a number of perspectives.
- Learn how to sort out relevant information.
- Extends their knowledge of a concept by classifying more than one example of that concept.
- Students go beyond merely associating a key term with a definition concept is learned more thoroughly and retention is improved

PRACTICALITIES

Set Up

- Give your students sets of materials that have been classified. You also tell them the names of the categories. For example, you could give your students fifteen rocks, and organized into three groups: five sedimentary rocks, five igneous, five metamorphic.
- Tell the students to find the characteristics that members of one group have in common that are different than the characteristics of members of other groups. In other words, they should try to figure out why the five sedimentary rocks have been put in one group, and why the five metamorphic rocks have been put in a different group than the sedimentary rocks. Etc.
- You might or might not have activities for the students to do with the materials so the students will study them in different ways. If you want them to focus on the results of these activities for attaining their concepts, you will ask them to focus on these results. For example, you might have them spill a little vinegar on their rock samples, you might have them hit their samples with another rock, etc.
- You will probably put your students into small groups. Choose groups so they will work effectively together.
- If you wish to minimize your supervisory role,

choose materials that are relatively safe to work with. If there will be some danger in working with the materials, visualize what sorts of mistakes your students are likely to make. Then warn them of the dangers in advance.

Carry Out

- The students study the materials, compare and contrast those that are in the same group and those that are in the different groups, attempting to determine the rationale that was used for the classification. As the students are comparing and contrasting, they will develop different hypotheses, and will have opportunities to test their hypotheses by further examination of their materials, and by discussion in their small groups.
- The teacher's role at this stage is to meander through the classroom, observing the students at work. You will act as referee and coach. If students are hesitant about Ataking initiative", or if they are not testing the materials in a way in which they could, you might encourage them to go on with more tests.
- During this time, you could make anecdotal records, or fill in checklists of student actions.

Debrief

For every teaching strategy involving a debrief, I will suggest a different method. There are a number of ways in which debriefs can be done. Please mix and match the different forms of debriefs you use. In all large group (six or more students), encourage your students to use their conversation skills. (Don't overteach this, though. Tell them only once or twice in the year. Remind them only when you see that they are really forgetting.) Their conversational skills are to listen carefully to what other speakers say.

Then when they talk, they build on what others have said, and demonstrate this by using phrases such as "What I think is similar to what (another student) said", or "I disagree with what (another student) said, because ..." Encourage them also to speak tentatively with phrases such as "I thought" or "it seems":

- Put pairs of small groups together, so that if you originally had ten small groups of 3 students, you now have five small groups of six people. The groups are to discuss their observations and the reasons they think the objects have been classified together. Limit the time they will have for this discussion. When their time is up, give them a limited amount of time to come up with a ten word (or twenty, whatever you think is appropriate) phrase to summarize what they think the rationale is for the classification scheme. Tell the group that they should select one member to be the presentor.
- Have each of the larger groups present their results to the class.
- If your students have not come up with the rationale they should have, think of why they haven't. What background knowledge were they lacking, or what background knowledge contributed in a non-science way? What other materials might have helped them to form the concept you wanted them to form?

Check Up

- Once your students have come up with their rationales for the classification scheme, give them a sample which is not labelled. They are to choose which category this non-labelled sample fits in, and explain why they have classified it with this group.
- You could then ask how many groups changed their categories.

Hints

- For this teaching model to work well, the teacher should ensure that the initial samples given to the students are the clearest possible prototypes. In other words, if you had given the students samples of vertebrate animals: mammals, birds, fish, reptiles and amphibians, you would not give them whales and duckbilled platypuses amongst the mammals. These mammals are not generally what is expected of mammals. After the students have come up with the description of Abasic" mammals, then you could supply the exotic ones.

- Give the students time to develop their definitions of each category. Do not interrupt them when their first hypotheses are wrong. If you have set the model up correctly, the students will come up with the correct rationales eventually.

METHOD AND PROCEDURE

Method and procedure of the study has been discussed under the following headings:

Sample

In the present study 240 students of ninth class, enrolled in Government Senior Secondary School, Kanganwal; Government High School, Jhuner, and Government Senior Secondary School, Sandaur were divided into three groups, two experimental groups and one control group.

Design

In the present study 'pre-test post-test control group quasi-experimental design' was employed. The statistical technique of 'three way analysis of variance' (3x2x2) was used on gain scores for finding out the main effect and interactional effect of teaching techniques, intelligence and achievement motivation on scholastic achievement in physics of ninth class students.

Tools Used

In order to collect the required data for the study, the various tools used were: Meenakshi's socio-economic Status Scale, Jalota'a Verbal Group Test of General Mental Ability, Achievement Motivation Test of Pratibha Deo and Asha

Mohan, Lesson plans and a criterion test in physics.

PROCEDURE

The experiment was conducted in three stages-pre-test treatment and post-test–in all the three groups.

Pre-Test Stage

The groups were matched on the basis of socio-economic status of the students. Meenakshi's SES was used. Information was collected from school records to match the students on the basis of age and marks secured in science of 8th class. The criterion test in physics was used to measure the initial behaviour of the students. Jalota's Verbal Group Test of General Mental Ability and Achievement Motivation Test of Pratibha Deo and Asha Mohan were used to classify the students on the basis of intelligence and achievement motivation respectively.

Treatment Stage

Experimental group A was treated by using the lesson plans prepared in accordance with the Bruner's concept attainment model, experiment group B was treated by using the lesson plans prepared in accordance with Ausubel's advance organiser model and the control group C was treated by using the lesson plans prepared in accordance with conventional method of teaching simultaneously with the other groups.

Post-Test Stage

This was the terminal stage in which criterion test in physics (post-test) was administered on group A, group B and group C, on the completion of the treatment. In this way the terminal behaviour of the sample was evaluated.

TECHNIQUES USED

The following statistical techniques were employed for analysing the data in the present study:

- The measures of central tendency, dispersion and

one- way Anova were employed for matching the experimental groups and control group.

- Significant F-ratios were followed by t- test.
- The technique 'three way analysis of variance' (3×2×2) was used.

RESULTS

The three groups did not differ significantly from each other in their age and matched on the basis of age. The difference in mean marks between the groups, was not found significant. This suggests that the students under investigation were not different on the basis of marks secured in science in class VIII exam.

The students of all the three groups were not different from each other on the basis of socio-economic status.All the three groups were found to be homogeneous with regard to their initial behaviour i.e. knowledge of physics.

There existed a significant difference with respect to learning of concepts in physics among subjects taught through three different techniques. Significant F-ratio was followed by t-test. So t- test was applied to test the significance of difference between means of gain scores of subjects on criterion test in physics, taking two treatments at the same time.

A statistically significant difference was found between high and low level intelligence groups for learning of concepts in physics (F=14.66) where high intelligence group is better in concept learning than low intelligence group. No statistically significant difference was found between the subjects belonging to high and low level of achievement motivation for learning of concepts in physics.

(F= 1.51). The result did not show any independent effect of achievement motivation on the gain scores of subjects for learning of concepts in physics. The teaching techniques, intelligence and achievement motivation were not found to have any statistically significant effect on scholastic achievement of students for learning of concepts in physics (F = 0.32). This result indicated that interaction effect between teaching techniques, intelligence and achievement motivation on scholastic achievement in learning of concepts in physics does not exist at all.

EXAMPLES OF CONCEPT ATTAINMENT MODELS

- Give your students pictures of animals which are classified as mammals, fish, reptiles, birds. If you add skin samples to your selections, you could also include amphibians.
- Give your students a magnet, and let the magnet choose the materials which are magnetic and which are not, and then the students attempt to determine what the qualities of magnetic materials are vs. non-magnetic.
- Any two or more categories, and science is full of them, will be appropriate.

ADVANCE ORGANISER MODEL

INTRODUCTION

Advance organizers can be thought of as extremely well-designed and thought out unit outlines. Presented before the actual topics to be learned (in advance of learned material), it is notable that the Advance Organizer model is designed to prepare students for how to think about the lessons to come, giving some detail about terminology and connections but not giving the entire unit content. Advance organizers are not designed for day-to-day use; instead, they are used to provide a structure at the beginning of a major unit of study.

Ausubel suggests 2 different types of organizers for 2 different purposesTthough others have suggested other organizers, they seem to fall within these categories:

- Comparative Organizers present a study of the differences between items the student already knows and what they are about to learn.
- Expository organizers present a basic concept at a very high, abstract level. They can be used in combination also, but it is more likely to be used separately as each has its own separate strength.

It is important to note that Ausubel's Advance Organizers provide a structure for student thinking, not just a structure for lessons themselves. In this way, students are engaged in active learning, adding to the existing lecture and other potentially passive activities that are offered in the classroom.

OVERVIEW

Advance Organizers are like that: they are simply devices used in the introduction of a topic which enable learners to orient themselves to the topic, so that they can locate where any particular bit of input fits in and how it links with what they already know. (The name was coined by Ausubel.) Ausubel's major principle — that the most important determinant of learning is what the learner already knows — calls for an image or example which directs the learner to relevant prior experience or learning (preferably of course live and significant experience) and also points forward to new material.

An advance organizer is a cognitive strategy proposed by Ausubel in his Subsumption Theory, which allows the learner to recall and transfer prior knowledge to the new information being presented. This theory is based on the idea that learning is facilitated, if the learner can find meaning in the new information. If a connection can be made between the new information and previous knowledge, the learning experience will become more meaningful to the learner. Therefore, the new information will be learned. The advance organizer is not a strategy used by the learner, but rather an instructional strategy used by the teacher.

In essence, the advance organizer is a brief, general speech prepared by the teacher, before presenting the new material, to introduce the new lesson. In designing the advance organizer recall of previous knowledge relevant to the new knowledge is important. It should provide a bridge that links the known to the unknown, by including an abstract outline of the new information and a restatement of old knowledge. Theoretically, this will encourage transfer and application of old knowledge, to make the new knowledge more meaningful to the learner. In SLA advance organizers could be used to help the learner categorize new learning, in relation to their native language. The learner could then distinguish similarities and differences in the target language and their native language, thus carrying out a cognitive comparison between deviant and correct target language, forms or utterances.

This may even reduce learners' errors as conscious attention is focused on these differences and similarities. The use of advance organizers does fit in with current teaching approaches, particularly with the communicative language approach. For in this approach, learners negotiate for meaning and the teacher acts as a facilitator of the communication process.

JURISPRUDENCE INQUIRY MODEL

INTRODUCTION

This model is designed for secondary students in the social studies and implies the case study method, reminiscent of legal education. Students study cases involving social problems in areas where public policy is to be made (justice and equality, poverty and power etc.) They are led to identify the public policy issues as well as options available for dealing with them and the values underlying those options. This model can be used in any area where there are public policy issues for instance ethics in science, business and sports etc.

TEACHING PREREQUISITES FOR MAXIMUM SUCCESS

The model presented in this chapter is somewhat complex and assumes that a number of teaching skills are understood, if not used by, the teacher. These include: cooperative learning strategies of Johnson, Grooker, Stutsman, Hultman, and Johnson (1985) and Slavin (1989); higher-order questioning skills; wait time; classroom organization and management skills. In addition, it helps to understand a constructivist approach to teaching and the need for student empowerment as both an approach to teaching and as an outcome of education. Also, the teacher must have enough content knowledge of the subject being taught so that he or she can concentrate on how to teach and not spend preparation time on what to teach. All of these characteristics must be blended with an understanding of how children learn and when to intercede for maximum learning.

THE JURISPRUDENTIAL MODEL OF TEACHING

Pedersen (1990) modified the original Joyce and Weil Jurisprudential Model (1986) to create a jurisprudential inquiyr model of teaching that effectively lends itself to the study of science, technology, and societal issues in the classroom. The jurisprudential inquiyr STS model approaches teaching issues by dividing a class into the issue viewpoints. Through the use of information-acquisition strategies and classmate interactions, students present their views to a class-selected board of arbiters. It is the board's responsibility to listen to the student arguments in a public hearing and render a decision on the issue.

The final phase of this and many other teaching strategies involves the creation and assessment of action plans. In many ways the actual action plans developed by students are just as important an outcome as the related science concepts they learned. What follows in an outline of the six phases of the jurisprudential inquiry model.

Phase I: Orientation to the Issue

The initial step of this model introduces students to the selected issue. This occurs on the very first day that the topic is being studied. During this initial stage, the teacher must accomplish several tasks. They include:

- Divide the class into teams of two or three students. Each team will be assigned a side of the issue to represent in their respective group. The purpose of the team is to cooperate in reading, researching, and interacting on the side of the issue that they have been assigned.
- Now arrange the teams into groups so that the number of teams in a group equals the number of

sides to the issue. For example, a recycling issue may have two sides – recycling and nonrecycling. Therefore each group would have two teams of two (or three) members, a total of four (six) in the group.
- Assign each team within a group one side of the issue to represent. It is important to do this randomly. Inevitably some students will be assigned to a side of an issue that they do not believe in, but this is perhaps desirable.

It is important to remember that the issue selected becomes the focus of the curriculum. The content becomes the support for the issue.

Phase II: Identifying and Defining the Issue

Students begin to use the content during the second phase of the model. The students, working in their cooperative teams, use the library and other resources to gather,

Clarify, and synthesize facts about the issue. The students begin to identify values and value conflicts and raise questions about opposing views. The following should be considered when entering Phase II.

- Prepare for an adequate number of days in the library or for working with other resources. The teacher should be prepared to give guidance to both the students and resource people when necessary. For example, the teacher may need to address interview techniques, help students learn to read for fact versus opinion, or assist with questionnaire design. The teacher may also find it necessary to touch base with resource personnel such as librarians to ensure that students get the information they need. (The reader will find Hungerford, Litherland, Peyton, Ramsey, and Volk, 1988, especially useful in developing this phase of the project.)
- Allow time for the teams to be together to research, read, interview, survey, telephone, meet , discuss the issues and what they have found, and prepare each other for a public meeting.

- Students can use encyclopedias, magazines, journal articles, government publications, people, special interest groups, and a host of other resources. Probably the most overlooked resource will be the local or regional newspaper. It is important for the students to understand, when reading the newspaper, the difference between fact and opinion. Students may assume that an editorial, because it is in the paper, is fact.

Phase III: Synthesizing the Research Information into Arguments

At least one day prior to the public meeting, the students get back together as an intact class. At this point, the teacher will allow all of the teams representing the same side of the issue to get together to share information and prepare for the public discussion. It is during this time that the students need to plan a strategy for the public meeting. The following can be used as a guide for the students when in the large groups.

- Establish a stance based on factual information.
- Point out the undesirable or desirable consequences of a position.
- Clarify the value conflict with analogies.
- Set priorities; assert priority of one value over another.
- Identify factual assumptions and determine if they are relevant.
- Determine the predicted consequences and examine their factual.
- Validity (will they occur?)

During Phase III, the teacher will also select from the class a board of arbiters, two newspaper reporters, and two camera crew members. Each of these positions should be represented by both or all sides of the issue if possible. The following instructions are used to guide each of these roles in the debate.

BOARD OF ARBITERS

- Prepare questions to ask each of the presenters.

(These questions should be used for clarifying points.)

- Plan a strategy for initiating and running the public meeting. This would include who will talk first, who will talk last, and how much time will be allotted for each side and each person. (It is suggested that each student present a part of the argument for his or her side of the issue. Approximately 2-3 minutes per student is adequate for this purpose.)
- Be able to summarize those points that persuaded you in making your decision.

Newspaper and Camera Crew:

- Prepare questions to ask selected members of the groups involved in the debate. (It will also be necessary to decide who to interview.)
- Be able to summarize the comments made during the interview.
- Be able to summarize the comments made during the meeting. (For the camera crew, editing the videotape and/or adding comments of their own will summarize the comments.)

Phase IV: The Public Meeting

The fourth phase of the jurisprudential inquiry STS model involves the students in a mock public meeting. This meeting involves all students in presenting the different sides of the issue being studied. During the debate it is important that the students on the board of arbiters initiate and oversee the meeting. It is important also for the teacher to see that the following guidelines are followed:

- Maintain a vigorous intellectual climate where all views are respected.
- Avoid the direct evaluation of each other's opinions.
- See that issues are thoroughly explored.
- Respect the authority of the board.

Phase V: Clarification and Consensus

During this phase, students spend two days clarifying and

arriving at a consensus on the issue. The first day is spent with the students still divided into the respective sides of the issue, the board, the newspaper crew, and the camera crew. During this time the students clarify their best arguments in support of the side of the issue they represented. The board will be responsible for clarifying why they rendered their decision. The newspaper crew and camera crew will work on preparing their respective reports.

On the second day, students separate into their original groups. The groups were originally constructed so that all perspectives of the issue would be represented. The purpose of these groups is to come to a consensus on the issue. The students should use all information available to them in drawing their conclusions. This would include information from the debate, the research done, other groups, the newspaper and camera crews' perspective, and the board's recommendations.

The students' cooperative effort should represent the opinions of all the students in the groups. Their goal is to write those arguments that justify the original group's position on the issue.

Phase VI: Application

The final phase of this model is the most important phase. It is in this phase that the students take what they have learned and apply it to their surroundings. Students must be able to see the value in the science they have learned and see that, with this knowledge, they can have an impact.

The first step of this process is for each student to propose an overall action plan with resolutions. Some of the ways students have applied what they have learned and became involved in community activities include:

- Writing letters to city council, state representatives, state senators, governors, or mayor.
- Leading or participating in activities such as community cleanups, recycling activities, or petition drives.

- Attending city council meetings or local environmental meetings

Whatever actions students take should be assessed in light of their action plan statements.

The key to this model of instruction is that students have opportunities to apply the investigation skills and action strategies to the community in which they live.

TEACHER'S ROLE

The teacher's role during this exercise is important. As the students are researching, discussing, and debating, the teacher should encourage the students to commit themselves to one side of the issue, but be supportive if they change their minds when confronted with new evidence, and encourage them to consider other points of view. At all times, the teacher should remain neutral on the issue, encourage differentiation of positions, and promote synthesis of the different positions presented to the class.

SUMMARY

It is important to remember that issues are not things that a teacher can pull out of a book, they are not simply newspaper articles about issues in science, and they are not "discussing" an issue for ten minutes once a week. It is the integration of societal and technological issues that makes science content much more meaningful. The jurisprudential inquiry model can be used to accomplish that integration. Students must see the value of science. By using issues in this manner, students see how the issue impacts them and also how they impact the issue.

Unit VIII

Computers in History of Education

COMPUTER-ASSISTED INSTRUCTION

INTRODUCTION

Not so long ago, the microcomputer was a rare and exotic sight in American classrooms. Then, during the 1970s, many schools began acquiring microcomputers and putting them to use for instruction, drill and practice, recordkeeping, and other applications.

The use of microcomputers expanded rapidly during the 1980s. Between 1981 and the end of the decade:

- American schools acquired over two million microcomputers.
- The number of schools owning computers increased from approximately 25 percent to virtually 100 percent.
- More than half the states began requiring—or at least recommending—preservice technology programs for all prospective teachers (Kinnaman 1990).

"The 'information age' has clearly arrived," notes Kinnaman, "and in the '90s the educational use of computer technology will surely continue to grow." While this is no doubt an accurate prediction, many educators, legislators, parents, and researchers have expressed concern about the educational effectiveness of using microcomputers in schools. Because the acquisition of computer hardware and educational software programs involves a considerable monetary investment, these groups want assurance that computers in the schools are more than expensive and entertaining toys; they desire evidence that educational microcomputer use truly enhances learning in demonstrable ways.

Fortunately, a great deal of research has been conducted during the 1970s, 1980s, and early 1990s on the effects of computer use on student achievement, attitudes, and other variables, such as learning rate. This research covers a wide range of topics, from computerized learning activities, which supplement conventional instruction, to computer programming, to computerized recordkeeping, to the development of databases, to writing using word processors, and other applications.

The main focus of this report is the most commonly used and most frequently researched kind of educational computer use—computer-assisted instruction (CAI). Findings about other educational computer applications are presented as they relate to this main focus.

DEFINITION

"Computer-assisted instruction" (CAI) refers to instruction or remediation presented on a computer. Many educational computer programs are available online and from computer stores and textbook companies. They enhance teacher instruction in several ways.

Computer programs are interactive and can illustrate a concept through attractive animation, sound, and demonstration. They allow students to progress at their own pace and work individually or problem solve in a group. Computers provide immediate feedback, letting students know whether their answer is correct. If the answer is not correct, the programme shows students how to correctly answer the question. Computers offer a different type of activity and a change of pace from teacher-led or group instruction.

Computer-assisted instruction improves instruction for students with disabilities because students receive immediate feedback and do not continue to practice the wrong skills. Computers capture the students' attention because the programs are interactive and engage the students' spirit of competitiveness to increase their scores. Also, computer-assisted instruction moves at the students' pace and usually does not move ahead until they have mastered the skill. Programs provide differentiated lessons to challenge students who are at risk, average, or gifted.

It will be helpful, before discussing the research findings, to offer some definitions of CAI and other kinds of learning activities involving computers. As Kulik, Kulik, and Bangert-Drowns point out in their 1985 research summary, "the terminology in the area is open to dispute". This is putting it mildly. Those seeking to make sense of the array of terms used by educators and researchers—computer-assisted instruction, computer-based education, computer-based instruction, computer-enriched instruction, computermanaged instruction—can easily become confused.

The following definitions are a synthesis of those offered by Bangert-Drowns, et al. (1985), Batey (1987), Grimes (1977), Samson et al. (1986), and Stennett (1985), and represent commonly accepted (though certainly not the only) definitions of these terms:

- Computer-based education (CBE) and computer-based instruction (CBI) are the broadest terms and can refer to virtually any kind of computer use in educational settings, including drill and practice, tutorials, simulations, instructional management, supplementary exercises, programming, database development, writing using word processors, and other applications. These terms may refer either to stand-alone computer learning activities or to computer activities which reinforce material introduced and taught by teachers.
- Computer-assisted instruction (CAI) is a narrower term and most often refers to drill-and-practice, tutorial, or simulation activities offered either by themselves or as supplements to traditional, teacherdirected instruction.
- Computer-managed instruction (CMI) can refer either

to the use of computers by school staff to organize student data and make instructional decisions or to activities in which the computer evaluates students' test performance, guides them to appropriate instructional resources, and keeps records of their progress.

- Computer-enriched instruction (CEI) is defined as learning activities in which computers (1) generate data at the students' request to illustrate relationships in models of social or physical reality, (2) execute programs developed by the students, or (3) provide general enrichment in relatively unstructured exercises designed to stimulate and motivate students.

WHAT DOES CAI LOOK LIKE FOR WRITING?

Computer-Assisted Writing Instruction

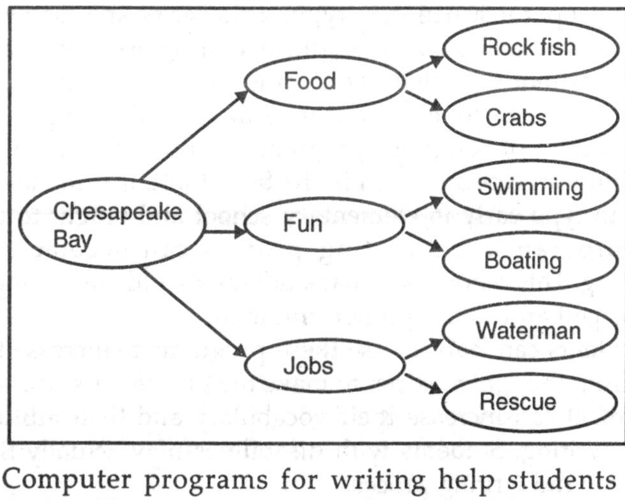

Computer programs for writing help students with developing ideas, organizing, outlining, and brainstorming. Templates provide a framework and reduce the physical effort spent on writing so that students can pay attention to organization and content.

The example at the right, similar to the programme Inspiration, demonstrates how a student has organized her writing. Her topic is the Chesapeake Bay. She thinks about three main ideas for her topic: food, fun, and jobs. Next, she adds supporting details for each of her three main ideas. Now she can compose her paragraph. Programs like Inspiration or Kidspiration are fun because students can use pictures, change the shape or colors of the circles, and change the chart into an outline. Word processors are excellent tools for students who find handwriting tedious.

Often, students with disabilities have difficulty with all the requirements for the writing process. They have trouble organizing their thoughts and then retaining those thoughts long enough to put them on paper. Their handwriting must be neat enough and their spelling and grammar correct enough to convey their message, tasks that they may find difficult.

But before word-processing can save time during the actual writing process, students must know how to type and how to use the computer. Typing speeds may be slower without proper instruction in typing; slower typing may lead to less quality and shorter length in writing assignments. If students cannot type fluently or must search for letters and numbers, the process may be slower than handwriting.

Examples of computer programs that assist students in the writing process are listed in the box at left. If students are taught to type early in elementary school and taught to use these programs, the writing process can become less frustrating. This is not to say that students should not be taught how to spell and to use proper grammar.

Students can learn to use these programs to increase the speed from thought to paper to make the process less stressful for them. It can increase their vocabulary and their attitude toward writing. Students with disabilities may actually find they enjoy the writing process.

HOW IS CAI IMPLEMENTED?

Teachers should review the computer programme or the online activity or game to understand the context of the lessons and determine which ones fit the needs of their students and how they may enhance instruction:

- Can this programme supplements the lesson, give

basic skills practice, or be used as an educational reward for students?

- Is the material presented so that students will remain interested yet not lose valuable instruction time trying to figure out how to operate the programme? Does the programme waste time with too much animation?
- Is the programme at the correct level for the class or the individual student?
- Does this programme do what the teacher wants it to do (help students organize the writing, speed up the writing process, or allow students to hear what they wrote for editing purposes)?

Teachers should also review all Web sites and links immediately before directing students to them. Web addresses and links frequently change and become inactive. Students might become frustrated when links are no longer available.

Writing programs are beneficial to writing instruction because they allow students to learn in a variety of ways and can speed up the writing process. With proper training, students can learn to focus on the message instead of the mechanics.

RESEARCH FINDINGS

The single best-supported finding in the research literature is that the use of CAI as a supplement to traditional, teacher-directed instruction produces achievement effects superior to those obtained with traditional instruction alone. Generally speaking, this finding holds true for students of different ages and abilities and for learning in different curricular areas. As summarized in Stennett's 1985 review of reviews, "well-designed and implemented D&P [drill-andpractice] or tutorial CAI, used as a supplement to traditional instruction, produces an educationally significant improvement in students' final examination achievement".

Some writers also reported on research which compared the effects of CAI alone with those produced by conventional instruction alone. Here, results are too mixed to permit any firm conclusion. Some inquires have found CAI superior, some have found conventional instruction superior, and still others have found no difference between them.

Other researchers and reviewers compared the achievement effects produced by all forms of computerbased instruction (sometimes alone and sometimes as a supplement to traditional instruction) as compared with the effects of traditional instruction alone. While the research support is not as strong as that indicating the superiority of CAI, the evidence nevertheless indicates that CBE approaches as a whole produce higher achievement than traditional instruction by itself.

This group of findings supports the conclusion drawn by Dalton and Hannafin in their 1988 study to the effect that "while both traditional and computer-based delivery systems have valuable roles in supporting instruction, they are of greatest value when complementing one another".

Researchers concerned with student writing outcomes have determined that writing performance is superior when the teaching approach emphasizes "writing as a process," rather than focusing only on the end product- -the finished composition. The writing-as-a-process approach encourages students to engage in prewriting activities, followed by drafting, revising, editing, and final publication, with each step receiving considerable attention and often feedback from teachers or peer editors.

Word processing programs, with their capability to add, delete, and rearrange text, are seen as being far more congruent with the writing process than more laborious pencil-and-paper approaches. And indeed, most research in this area indicates that the use of word processors in writing programs leads to better writing outcomes than the use of paper-and-pencil or conventional typewriters. Specific positive outcomes associated with the use of word processors in writing include:

- Longer written samples.
- Greater variety of word usage.
- More variety of sentence structure.
- More accurate mechanics and spelling.
- More substantial revision.

- Greater responsiveness to teacher and peer feedback.
- Better understanding of the writing process.
- Better attitudes toward writing.
- Freedom from the problem of illegible handwriting.

Researchers are careful to point out that these desirable outcomes are obtained when computers are used as part of a holistic, writing-as-a-process approach. Only using computers for drill and practice on isolated subskills, such as grammar and mechanics, is not associated with improved writing achievement. As expressed by Sommers and Collins in their 1984 article on computers and writing, "microcomputers are counterproductive when used in a theoretical vacuum"

LEARNING RATE

As well as enabling students to achieve at higher levels, researchers have also found that CAI enhances learning rate. Student learning rate is faster with CAI than with conventional instruction. In some research studies, the students learned the same amount of material in less time than the traditionally instructed students; in others, they learned more material in the same time. While most researchers don't specify how much faster CAI students learn, the work of Capper and Copple (1985) led them to the conclusion that CAI users sometimes learn as much as 40 percent faster than those receiving traditional, teacher-directed instruction.

RETENTION OF LEARNING

If students receiving CAI learn better and faster than students receiving conventional instruction alone, do they also retain their learning better? The answer, according to researchers who have conducted comparative studies of learning retention, is yes. In this research, student scores on delayed tests indicate that the retention of content learned using CAI is superior to retention following traditional instruction alone.

ATTITUDES

- Much of the research that examines the effects of CAI

and other microcomputer applications on student learning outcomes also investigates effects upon student attitudes. This line of inquiry has brought most researchers to the conclusion that the use of CAI leads to more positive student attitudes than the use of conventional instruction. This general finding has emerged from studies of the effects of CAI on student attitudes toward:

OTHER BENEFICIAL EFFECTS

The effects of CAI on other student outcomes have not been as extensively researched as CAI's effects on achievement, learning rate, retention, and attitudes. Some researchers have, however, investigated CAI's influence on other variables and found it to confer benefits on:

- Locus of control. We find that CAI students have more of an internal locus of control/sense of self-efficacy than conventionally instructed students.
- Attendance. CAI students had better attendance in Capper and Copple's study.
- Motivation/time-on-task.
- Cooperation/collaboration. Cooperative, prosocial behaviour was greater with CAI in the work of Dickinson.

CAI AND DIFFERENT STUDENT POPULATIONS

Is CAI more effective with some student populations than others? Many researchers have conducted comparative analyses to answer this question and have produced findings in several areas.

Younger versus older students. Most comparative studies have shown that CAI is more beneficial for younger students than for older ones. While research shows CAI to be beneficial to students in general, the degree of impact decreases from the elementary to secondary to postsecondary levels.

Lower-achieving versus higher-achieving students. These comparisons show that CAI is more effective with lower-achieving students than with higher-achieving ones. Again, both lower- and higher-achieving students benefit from CAI. However, the comparatively greater benefits experienced by lower-achieving students, like those experienced by younger students, are largely due to the need these groups have for elements common to the majority of CAI programs—extensive drill and practice, privacy, and immediate feedback and reinforcement.

Economically disadvantaged versus higher-SES students. Researchers note that CAI confers greater benefits on economically disadvantaged students than those from more privileged backgrounds. Lower SES students, too, benefit greatly from opportunities to interact privately with CAI drill-and-practice and tutorial programs.

Lower- versus higher-cognitive outcomes. Closely related to the above is the finding that CAI is more effective for teaching lower-cognitive material than higher-cognitive material. This research makes essentially the same point—that CAI is particularly effective for reinforcing the basic, fact-oriented learning most often engaged in by younger, lowerachieving, and/or lower SES students.

Handicapped learners. Research conducted with learning disabled, mentally retarded, hearing impaired, emotionally disturbed, and language disordered students indicates that their achievement levels are greater with CAI than with conventional instruction alone. In some of this research, handicapped CAI students even outperformed conventionally taught, nonhandicapped students.

Males versus females. This comparison was not addressed by enough researchers to draw firm conclusions. The 1988 meta-analysis of 82 studies of CBE conducted by Roblyer, et al. concluded that effect differences slightly favour boys over girls, with differences falling short of statistical significance.

CAI AND DIFFERENT CURRICULAR AREAS

A few researchers undertook to compare the effectiveness of CAI in different curricular areas. Their findings, though not conclusive, indicate that CAI activities are most effective in the areas of science and foreign languages, followed, in descending order of effectiveness, by activities in mathematics, reading, language arts, and English as a Second Language, with CAI activities in ESL found to be largely ineffective.

STUDENTS LIKE CAI

An earlier section of this report offers research evidence showing that CAI enhances student attitudes toward several aspects of schooling. Some researchers took these investigations a step further by asking students what it is about CAI that they like. The following is a list of reasons given by students for liking CAI activities and/or favoring them over traditional learning. These student preferences also contribute to our understanding of why CAI enhances achievement.

Students say they like working with computers because computers:

- Are infinitely patient.
- Never get tired.
- Never get frustrated or angry.
- Allow students to work privately.
- Never forget to correct or praise.
- Are fun and entertaining.
- Individualize learning.
- Are self-paced.
- Do not embarrass students who make mistakes.
- Make it possible to experiment with different options.
- Give immediate feedback.
- Are more objective than teachers.
- Free teachers for more meaningful contact with students.
- Are impartial to race or ethnicity.
- Are great motivators.
- Give a sense of control over learning.
- Are excellent for drill and practice.
- Call for using sight, hearing, and touch.
- Teach in small increments.
- Help students improve their spelling.
- Build proficiency in computer use, which will be valuable later in life.

- Eliminate the drudgery of doing certain learning activities by hand (e.g., drawing graphs).
- Work rapidly—closer to the rate of human thought.

Many of these items point to students' appreciation of the immediate, objective, and positive feedback provided by computer learning activities by comparison with teacher-directed activities. As Robertson, et al. (1987) point out:

"This reduction in negative reinforcement allows the student to learn through trial and error at his or her own pace. Therefore, positive attitudes can be protected and enhanced".

COST-EFFECTIVENESS

While cost considerations are not a major focus of this report, it is worth noting that some of the research on effectiveness also addressed the cost-effectiveness of CAI and other computer applications. Ragosta, Holland, and Jamison (1982) concluded that equal amounts of time of CAI reinforcement and the more-expensive one-to-one tutoring produced equal achievement effects.

Niemiec, Sikorski, and Walberg (1989) also found CAI activities significantly more cost-effective than tutoring and suggested that computers be used more extensively in schools. And in their 1986 study of costs, effects, and utility of CAI, Hawley, Fletcher, and Piele noted that the cost differences between CAI and traditional instruction were insignificant and concluded that "the microcomputer-assisted instruction was the costeffective alternative of choice" for both grades addressed in the study.

MULTIMEDIA PRESENTATION

OVERVIEW

Multimedia presentations provide you an ideal platform to stand out from clutter. Your clients and prospects are bombarded everyday by messages and advertising through print and other traditional media.

Burgeoning competition and the accompanying clamour to get noticed, have necessitated a form of communication that can present exhaustive information in an interactive and engaging way. Interactive CD-ROM based multimedia corporate presentations, CBTs, new product launch info CDs and multimedia CD catalogs can give you the edge that can help attain higher recall and recognition from your prospects. Not yet convinced?

We can help you convert your:

- Print catalog.
- Web site.
- Your product photographs.
- Your company profile into a CD.

We can create stunning cd presentation design and engaging cd catalog designs - designs that are sure to generae your clients' interest in your products. We can either place your data in static or in a dynamic manner onto a CD. You get a master CD-ROM or a digital card, which is basically an electronic business card, shaped CD-ROM, also called a CD card. Your presentation or cd catalogue is written onto this cd. It also has an auto-run file and a cdicon customised for you. You could replicate as and when you need more copies. You will be surprised to find out how cheap it works out in comparison to print catalogues and how easy it is to make changes.

If you already have a website we can put it on a CD, design a website intro and make it auto-run and launch your website after the intro is over. Such a cd presentation design would cost as little as Rs. 5000/- or USD 120/-.

If you want to know more about how a cd presentation can help your business or just want more info on our CD presentation/ cd catalogue designing process, click here. To get a quote, mail us your requirements.

If you are looking for a company that can provide your organization with a multimedia presentation, which can enable you to put across your services/products to customers or clients in the best possible manner, then get in touch with us today! We develop multimedia presentation on CD ROMs in the best medium to combine sight, sound, motion, and emotion to motivate consumer or business action. It positively stimulates and expedites the buying decision. It has been observed that an interactive multimedia presentation can lay a very deep impact on your target audience's mind and can help you do business well. Our experts can create a multimedia presentation for your company that you would surely find most appealing and very useful indeed.

It has been seen that 90% of all computers have CD- ROM capabilities. If this is the case, then why not get a multimedia presentation created by experts like us. We design a presentation well aligned with the nature of your business or services. We design multimedia presentation, which can easily capture the attention of your key audience. CD ROM presentations are the ideal platform to help you stand out from the rest. Effective CD ROM presentations can give you an edge that can help achieve higher recall and recognition from your prospects.

Allow our experts to create a multimedia presentation to go hand in hand with your marketing strategies. Information as depicted on the multimedia presentation we create is sure to drive positive results. We have the ability to create stunning presentations which is sure to arouse an interest in your customer's mind regarding your products or services.

We have the expertise to convert your website, product catalogue, company profile into a well structured presentation onto a CD ROM. We can also design multimedia presentation for new product launches, learning solutions, orientation programs and magazine or periodicals. ISHIR Digital has the expertise to create presentations in a highly professional, specialized and adept manner. We focus on an intelligent combination of sound, videos and stills. We can take care of your requirements and bring about a creative multimedia design to suffice your business needs.

DEFINITION

Multimedia presentation is a way of conveying information using interactive mode of media like text, audio, animation, video, graphics, etc. It is an effective way to capture the interest of viewers besides furnishing them with essentials of your presentation. Multimedia presentations are so enticing that they leave a lasting impression on the viewers.

Binarysoft is committed to deliver high-end Multimedia solutions at fair cost. We create presentations keeping in mind the fact that marketing is an important investment for you. We work in tight collaboration with your suggestions, your style, your content and your budget. Our products have a right mixture of technical knick-knacks in terms of programming skills, graphics, layouts, animations and script, etc. that seize the interest of the viewers.

TYPES OF MULTIMEDIA PRESENTATION

Depending on your requirements, we create following types of multimedia presentations:

- *Linear Presentations:* If your requirement is to play an intro of your company on website or display non-stop information about your products and services; then linear presentation is an optimum solution for you. These presentations do not require anyone to control its workings and are displayed with minimum user interactions.
- *Non-Linear Presentations:* If you have to give lecture in a seminar; or present your company's profile to large number of audience; or informing clients about your products and services. Then your presentation should be controlled by the speaker. In this case Non-Linear presentation is what you should opt for. These presentations are managed by the orator. It also enables you to shuffle through the pages as per the requirements.

Over the years, we follow a preset methodology to ensure that each web/multimedia project flows smoothly. Binarysoft's working process comprise of 3-phases:

- *Planning:* Our clients come to us with a vision of what they need to build. This vision is then translated into a user-centered information architect and project plan. The project plan includes all the specifications like target audience, time-frame of the presentation, the need for presentation, place where it is going to be presented, budget and many more. This initial information helps us to plan-out the development of your presentation.

- *Preparing:* Developing process initiates with outlining the specifications. We take care of all ins and outs of the project that includes audio-visual aids, animations, content, colors, fonts, graphics and the likes. We welcome any number of amendments and alterations from client's side to ensure that *we are building a product that meets the project goal.*

Delivering: The last phase is to deliver you the final product with specifications and the on specified time. But it doesn't end our development-cycle. We aim at complete customer satisfaction.

WEBSITES

INTRODUCTION

Websites as we generally know is a web portal which stores information that can be read by anyone who has *Internet access*.

Those were the basic laws of a website during the advent of the Internet. Gradually it become a source of *communication, entertainment and platform* for many people to establish their interest to become what we call as Internet-celebrities. Well they did not act in any movies or released an album like the Hollywood celebs. They just created websites which appealed to the mass. And those were not an instant hit. But soon they became the pioneers in the field of Internet.

You might have heard people saying this on the WWW. That the dot com boom is over and out. And the people who chose to ride by the train are long gone ahead of you. Well, I would agree to that for the fact that Internet is not like what it used to be 10 years back. But comeon, nothing is too late. Unless you are just too lazy, out of ideas or just don't know where to put your feet on.

Website are also called as collection of interlinked web

pages with a related topic, usually under a single domain name, which includes an intended starting file called a "home page". From the home page, you can get to all the other pages on the website. Also called a "web presence".

DEFINITION

A website or web site (often shortened to a site) is a collection of web pages, that is, documents accessible via the World Wide Web on the Internet. The pages of a website will be accessed from a common root URL, the homepage, and usually reside on the same physical server. The URLs of the pages organize them into a hierarchy, although the hyperlinks between them control how the reader perceives the overall structure.

A website will often be the work of one person, one organization, or on a particular topic, or have a particular purpose. This is quite a blurry definition, given the hypertext nature of the web: the whole of Wikipedia forms a website, but whether the Meta-Wikipedia pages are part of the same website or a sister website is open to debate.

Web sites are written in HTML (Hyper Text Markup Language) and are accessed using special software called web browsers. Plugins are available for browsers which allow them to show active content, such as Flash, Shockwave or applets written in Java. Some interactive content may also be generated with JavaScript, support for which is built-in for most browsers. An emerging standard called Dynamic HTML is starting to make an appearance, though no standard has been formally adopted yet.

TYPES OF WEBSITES

There are numerous types of websites, each specializing in a particualr service or use. A few types of websites include:

Business site: Used for promoting a business or service

Commerce site or eCommerce sites: for purchasing goods, such as Amazon.com

Download site: Strictly used for downloading electronic content, such as software, game demos or computer wallpaper

Information site: contains content that is intended merely to inform visitors, but not necessarily for commercial purposes; such as: RateMyProfessors.com

Shock site: Includes images or other material that is intended to be offensive to most viewers

Vanity site: Run by an individual or a small group (such as a family) that contains information or any content that the individual wishes to include

Many websites are a mixture of types.

For example, a business web site may promote the business's products, but may also host informative documents, such as white papers. There are also numerous sub-categories to the ones listed above. For example, a porn site is a specific type of eCommerce site or business site (that is, it is trying to sell memberships for access to its site). A fan site may be a vanity site on which the administrator is paying homage to a celebrity.

Many business websites, have all the appearance of brochures—that is an advertisement that can be strolled around. Some websites act as vehicles to communicate with other people: Webchat.

The content of a website is constrained by the hosting computer's power, and also legally, e.g. by copyright, pornography laws, etc.

INTERNET

OVERVIEW

Believe it or not, the Internet was created way back in 1969, during the Cold War, by the United States military. It was meant to be a "nuke-proof" communications network. Today, the Internet spreads across the globe and consists of countless networks and computers, allowing millions of people to share information. Data that travels long distances on the Internet is transferred on huge lines known collectively as the Internet backbone. The Internet is now maintained by the major Internet service providers such as MCI Worldcom, Sprint, GTE, ANS, and UUNET. Because these providers make huge amounts of revenue off the Internet, they are motivated to maintain consistent and fast connections which benefits everyday Internet users like you and me.

Many people think the Internet and the World Wide Web are the same thing. They're not! The World Wide Web is what you are browsing right now. It is one of the many features of the Internet. E-mail, FTP, and Instant Messaging are also features of the Internet.

HISTORY OF INTERNET

Some thirty years ago, the RAND Corporation, America's foremost Cold War think-tank, faced a strange strategic problem. How could the US authorities successfully communicate after a nuclear war?

Postnuclear America would need a command-and-control network, linked from city to city, state to state, base to base. But no matter how thoroughly that network was armored or protected, its switches and wiring would always be vulnerable to the impact of atomic bombs. A nuclear attack would reduce any conceivable network to tatters.

And how would the network itself be commanded and controlled? Any central authority, any network central citadel, would be an obvious and immediate target for an enemy missile. The centre of the network would be the very first place to go. RAND mulled over this grim puzzle in deep military secrecy, and arrived at a daring solution. The RAND proposal (the brainchild of RAND staffer Paul Baran) was made public in 1964. In the first place, the network would *have no central authority.* Furthermore, it would be *designed from the beginning to operate while in tatters.*

The principles were simple. The network itself would be assumed to be unreliable at all times. It would be designed from the get-go to transcend its own unreliability. All the nodes in the network would be equal in status to all other nodes, each node with its own authority to originate, pass, and receive messages. The messages themselves would be divided into packets, each packet separately addressed. Each packet would begin at some specified source node, and end at some other specified destination node. Each packet would wind its way through the network on an individual basis.

The particular route that the packet took would be unimportant. Only final results would count. Basically, the packet would be tossed like a hot potato from node to node to node, more or less in the direction of its destination, until it ended up in the proper place. If big pieces of the network had been blown away, that simply wouldn't matter; the packets would still stay airborne, lateralled wildly across the field by whatever nodes happened to survive. This rather haphazard delivery system might be "inefficient" in the usual sense (especially compared to, say, the telephone system) — but it would be extremely rugged.

During the 60s, this intriguing concept of a decentralized, blastproof, packet-switching network was kicked around by RAND, MIT and UCLA. The National Physical Laboratory in Great Britain set up the first test network on these principles in 1968. Shortly afterward, the Pentagon's Advanced Research Projects Agency decided to fund a larger, more ambitious project in the USA. The nodes of the network were to be high-speed supercomputers (or what passed for supercomputers at the time). These were rare and valuable machines which were in real need of good solid networking, for the sake of national research-and-development projects.

In fall 1969, the first such node was installed in UCLA. By December 1969, there were four nodes on the infant network, which was named ARPANET, after its Pentagon sponsor. The four computers could transfer data on dedicated high-speed transmission lines. They could even be programmed remotely from the other nodes. Thanks to ARPANET, scientists and researchers could share one another's computer facilities by long-distance. This was a very handy service, for computer-time was precious in the early '70s. In 1971 there were fifteen nodes in ARPANET; by 1972, thirty-seven nodes. And it was good.

By the second year of operation, however, an odd fact became clear. ARPANET's users had warped the computer-sharing network into a dedicated, high-speed, federally subsidized electronic post- office. The main traffic on ARPANET was not long-distance computing. Instead, it was news and personal messages. Researchers were using ARPANET to collaborate on projects, to trade notes on work, and eventually, to downright gossip and schmooze. People had their own personal user accounts on the ARPANET computers, and their own personal addresses for electronic mail. Not only were they using ARPANET for person-to-person communication, but they were very enthusiastic about this particular service — far more enthusiastic than they were about long-distance computation.

It wasn't long before the invention of the mailing-list, an ARPANET broadcasting technique in which an identical message could be sent automatically to large numbers of network subscribers. Interestingly, one of the first really big mailing-lists was "SF- LOVERS," for science fiction fans. Discussing science fiction on the network was not work-related and was frowned upon by many ARPANET computer administrators, but this didn't stop it from happening.

Throughout the '70s, ARPA's network grew. Its decentralized structure made expansion easy. Unlike standard corporate computer networks, the ARPA network could accommodate many different kinds of machine. As long as individual machines could speak the packet-switching lingua franca of the new, anarchic network, their brand-names, and their content, and even their ownership, were irrelevant.

The ARPA's original standard for communication was known as NCP, "Network Control Protocol," but as time passed and the technique advanced, NCP was superceded by a higher-level, more sophisticated standard known as TCP/IP. TCP, or "Transmission Control Protocol," converts messages into streams of packets at the source, then reassembles them back into messages at the destination.

IP, or "Internet Protocol," handles the addressing, seeing to it that packets are routed across multiple nodes and even across multiple networks with multiple standards — not only ARPA's pioneering NCP standard, but others like Ethernet, FDDI, and X.25.

As early as 1977, TCP/IP was being used by other networks to link to ARPANET. ARPANET itself remained fairly tightly controlled, at least until 1983, when its military segment broke off and became MILNET. But TCP/IP linked them all. And ARPANET itself, though it was growing, became a smaller and smaller neighborhood amid the vastly growing galaxy of other linked machines.

As the '70s and '80s advanced, many very different social groups found themselves in possession of powerful computers. It was fairly easy to link these computers to the growing network-of- networks. As the use of TCP/IP became more common, entire other networks fell into the digital embrace of the Internet, and messily adhered. Since the software called TCP/IP was public-domain, and the basic technology was decentralized and rather anarchic by its very nature, it was difficult to stop people from barging in and linking up somewhere-or-other. In point of fact, nobody *wanted* to stop them from joining this branching complex of networks, which came to be known as the "Internet."

Connecting to the Internet cost the taxpayer little or nothing, since each node was independent, and had to handle its own financing and its own technical requirements. The more, the merrier. Like the phone network, the computer network became steadily more valuable as it embraced larger and larger territories of people and resources.

A fax machine is only valuable if *everybody else* has a fax machine. Until they do, a fax machine is just a curiosity. ARPANET, too, was a curiosity for a while. Then computer-networking became an utter necessity.

In 1984 the National Science Foundation got into the act, through its Office of Advanced Scientific Computing. The new NSFNET set a blistering pace for technical advancement, linking newer, faster, shinier supercomputers, through thicker, faster links, upgraded and expanded, again and again, in 1986, 1988, 1990. And other government agencies leapt in: NASA, the National Institutes of Health, the Department of Energy, each of them maintaining a digital satrapy in the Internet confederation.

The nodes in this growing network-of-networks were divvied up into basic varieties. Foreign computers, and a few American ones, chose to be denoted by their geographical locations. The others were grouped by the six basic Internet "domains": gov, mil, edu, com, org and net. (Graceless abbreviations such as this are a standard feature of the TCP/IP protocols.) Gov, Mil, and Edu denoted governmental, military and educational institutions, which were, of course, the pioneers, since ARPANET had begun as a high-tech research exercise in national security.

Com, however, stood for "commercial" institutions, which were soon bursting into the network like rodeo bulls, surrounded by a dust-cloud of eager nonprofit "orgs." (The "net" computers served as gateways between networks.)

ARPANET itself formally expired in 1989, a happy victim of its own overwhelming success. Its users scarcely noticed, for ARPANET's functions not only continued but steadily improved. The use of TCP/IP standards for computer networking is now global. In 1971, a mere twenty-one years ago, there were only four nodes in the ARPANET network. Today there are tens of thousands of nodes in the Internet, scattered over forty-two countries, with more coming on-line every day. Three million, possibly four million people use this gigantic mother-of-all-computer-networks.

The Internet is especially popular among scientists, and is probably the most important scientific instrument of the late twentieth century. The powerful, sophisticated access that it provides to specialized data and personal communication has sped up the pace of scientific research enormously.

The Internet's pace of growth in the early 1990s is spectacular, almost ferocious. It is spreading faster than cellular phones, faster than fax machines. Last year the Internet was growing at a rate of twenty percent a *month.* The number of "host" machines with direct connection to TCP/IP has been doubling every year since 1988. The Internet is moving out of its original base in military and research institutions, into elementary and high schools, as well as into public libraries and the commercial sector.

Why do people want to be "on the Internet?" One of the main reasons is simple freedom. The Internet is a rare example of a true, modern, functional anarchy. There is no "Internet Inc." There are no official censors, no bosses, no board of directors, no stockholders. In principle, any node can speak as a peer to any other node, as long as it obeys the rules of the TCP/IP protocols, which are strictly technical, not social or political. (There has been some struggle over commercial use of the Internet, but that situation is changing as businesses supply their own links).

The Internet is also a bargain. The Internet as a whole, unlike the phone system, doesn't charge for long-distance service. And unlike most commercial computer networks, it doesn't charge for access time, either. In fact the "Internet" itself, which doesn't even officially exist as an entity, never "charges" for anything. Each group of people accessing the Internet is responsible for their own machine and their own section of line.

The Internet's "anarchy" may seem strange or even unnatural, but it makes a certain deep and basic sense. It's rather like the "anarchy" of the English language. Nobody rents English, and nobody owns English. As an English-speaking person, it's up to you to learn how to speak English properly and make whatever use you please of it (though the government provides certain subsidies to help you learn to read and write a bit).

Otherwise, everybody just sort of pitches in, and somehow the thing evolves on its own, and somehow turns out workable. And interesting. Fascinating, even. Though a lot of people earn their living from using and exploiting and teaching English, "English" as an institution is public property, a public good. Much the same goes for the Internet.

Would English be improved if the "The English Language, Inc." had a board of directors and a chief executive officer, or a President and a Congress? There'd probably be a lot fewer new words in English, and a lot fewer new ideas.

People on the Internet feel much the same way about their own institution. It's an institution that resists institutionalization. The Internet belongs to everyone and no one. Still, its various interest groups all have a claim. Business people want the Internet put on a sounder financial footing. Government people want the Internet more fully regulated. Academics want it dedicated exclusively to scholarly research. Military people want it spy-proof and secure. And so on and so on.

All these sources of conflict remain in a stumbling balance today, and the Internet, so far, remains in a thrivingly anarchical condition. Once upon a time, the NSFnet's high-speed, high-capacity lines were known as the "Internet Backbone," and their owners could rather lord it over the rest of the Internet; but today there are "backbones" in Canada, Japan, and Europe, and even privately owned commercial Internet backbones specially created for carrying business traffic. Today, even privately owned desktop computers can become Internet nodes. You can carry one under your arm. Soon, perhaps, on your wrist.

But what does one *do* with the Internet? Four things, basically: mail, discussion groups, long-distance computing, and file transfers.

Internet mail is "e-mail," electronic mail, faster by several orders of magnitude than the US Mail, which is scornfully known by Internet regulars as "snailmail." Internet mail is somewhat like fax. It's electronic text. But you don't have to pay for it (at least not directly), and it's global in scope. E-mail can also send software and certain forms of compressed digital imagery. New forms of mail are in the works.

The discussion groups, or "newsgroups," are a world of their own. This world of news, debate and argument is generally known as "USENET. " USENET is, in point of fact, quite different from the Internet. USENET is rather like an enormous billowing crowd of gossipy, news-hungry people, wandering in and through the Internet on their way to various private backyard barbecues. USENET is not so much a physical network as a set of social conventions. In any case, at the moment there are some 2,500 separate newsgroups on USENET, and their discussions generate about 7 million words of typed commentary every single day. Naturally there is a vast amount of talk about computers on USENET, but the variety of subjects discussed is enormous, and it's growing larger all the time. USENET also distributes various free electronic journals and publications.

Both netnews and e-mail are very widely available, even outside the high-speed core of the Internet itself. News and e-mail are easily available over common phone-lines, from Internet fringe- realms like BITnet, UUCP and Fidonet. The last two Internet services, long-distance computing and file transfer, require what is known as "direct Internet access" – using TCP/IP.

Long-distance computing was an original inspiration for ARPANET and is still a very useful service, at least for some. Programmers can maintain accounts on distant, powerful computers, run programs there or write their own. Scientists can make use of powerful supercomputers a continent away. Libraries offer their electronic card catalogs for free search. Enormous CD-ROM catalogs are increasingly available through this service. And there are fantastic amounts of free software available.

File transfers allow Internet users to access remote machines and retrieve programs or text. Many Internet computers – some two thousand of them, so far – allow any person to access them anonymously, and to simply copy their public files, free of charge.

This is no small deal, since entire books can be transferred through direct Internet access in a matter of minutes. Today, in 1992, there are over a million such public files available to anyone who asks for them (and many more millions of files are available to people with accounts).

Internet file-transfers are becoming a new form of publishing, in which the reader simply electronically copies the work on demand, in any quantity he or she wants, for free. New Internet programs, such as "archie," "gopher," and "WAIS," have been developed to catalog and explore these enormous archives of material.

The headless, anarchic, million-limbed Internet is spreading like bread-mold. Any computer of sufficient power is a potential spore for the Internet, and today such computers sell for less than $2,000 and are in the hands of people all over the world.

ARPA's network, designed to assure control of a ravaged society after a nuclear holocaust, has been superceded by its mutant child the Internet, which is thoroughly out of control, and spreading exponentially through the post-Cold War electronic global village. The spread of the Internet in the 90s resembles the spread of personal computing in the 1970s, though it is even faster and perhaps more important. More important, perhaps, because it may give those personal computers a means of cheap, easy storage and access that is truly planetary in scale.

The future of the Internet bids fair to be bigger and exponentially faster. Commercialization of the Internet is a very hot topic today, with every manner of wild new commercial information- service promised. The federal government, pleased with an unsought success, is also still very much in the act.

NREN, the National Research and Education Network, was approved by the US Congress in fall 1991, as a five-year, $2 billion project to upgrade the Internet "backbone." NREN will be some fifty times faster than the fastest network available today, allowing the electronic transfer of the entire Encyclopedia Britannica in one hot second.

Computer networks worldwide will feature 3-D animated graphics, radio and cellular phone-links to portable computers, as well as fax, voice, and high- definition television. A multimedia global circus!

Or so it's hoped — and planned. The real Internet of the future may bear very little resemblance to today's plans. Planning has never seemed to have much to do with the seething, fungal development of the Internet. After all, today's Internet bears little resemblance to those original grim plans for RAND's post- holocaust command grid. It's a fine and happy irony.

How does one get access to the Internet? Well — if you don't have a computer and a modem, get one. Your computer can act as a terminal, and you can use an ordinary telephone line to connect to an Internet-linked machine.

These slower and simpler adjuncts to the Internet can provide you with the netnews discussion groups and your own e-mail address. These are services worth having — though if you only have mail and news, you're not actually "on the Internet" proper.

If you're on a campus, your university may have direct "dedicated access" to high-speed Internet TCP/IP lines. Apply for an Internet account on a dedicated campus machine, and you may be able to get those hot-dog long-distance computing and file-transfer functions. Some cities, such as Cleveland, supply "freenet" community access. Businesses increasingly have Internet access, and are willing to sell it to subscribers. The standard fee is about $40 a month — about the same as TV cable service.

As the Nineties proceed, finding a link to the Internet will become much cheaper and easier. Its ease of use will also improve, which is fine news, for the savage UNIX interface of TCP/IP leaves plenty of room for advancements in user-friendliness. Learning the Internet now, or at least learning about it, is wise. By the turn of the century, "network literacy," like "computer literacy" before it, will be forcing itself into the very texture of your life.

ADVANTAGES OF INTERNET

Communication

The foremost target of internet has always been the communication. And internet has excelled beyond the expectations .Still; innovations are going on to make it faster, more reliable. By the advent of computer's Internet, our earth has reduced and has attained the form of a global village.

Now we can communicate in a fraction of second with a person who is sitting in the other part of the world. Today for better communication, we can avail the facilities of e-mail; we can chat for hours with our loved ones. There are plenty messenger services in offering. With help of such services, it has become very easy to establish a kind of global friendship where you can share your thoughts, can explore other cultures of different ethnicity.

Information

Information is probably the biggest advantage internet is offering. The Internet is a virtual treasure trove of information. Any kind of information on any topic under the sun is available on the Internet. The search engines like Google, yahoo is at your service on the Internet.

You can almost find any type of data on almost any kind of subject that you are looking for. There is a huge amount of information available on the internet for just about every subject known to man, ranging from government law and services, trade fairs and conferences, market information, new ideas and technical support, the list is end less.

Students and children are among the top users who surf the Internet for research. Today, it is almost required that students should use the Internet for research for the purpose of gathering resources. Teachers have started giving assignments that require research on the Internet.

Almost every coming day, researches on medical issues become much easier to locate. Numerous web sites available on the net are offering loads of information for people to research diseases and talk to doctors online at sites such as, America's Doctor. During 1998 over 20 million people reported going online to retrieve health information.

Entertainment

Entertainment is another popular raison d'être why many people prefer to surf the Internet. In fact, media of internet has become quite successful in trapping multifaceted entertainment factor.

Downloading games, visiting chat rooms or just surfing the Web are some of the uses people have discovered. There are numerous games that may be downloaded from the Internet for free.

The industry of online gaming has tasted dramatic and

phenomenal attention by game lovers. Chat rooms are popular because users can meet new and interesting people. In fact, the Internet has been successfully used by people to find life long partners. When people surf the Web, there are numerous things that can be found. Music, hobbies, news and more can be found and shared on the Internet.

Services

Many services are now provided on the internet such as online banking, job seeking, purchasing tickets for your favourite movies, guidance services on array of topics engulfing the every aspect of life, and hotel reservations. Often these services are not available off-line and can cost you more.

E-Commerce

Ecommerce is the concept used for any type of commercial maneuvering, or business deals that involves the transfer of information across the globe via Internet. It has become a phenomenon associated with any kind of shopping, almost anything. You name it and Ecommerce with its giant tentacles engulfing every single product and service will make you available at your door steps. It has got a real amazing and wide range of products from household needs, technology to entertainment.

DISADVANTAGES

Theft of Personal Information

If you use the Internet, you may be facing grave danger as your personal information such as name, address, credit card number etc. can be accessed by other culprits to make your problems worse.

Spamming

Spamming refers to sending unwanted e-mails in bulk, which provide no purpose and needlessly obstruct the entire system. Such illegal activities can be very frustrating for you, and so instead of just ignoring it, you should make an effort to try and stop these activities so that using the Internet can become that much safer.

Virus Threat

Virus is nothing but a programme which disrupts the normal functioning of your computer systems. Computers attached to internet are more prone to virus attacks and they can end up into crashing your whole hard disk, causing you considerable headache.

Pornography

This is perhaps the biggest threat related to your children's healthy mental life. A very serious issue concerning the Internet. There are thousands of pornographic sites on the Internet that can be easily found and can be a detrimental factor to letting children use the Internet.

Though, internet can also create havoc, destruction and its misuse can be very fatal, the advantages of it outweigh its disadvantages.

Unit IX

Professional Growth

OVERVIEW OF PROFESSIONAL GROWTH

How does educational change occur for staff in the early childhood field when the curriculum content is not centrally mandated and the people involved have varying employer and work contexts? To explore that question, this paper reviews the early childhood professional development literature and proposes alternative perspectives that recognize staff as empowered learners who build their working knowledge through spirals of engagement over time.

The issues raised by different perspectives are illustrated by a study that relates to the nature of curriculum decision-making in settings for children ages 0-5 years in the Sydney region of New South Wales, Australia. The research has provided an impetus for rethinking early childhood professional development. Insights gained from involvement in the study reinforce the importance of recognizing the complexity of personal professional growth, particularly in the context of philosophical and pedagogical challenges from a rapidly changing field.

The current Australian sociopolitical context has tended to create an early childhood field in which staff feels underpaid and demoralized. It is therefore surprising to find—at the same time—a climate of intellectual inquisitiveness generating engagement with the complexities of reconceptualizing teachers' work. Dissatisfaction with current practices has provoked a wave of interest in alternative approaches to teacher planning that transcend the technicalities of simple record keeping. This practitioner energy inspired the researchers to participate in the dialogue about planning with practitioners in the field while investigating the context of professional growth.

LINEAR PERSPECTIVES

Spodek (1996) notes that the term "professional development" is ambiguous (p. 115). In an attempt to confront this ambiguity, it is valuable to review several dominant models of early childhood professional development. Several authors are key reference points.

These include Katz (1977), VanderVen (1988, 1990), and the National Association for the Education of Young Children (NAEYC, 1994), each with a slightly different perspective. Katz (1977) described teachers in terms of their predominant concerns, in sequential order from self through to the profession at large. This *concerns-based model* of teacher development described teachers in terms of four stages from survival to maturity.

Rather than using individual concerns as the frame of reference, NAEYC (1994) focused on *qualifications* as a key discriminator. It proposed six levels of professional development from that of people starting competency-based or degree-oriented training through to the achievement of doctoral-level qualifications. NAEYC (1994) also offered nine principles of effective professional development.

In 1988, VanderVen described a five-stage *developmental sequence* towards professionalism (from novice to influential). She argued that the "development of professionalism is related to practitioner ability to assume the roles necessary to deliver the various functions of the field". This conceptualization focused on the differentiation of roles and the amount of supervision required for effective practice, while proposing a sequential model of the development of "professionalism."

Spodek (1996) described VanderVen's stages of professional development as "ecologically based," building on Bronfenbrenner's conception of systems (e.g., orientation to the micro or the macro). VanderVen (1990) later proposed sets of adjectives that describe different responsibilities of staff on a three-stage career development track. The definition of "professionalism" vis-à-vis "professional development" is, at this point, problematic.

CHALLENGING THE LINEAR PERSPECTIVE

The conceptualizations in VanderVen's papers (1988, 1990) seem to be framed by (and perhaps limited by) the American experience. "Professional development" carries different meanings in different circumstances. American early childhood settings have strikingly different cultural and contextual frames of reference than do those in Australia.

For example, while it is easy to agree that "there are many gaps and discontinuities in the development of professionalism vis-à-vis today's workforce in early childhood education" , it is more difficult to agree with the subsequent claim that "this is particularly apparent for the large novice-stage group, whose members provide a great amount of direct service, but whose potential for professional growth is in many instances modest" (p. 157). This statement seems a damning indictment of human potential, but it may be relevant for the context in which it was written.

Across the centers involved in the research reported later in this paper, there are staff members with minimal "professional preparation" or qualifications who, nevertheless, demonstrate insight and commitment to engage in ideas that are synonymous with professional growth. This situation is not a claim that the networked, informal professional involvement described in this study should replace or be equated with more formal study to gain qualifications. There is, however, an argument that a linear conception of professional development that equates with such study and qualifications is overly simplistic.

Saracho and Spodek (1993) analyzed and reviewed literature in the field of early childhood teacher professional development. While proposing suggestions for improvement in the existing conceptualizations, they did not offer a critique of the assumptions underlying the dominant "stages" conceptions. VanderVen (1994) analyzed and redefined the early childhood profession as contextual rather than linear. Nevertheless, the concept of professional development that she advocated still has a focus on the "transfer of knowledge and skills"rather than having a priority on socially constructed knowledge.

Rodd (1997) took on this challenge and argued:

Some current approaches to professional development, such as those of Katz (1977) and VanderVen (1990), appear to take a Piagetian perspective, arguing that early childhood professionals need to develop in order to learn. Yet it could be argued that continued improvement in the quality of early childhood service provision appears to be more related to the Vygotskian (1962) perspective, where early childhood professionals.are supported by their colleagues, to learn in order to develop.

Piagetian conceptions suggest individuals in isolation moving along a qualification track, assuming a logical sequence of steps that require the transmission of skills to "develop." These seem to underestimate the complexity of possible processes and variation in individual experience. There are, however, other frames of reference that provide alternative perspectives to the concept of professional development.

CLASSROOM CLIMATE

OVERVIEW

Classroom climate should not be confused with classroom culture or conditions.

Certain classroom climate are needed to enhance teaching and learning and could also enhance a positive classroom culture and climate, e.g.:

- Authentic relationships, based on quality, openness and consistency which influence existing relationships in class.
- Rules and boundaries, set by the educator, which inform learners what is expected of them in class.

- Planning, resources and preparation, which include planning for a diverse group of learners, access to Learning and Teaching Support Material and the ability to use Learning And Teaching Support Material creatively in a variety of ways.
- Educator repertoire, the variety of teaching styles and models the educator feels comfortable with and can apply in class in different contexts, with diverse learners to achieve the outcomes as stated in the Revised National Curriculum Statement.
- Pedagogic partnerships, meaning the educator's ability to forge professional relationships with colleagues in order to better their own teaching practice.
- Reflection on teaching, which points to the ability of the educator to reflect on own practice and to try out new styles and models recommended by other educators.

It is evident from the previous paragraphs that a positive classroom culture and climate could play a positive role in building a productive classroom. A positive classroom culture and climate conducive to an effective learning classroom requires however, classroom management practices to direct and manage the development of a productive classroom.

Classroom management is at the heart of the educator's work. The educator must be able to organize and manage learners in a confined space in order to enable learners to feel safe and concentrate on tasks.

Moyles describes classroom management as:"what teachers do once they have considered their organization in order to ensure both the smooth running of the learning environment and fulfillment of intentions."

According to Kruger & Schalkwyk classroom management includes all the activities needed for the main task, namely teaching and learning, to happen effectively. It deals with management of tasks as well as people. Effective classroom management helps to establish and maintain conditions in the classroom which enhances effective teaching and learning. To succeed at this an educator will need good skills in long-term planning as well as short-term planning.

CLASSROOM INTERACTION ANALYSIS

OVERVIEW

Interaction between teacher and students is an essential part of teaching learning process. An educationist, Flanders originally developed an instrument called Flanders Interaction Analysis. FIA system was designed to categorize the types and quantity of verbal interaction in the classroom and to plot the information on a matrix so that it could be analyzed and interpreted. The results gave a picture as to who was talking in the classroom, how much and kind of talking that took place.

This system consists of ten categories, namely, accepting feelings, praising for encouraging, using ideas of students, asking questions, lecturing, giving directions, criticizing or justifying student talk-response, student talk initiation and silence or confusion.

FIA became o widely used coding system to analyse and improve teacher student interaction pattern. Perhaps few studies have been carried out regarding classroom interaction in Pakistan on this vital aspect of teaching learning process.

The main objective of proposed study was explore patterns of classroom interaction of secondary and tertiary levels in the North West Frontier using Interaction Analysis system. This study was significant because its findings and conclusions may stimulate teachers to improve their teaching behaviour in order to maximize students learning.

To achieve the above study objectives, six hypotheses were formulated in the light of Flanders Two third rule of teacher student class room interaction, both at secondary and tertiary level, namely, about two-third of the class room time is devoted to talking, about two-third of this time the person talking is the teacher and two-third of the s talk is talk. In order to compare the interaction patterns at secondary and tertiary level, three additional hypotheses were framed, namely, there is significant difference between teacher talking time at secondary and tertiary levels, there is significant difference between silence time at secondary and higher level.

Thus the number of all the hypotheses was nine. Twenty-five classrooms at secondary and twenty-five at tertiary level were randomly selected as a sample of this study. Fifty observations were carried out, each in one classroom, using Flanders Interaction Analysis system to secure the data. To do this, time sampling was used and each classroom was observed for 810 second in a 45-minutes class. After obtaining and encoding the data, it was tabulated, analyzed and interpreted by using percentage, means, standard deviations and t-test.

All the nine hypotheses were supported and it was concluded that, both at secondary and tertiary level, more than two-third of classroom time was devoted to talking, thus talk method dominated in classes. More than two third of the classroom talking time was devoted to teachers talking at secondary and tertiary levels, the teachers playing the dominant role. More than two-third of the teacher s talking time was devoted for direct talk, which showed the directive role of the teacher at secondary and tertiary levels.

Students talk time at secondary and tertiary level differed in favour of secondary level classes where students talk time was greater than at tertiary level. The talk time of teacher at tertiary level was greater than that of the teacher s at secondary level. Silence time at secondary level was significantly greater than at tertiary level.

FACTORS IN SHAPING STRUCTURE OF CLASSROOM INTERACTION

- Students' prior world knowledge and learning experiences;
- Students' *interim* grammar;
- Teacher's style;
- Teacher's methodological knowledge and expertise;
- The curriculum;
- Traditional views on classroom conventions;
- Classroom struggle for power;
- Teacher's control of topic and interaction;

- The way teacher and students feel about each other;
- The teacher's greater knowledge;
- Learner expectations regarding use in class and task completion;
- Student comprehension of what the teacher says and does;

NORMS GOVERNING CLASSROOM INTERACTION

- The co-operative principle of conversation (Grice's maxims)
- Norms that regulate personal and social distance;
- Norms that regulate language usage;
- Norms that regulate content and thematic development;
- Norms that regulate discourse structure;
- Norms that regulate social behaviour in the classroom;
- Norms that regulate affects in the FL classroom;

PATTERNS OF CLASSROOM INTERACTION

- Classroom communicative competence;
- Intellectual development;
- Met linguistic knowledge.

Briefly design an activity that best suits a particular pattern. Patterns in EFL classroom can be grouped as follows:

- Lockstep (teacher / student , teacher / whole class);
- Pair work (closed pairs);
- Pair work (open pairs);
- Mingles;
- Small Groups;
- Groups;

FEATURES

Pattern A

- Teacher acts as a linguistic model and informant, as a corrector, as a provider of feedback on choral and individual performance. pronunciation, streess, intonation, usage.

- Teacher controls thematic and social structure of student participation.
- Learner exposure to linguistic input opportunity to developed comprehension of the foreign language (classroom language instruction)
- Opportunity to develop comprehension of classroom social rules and conventions.
- Reduced amount of student talking time.
- Teacher leads students towards convergent thinking.

Pattern B

- Teacher controls students output and participants in the interaction (accuracy - oriented, teacher - directed).
- Teacher sets communicative tasks (fluency-oriented, teacher-directed).
- Learners practice language patterns (repetition, transformation, expansion).
- Learners develop communicative competence - choice of language, use of discourse markers, turn- taking mechanisms, paralinguistic features, registers and styles (Information and opinion gaps , problem-solving activities).
- Learners apply / develop cooperative principles.
- Learners activate their world knowledge and their cognitive affective , meta-cognitive and meta-communicative strategies.
- Learners may eventually develop divergent thinking.

Pattern C

- Teacher exerts less control of student output and social structure of communication.
- Teacher sets up communicative tasks. (Fluency-oriented activities).
- Learners practice language patterns (repetition, transformation, expansion).
- Learners develop communicative competence - choice

of language, use of discourse markers, turn- taking mechanisms, paralinguistic features, registers and styles (Information and opinion gaps , problem-solving activities).

- Learners apply / develop cooperative principles.
- Learners activate their world knowledge and their cognitive affective , meta-cognitive and meta-communicative strategies.
- Learners have a choice of addressee.
- Learners may eventually develop divergent thinking.
- Learners develop clarity of diction and alertness (reaction time).

Pattern D

- Teacher controls student's output (accuracy - oriented, teacher - directed).
- Teacher sets up communicative tasks (fluency-oriented, teacher-directed).
- Learners practice language patterns repetition, transformation, expansion).

Learners develop communicative competence -choice of language, use of discourse markers, turn-taking mechanisms, paralinguistic features, registers and styles (Information and opinion gaps, problem-solving activities).

- Learners apply / develop cooperative principles.
- Learners activate their world knowledge and their cognitive affective, meta-cognitive and meta-communicative strategies.
- Learners may eventually develop divergent thinking.
- Learners have more freedom of movement.
- Learners develop self-confidence.
- Class-hours can be more joyful for the learners.

Pattern E

- Teacher exerts less control of student output and social structure of communication.
- Teacher sets up communicative tasks. (Fluency-oriented activities).

- Learners develop communicative competence - choice of language, use of discourse markers, turn-taking mechanisms, paralinguistic features, registers and styles (Information and opinion gaps , problem-solving activities).
- Learners apply / develop cooperative principles.
- Learners activate their world knowledge and their cognitive affective , meta-cognitive and meta-communicative strategies.
- Learners have a choice of addressee.
- Learners may eventually develop divergent thinking.

Pattern F

- All features of pattern E.
- Group dynamics gets importance.

Unit X

Action Research in History

PROBLEM IDENTIFICATION

INTRODUCTION

It is assumed that you have already identified a particular site as requiring a RA. The objective of Problem Identification is to 'take stock' of the problem for a particular site, and answer the question:

- 'What do we think the problem is?'
- "What information should be collected and assessed to confirm our understanding of the problem?"

The main outcome of the Problem Identification stage is to set the overall purpose and objectives of the RA and to determine the likely data requirements. This step should:

- Clearly identify what aspect of the RA needs to be addressed;
- Set the objectives of the RA (what will and will not be considered), and
- Identify what information needs to be collected, analysed and assessed.

RISK ASSESSMENT OBJECTIVES

The specific objectives of the assessment will depend on the state of knowledge about the site:

- If no previous studies or sampling have been undertaken, the objectives may relate to establishing whether contamination is present, at what concentrations and in what media.

- If there has been a previous investigation, this step may identify that a particular contaminant pathway needs to be further assessed.
- If previous Tiers of a RA have been completed, this step may address a particular information gap.

The objectives of a Risk Assessment will vary depending on the nature of the site and the Tier at which the Risk Assessment is being undertaken.

Tier 1 - Problem Identification

The first part of this step is to assess existing information and identify the problem that the RA is trying to address. Any preliminary findings about the site should be documented. Care should be taken to make sure that all available information is carefully assessed before the next stages of the RA are undertaken. At this stage it is important to identify and document the following details:

- Current and historic land uses.
- Potential/actual contaminants of concern.
- Potential pathways.
- Potential receptors.
- Areas of uncertainty.

Problem Identification should consider a wide range of possible contaminants, receptors, and pathways. This should lead to the formulation of a conceptual site model that can be tested through the RA process, and provide the basis for developing the objectives for undertaking a Tier 1 assessment. In most cases some general information about the site should be available from the Initiation stage. This should include current and past land uses, consent information, and site records. Further information is generally necessary to undertake a full site characterisation, including:

- Land use and land-use history:
  - Identify existing and past land uses on site
  - Identify nearby existing and past land uses
  - Document any gaps in these records
  - Identify what chemicals or materials were used at the site (types, quantities, processes, storage, and disposal).

- Identify and document any incidents of chemical releases and possible release mechanisms.

- Identify potential or possible contaminants of concern.
- Identify other contaminant sources (e.g. nearby factory, natural contaminant source), and
- Broadly define the surrounding environment and identify:
  - Potential ecological values.
  - Buildings or heritage sites.
  - Sensitive land uses (e.g. school) or human receptors, and
  - Cultural sites.

Using this information, you should draw preliminary conclusions on the following key factors:

- Contaminants of concern;
- Potential receptors; and
- Main pathways (contaminants release, transport and fate mechanisms).

Any assumptions used in completing the site characterisation, and any information gaps should be clearly documented.

WHY DO WE NEED TO IDENTIFY PROBLEMS?

A clearly specified list of problems is the most suitable basis for identifying potential solutions. Problems can be identified, both now and in the future, as evidence that objectives are not being achieved. However, objectives are often rather abstract, and it may be easier for members of the public to understand a strategy based on clearly identified problems. This problem-oriented approach to strategy formulation is an alternative to starting with objectives, but does still need to be checked against the full list of objectives.

OBJECTIVE ANALYSIS

Objective analysis of problems requires the adoption of an appropriate set of indicators and targets. When a condition is measured or predicted to differ from a threshold, then a problem is said to exist. A range of thresholds can be set, so that problems may be graded by severity. Thus, for example, noise levels which exceed, say, could be classed as 'slight', 'moderate' and 'severe' noise problems. When thresholds are defined, they can be used, with current data, to identify current problems. Given an appropriate predictive model, a similar exercise can be conducted for a future year.

WHY IS IT USEFUL TO DETERMINE THE SEVERITY OF PROBLEMS NOW AND IN THE FUTURE?

If problems are identified through consultation, the city authority is able to determine the areas of concern for citizens. This will in turn help to confirm that they have selected the right objectives, and to indicate the basis on which targets might be set. Identification through objective analysis and monitoring enables cities, and citizens, to compare problems in different areas and in different years on a consistent basis. Comparison of predicted problems if nothing further is done with predictions of the impacts of possible solutions provides an immediate indication of the scale of the predicted improvement, and also highlights any possible adverse effects.

WHAT ARE THE WEAKNESSES OF THIS APPROACH?

It is essential to start with a comprehensive list of indicators, which cover all the objectives. Without this, some types of problem will be overlooked. If problems are judged analytically by reference to thresholds, there is a danger that the thresholds set will be somewhat arbitrary. It will be important to check that problems are not occurring at levels below the threshold. Where thresholds are set for different indicators, this will imply that problems of that severity are equally serious. Thus, for example: if a noise level in excess of 65dB(A) and a carbon monoxide level in excess of 8.5ppm were both to be classed as 'slight' problems, this would imply an equivalent severity.

The approach may only show problems as symptoms. Some analysis of the underlying causes of the problems should always be considered. For example, it would not be safe to assume that adding extra capacity at the location concerned should solve a congestion problem. It may be that land use patterns are encouraging longer distance travel, or that inadequate public transport is forcing people to drive. Other solutions, such as travel demand management or public transport improvements may be more appropriate and may only be revealed by analysis of the causes of the problem.

PROBLEM IDENTIFICATION

The provider should try to make a distinction between those adolescents who are depressed and those who are at high suicide risk. Clearly, such screening is difficult. A less experienced health provider may want to consult or refer to a mental health professional who has experience and expertise in working with adolescents to help decide what kind of intervention and subsequent treatment is needed. The provider and adolescent should work together to reach an agreement that a problem exists.

The adolescent may deny that depression or suicide ideation are problems or that these feelings interfere with activities of daily living. Because depression may be present in numerous forms, from withdrawal to extreme behavioral changes, providers may have to clearly outline for the adolescent what they believe the problem is, what the risks are, and what needs to be changed. For example, providers might advise an adolescent that it is not a problem to skip a meal once in a while, but a loss of appetite due to depression can be much more serious. Mild Depression

Mild depression can be caused by several factors, including an interpersonal situation that is causing the adolescent difficulty, a personal loss that the adolescent has experienced, or a stressful or humiliating event. Mild depression is usually transient and not accompanied by feelings of hopelessness, a drop in school grades, loss of friends, or by high-risk behaviour, such as drinking and driving, unprotected sexual intercourse, or using drugs. However, a mild depression coupled with substance abuse or a personality disorder can result in suicide. Moderate to Severe Depression Moderate to severe depression is typified by prolonged symptoms, accompanied by mild behavioral changes and/or other symptoms, such as spending a lot of time alone or being chronically bored.

Evidence of dysfunction or other concerns include an absence of an appropriate response to pleasurable activities, changes in sleep patterns, crying easily, isolation or feeling worthless, drug or alcohol use, and difficulty with family relations. The adolescent should be referred for an evaluation by a psychiatrist skilled in working with adolescents and their families. Parents should be advised to remove firearms and other weapons.

STATEMENT OF OBJECTIVES

OVERVIEW

Based on a model conceived by John Bird when in 1991, he founded a street newspaper that was to be sold by the homeless themselves. He reckoned if this was fruitful, the homeless would rather sell than beg. It was a way of encouraging and supporting homeless people to gain a level of independence and income, placing the emphasis on self-support. This became the talk of many countries including South Africa. Indeed with the country's new political dispensation in 1994, our cities began experiencing a mass rural or informal settlement to urban migration. Those that came wanted food, shelter and work. Churches, governmental and non-governmental organizations started soup kitchens whose queues were usually kilometers long.

But as the years went by, these services soon realized they could only provide the "daily bread" of the hungry and hardly anything more. It was soon realized something had to be done to bridge the gaps between food, shelter and employment. After several workshops, meetings and consultations Homeless Talk was born.It was the work among many others of Judy Bassingwaithe of the Central Methodist Mission, Rev Diane Wicks of the St George's United Church, the Homeless community of Johannesburg, the Central Johannesburg Partnership as well as the Johannesburg Housing Association.

WHY A NEWSPAPER AND NOT SOME OTHER PROJECT?

Founders of Homeless Talk had always held the view that the media was biased when it came to addressing the plight of the homeless and because of this, the general public was ignorant about who the homeless are and what their needs are. Because of this ignorance, the homeless were left to fend for themselves with little or no assistance for either the government or the general public.

With the establishment of a paper to serve as the voice of the homeless, it was expected that this ignorance would be addressed. Thirteen years later, although the battle still continues, from public response so far it could be said that perceptions have changed remarkably as far as issues of homelessness are concern.

MISSION STATEMENT

We improve the quality of life of street people by empowering them to be self-reliant and to positively contribute to the society. Through the help of stakeholders we aim to minimize poverty, unemployment, homelessness and to improve the sustenance of healthy environmental living.

AIMS & OBJECTIVES

It has always remained the aim of the publication to be used as a tool in "Helping the Homeless Help Themselves". Through this lies a form of empowerment that has seen many writers and vendors use the paper to save money and start their own businesses or move to other mainstream publications. We still continue to open doors for new aspiring writers from the street, offering training and increasing our resource data base through research.

HYPOTHESIS

Explanation: *Hypothesis* invites authors to submit new and

thought-provoking predictions based on scientific findings or theories from any field. We aim to establish an interdisciplinary journal that swiftly publishes new, provocative, and sometimes currently untestable ideas, while preserving the freethinking nature of the earliest scientific publications. Thus, *Hypothesis* favours publication of articles that go beyond reporting data or summarizing a body of work, providing a vessel for thoughtful speculation and healthy debate where authors can freely articulate their most exciting ideas. Moreover, by challenging authors to create intriguing hypotheses concerning their reviewed or original research, *Hypothesis* is committed to publishing entertaining articles suitable for all readers.

An hypothesis is a specific statement of prediction. It describes in concrete (rather than theoretical) terms what you expect will happen in your study. Not all studies have hypotheses. Sometimes a study is designed to be exploratory (see inductive research). There is no formal hypothesis, and perhaps the purpose of the study is to explore some area more thoroughly in order to develop some specific hypothesis or prediction that can be tested in future research. A single study may have one or many hypotheses.

Actually, whenever I talk about an hypothesis, I am really thinking simultaneously about *two* hypotheses. Let's say that you predict that there will be a relationship between two variables in your study. The way we would formally set up the hypothesis test is to formulate two hypothesis statements, one that describes your prediction and one that describes all the other possible outcomes with respect to the hypothesized relationship. Your prediction is that variable A and variable B will be related (you don't care whether it's a positive or negative relationship).

Then the only other possible outcome would be that variable A and variable B are *not* related. Usually, we call the hypothesis that you support (your prediction) the *alternative* hypothesis, and we call the hypothesis that describes the remaining possible outcomes the *null* hypothesis. Sometimes we use a notation like H_A or H_1 to represent the alternative hypothesis or your prediction, and H_O or H_0 to represent the null case. You have to be careful here, though. In some studies, your prediction might very well be that there will be no difference or change. In this case, you are essentially trying to find support for the null hypothesis and you are opposed to the alternative.

If your prediction specifies a direction, and the null therefore is the no difference prediction and the prediction of the opposite direction, we call this a *one-tailed hypothesis*. For instance, let's imagine that you are investigating the effects of a new employee training programme and that you believe one of the outcomes will be that there will be *less* employee absenteeism. Your two hypotheses might be stated something like this:

The null hypothesis for this study is:

H_O: As a result of the XYZ company employee training programme, there will either be no significant difference in employee absenteeism or there will be a significant *increase*.

Which is tested against the alternative hypothesis:

H_A: As a result of the XYZ company employee training programme, there will be a significant *decrease* in employee absenteeism.

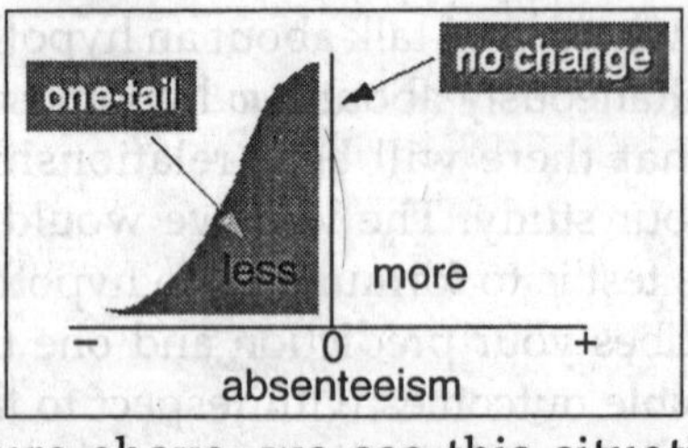

In the figure above, we see this situation illustrated graphically. The alternative hypothesis — your prediction that the programme will decrease absenteeism — is shown there. The null must account for the other two possible conditions: no difference, or an increase in absenteeism. The figure shows a hypothetical distribution of absenteeism differences. We can see that the term "one-tailed" refers to the tail of the distribution on the outcome variable.

When your prediction does *not* specify a direction, we say

you have a *two-tailed hypothesis*. For instance, let's assume you are studying a new drug treatment for depression. The drug has gone through some initial animal trials, but has not yet been tested on humans. You believe (based on theory and the previous research) that the drug will have an effect, but you are not confident enough to hypothesize a direction and say the drug will reduce depression (after all, you've seen more than enough promising drug treatments come along that eventually were shown to have severe side effects that actually worsened symptoms). In this case, you might state the two hypotheses like this:

The null hypothesis for this study is:

H_O: As a result of 300mg./day of the ABC drug, there will be no significant difference in depression.

Which is tested against the alternative hypothesis:

H_A: As a result of 300mg./day of the ABC drug, there will be a significant difference in depression.

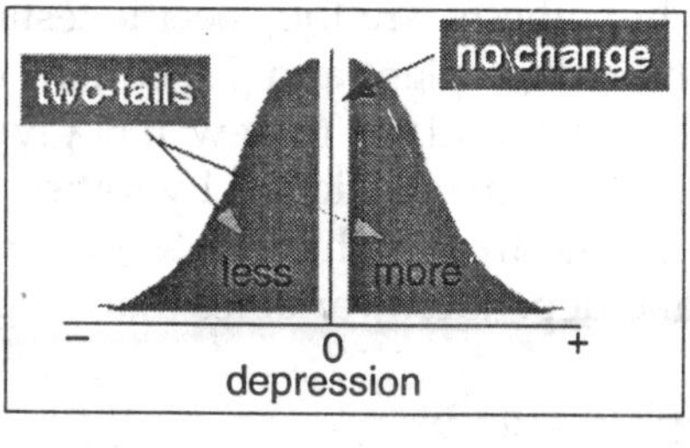

The figure above illustrates this two-tailed prediction for this case. Again, notice that the term "two-tailed" refers to the tails of the distribution for your outcome variable.

The important thing to remember about stating hypotheses is that you formulate your prediction (directional or not), and then you formulate a second hypothesis that is mutually exclusive of the first and incorporates all possible alternative outcomes for that case. When your study analysis is completed, the idea is that you will have to choose between the two hypotheses.

If your prediction was correct, then you would (usually) reject the null hypothesis and accept the alternative. If your original prediction was not supported in the data, then you will accept the null hypothesis and reject the alternative. The logic of hypothesis testing is based on these two basic principles:

- The formulation of two mutually exclusive hypothesis statements that, together, exhaust all possible outcomes.
- The testing of these so that one is necessarily accepted and the other rejected.

OK, I know it's a convoluted, awkward and formalistic way to ask research questions. But it encompasses a long tradition in statistics called the *hypothetical-deductive model,* and sometimes we just have to do things because they're traditions. And anyway, if all of this hypothesis testing was easy enough so anybody could understand it, how do you think statisticians would stay employed?

RESEARCH HYPOTHESIS

Research hypotheses are the specific testable predictions made about the independent and dependent variables in the study. Usually the literature review has given background material that justifies the particular hypotheses that are to be tested. Hypotheses are couched in terms of the particular independent and dependent variables that are going to be used in the study.

An example would be

"Children who are exposed to regular singing of the alphabet will show greater recognition of letters than children who are exposed to regular pronouncing of the alphabet"

Notice the IV is specified (singing compared to pronouncing) and the DV is specified (recognition of letters is what will be measured). Notice also that this research hypothesis specifies a direction in that it predicts that the singing group will recognise more letters than the pronouncing group. This is not always the case. Research hypotheses can also specify a difference without saying which group will be better than the other. In general, it is considered a better hypothesis if you can specify a direction.

Finally, note the deductive reasoning principle of the

scientific method when we test hypotheses. If our theories and ideas are the truth we can devise controlled experiments and find evidence to support them.

This gives considerable credence to our theories. If we work the other way, and gather data first and then try to work out what happened (inductive reasoning) we could be faced with a large number of competing theories all of which could be true or not true.

This is sometimes called posthoc theorising and is a common way in which people explain events in their world. But we have no way of knowing which one is correct, we have no way of ruling out the competing reasons and we usually end up with choosing the one that fits best with our existing biases.

Inductive reasoning does have a role in exploratory research in order to develop initial ideas and hypotheses, but in the end the hypotheses have to be tested before they can have scientific credence.

DATA COLLECTION AND ANALYSIS

DESCRIPTION

Surveys collect data from a targeted group of people about their opinions, behaviour or knowledge. Common types of surveys are written questionnaires, face-to-face or telephone interviews, focus groups and electronic (e-mail or Web site) surveys.

Surveys are commonly used with key stakeholders, especially customers and employees, to discover needs or assess satisfaction.

WHEN TO USE A SURVEY

- When identifying customer requirements or preferences.
- When assessing customer or employee satisfaction, such as identifying or prioritizing problems to address.
- When evaluating proposed changes.

- When assessing whether a change was successful.
- Periodically, to monitor changes in customer or employee satisfaction over time.

SURVEY BASIC PROCEDURE

Note: It's often worthwhile to have a survey prepared and administered by a research organization. However, you will still need to work with them on the following steps so that the survey will be most useful.

- Decide what you want to learn from the survey and how you will use the results.
- Decide who should be surveyed. Identify population groups; if they are too large to permit surveying everyone, decide how to obtain a sample. Decide what demographic information is needed to analyse and understand the results.
- Decide on the most appropriate type of survey.
- Decide whether the survey's answers will be numerical rating, numerical ranking, yes–no, multiple choice or open-ended—or a mixture.
- Brainstorm questions and, for multiple choice, the list of possible answers. Keep in mind what you want to learn, and how you will use the results. Narrow down the list of questions to the absolute minimum that you must have to learn what you need to learn.
- Print the questionnaire or interviewers' question list.
- Test the survey with a small group. Collect feedback.
  - Which questions were confusing?
  - Were any questions redundant?
  - Were answer choices clear? Were they interpreted as you intended?
  - Did respondents want to give feedback about topics that were not included? (Open-ended questions can be an indicator of this.)
  - On the average, how long did it take for a respondent to complete the survey?
  - For a questionnaire, were there any typos or printing errors?

Also test the process of tabulating and analyzing the results. Is it easy? Do you have all the data you need?

- Revise the survey based on test results.
- Administer the survey.
- Tabulate and analyse the data. Decide how you will follow through. Report results and plans to everyone involved. If a sample was involved, also report and explain the margin of error and confidence level.

SURVEY CONSIDERATIONS

- Conducting a survey creates expectations for change in those asked to answer it. Do not survey if action will not or cannot be taken as a result.
- Satisfaction surveys should be compared to objective indicators of satisfaction, such as buying patterns for customers or attendance for employees, and to objective measures of performance, such as warranty data in manufacturing or re-admission rates in hospitals. If survey results do not correlate with the other measures, work to understand whether the survey is unreliable or whether perceptions are being modified, for better or worse, by the organization's actions.
- Surveys of customer and employee satisfaction should be ongoing processes rather than one-time events.
- Get help from a research organization in preparing, administering and analyzing major surveys, especially large ones or those whose results will determine significant decisions or expenditures.

Bibliography

Dikshit, D.P. *Political History of the Chalukyas of Badami*. New Delhi: 1980.

Dixit, Prabla. *Communalism: A Struggle for Power*. New Delhi: 1981.

Doniger, Wendy, trans. *Laws of Manu*. 1992.

Doshi, Saryu, ed. *India and Greece*. New Delhi: 1985.

Dunn, Rose E. *The Adventures of Ibn Battuta*. 1986.

Dutt, Ashok K., and Allen G. Noble. "The Culture of India in a Spatial Perspective: An Introduction." Pages 1-28 in Allen G. Noble and Ashok K. Dutt, eds., *India: Cultural Patterns and Processes*. 1982.

Eaton, Richard M. *The Rise of Islam and the Bengal Frontier, 1204-1760*. Comparative Studies on Muslim Societies, No. 17. Berkeley: 1993.

Eaton, Richard M. *Sufis of Bijapur, 1300-1700: Social Roles of Sufis in Medieval India*. 1978.

Eldridge, P.J. *The Politics of Foreign Aid in India*. 1970.

Ellinwood, DeWitt C., and S.P. Pradhan. *India and World War I*. New Delhi 1978.

Embree, Ainslie T. *1857 in India: Mutiny or War of Independence*. Lexington, 1963.

Embree, Ainslie T., ed. *Alberuni's India*. New York: 1971.

Embree, Ainslie T., ed. *Encyclopedia of Asian History*. 4 vols. The Asia Society. New York: 1988.

Embree, Ainslie T., ed. *Sources of Indian Tradition, 1: From the Beginning to 1800*. 2d ed. Introduction to Oriental Civilization Series. New York: 1988.

Erickson, Erik H. *Gandhi's Truth: On the Origins of Militant Nonviolence.* New York: 1970.

Fairservis, Walter A. *The Roots of Ancient India: The Archaeology of Early Indian Civilization.* New York: 1971.

Farmer, Edward L., Gavin R.G. Hambly, David Kopf, Byron K. Marshall, and Romeyn Taylor. *Comparative History of Civilizations in Asia.* 2 vols. Reading, Massachusetts: 1977.

Featherstone, Donald F. *Victorian Colonial Warfare, India: From the Conquest of Sind to the Indian Mutiny.* London: 1992.

Fischer, Louis. *The Life of Mahatma Gandhi.* New York: 1950.

Fisher, Michael. *A Clash of Cultures: Awadh, the British, and the Mughals.* New Delhi: 1987.

Fisher, Michael. *Indirect Rule in India: Residents and the Residency System, 1764-1857.* New Delhi: 1991.

Index

U

V

W

X